The Essence of Psychotherapy

Reinventing the Art
in the New Era of Data

The Essence of Psychotherapy

Reinventing the Art
in the New Era of Data

NICHOLAS A. CUMMINGS
JANET L. CUMMINGS

Academic Press
San Diego   London   Boston   New York   Sydney   Tokyo   Toronto

Cover: Image of a statuette of the Grecian goddess Psyche created by artist Maxi Harper of Burlingame, California in 1995.

Academic Press
A Harcourt Science and Technology Company
525 B Street, Suite 1900, San Diego, California 92101-4495, USA
http://www.academicpress.com

Academic Press
24-28 Oval Road, London NW1 7DX
http://www.hbuk.co.uk/ap/

Library of Congress Cataloging Card Number: 99-68193

International Standard Book Number: 0-12-198760-4

PRINTED IN THE UNITED STATES OF AMERICA
00 01 02 03 04 05 MM 9 8 7 6 5 4 3 2 1

ACKNOWLEDGMENTS

The authors are grateful to the following contemporary master therapists who contributed cases illustrating their psychotherapeutic orientation:

Simon H. Budman, Ph.D.
Innovative Training Systems, Newton, MA

Elizabeth and James F.T. Bugental, Ph.D.
Novato, CA

Paula Hartman-Stein, Ph.D.
Center for Healthy Aging, Akron, OH

Steven C. Hayes, Ph.D.
University of Nevada, Reno

Michael F. Hoyt, Ph.D.
Kaiser Permanente Medical Center, Hayward, CA

Arnold A. Lazarus, Ph.D.
Rutgers University, New Jersey

Leigh McCullough, Ph.D.
Beth Israel Medical Center, Boston

Kirk J. Schneider, Ph.D.
Center for Existential Therapy, San Francisco, CA

Jeffrey K. Zeig, Ph.D.
The Milton H. Erickson Foundation, Phoenix, AZ

ABOUT THE AUTHORS

Nicholas A. Cummings, Ph.D., Sc.D. President, Foundation for Behavioral Health and Chairman, The Nicholas & Dorothy Cummings Foundation, Inc. Founding CEO, American Biodyne (MedCo/Merck, then Merit, now Magellan Behavioral Care). Former President, American Psychological Association. Founder of the four campuses of the California School of Professional Psychology. Chief Psychologist (Retired), Kaiser Permanente. Founder, National Academies of Practice. Founder, American Managed Behavioral Healthcare Association. Founder, National Council of Professional Schools of Psychology. Former Executive Director, Mental Research Institute, Palo Alto. Currently Distinguished Professor, University of Nevada, Reno.

Janet L. Cummings, Psy.D. President, The Nicholas & Dorothy Cummings Foundation, Inc. and independent practice, Scottsdale, Arizona. Former staff psychologist, American Biodyne (MedCo/Merck, then Merit, now Magellan Behavioral Care). Doctorate, School of Professional Psychology, Wright State University, 1992.

RECENT BOOKS BY THE AUTHORS

N.A. Cummings & M. Sayama (1995). *Focused Psychotherapy: A Casebook of Brief, Intermittent Psychotherapy Throughout the Life Cycle.*

N.A. Cummings, M.S. Pallak, J.L. Cummings (Eds.) (1996). *Surviving the Demise of Solo Practice: Mental Health Practitioners Prospering in the Era of Managed Care.*

N.A. Cummings, J.L. Cummings, & J.N. Johnson (Eds.) (1997). *Behavioral Health in Primary Care: A Guide for Clinical Integration.*

J.L. Thomas & J.L. Cummings, (Eds.) (1999). *The Importance of Psychological Treatment: The Collected Papers of Nicholas A. Cummings, Vol. 1.*

CONTENTS

Acknowledgments   v

About the Authors   vii

1 **What Are "Best Practices," Anyway?**   1

Manuals, Manuals Everywhere, for Every Type of Shrink   3
Guidelines versus Standards   4
Advantages and Disadvantages of Standardization   5
Garbage in, Garbage out   8
Not all Psychological Procedures Are Psychotherapy   11
Will Medication Replace Psychotherapy?   14
Will Other Psychological Treatments Replace Psychotherapy?   15
The Death and Resurrection of Clinical Romanticism   16
The Best a Profession Can Be   18

2 **Psychotherapy Is an Amalgam of All Techniques
   and Competencies**   21

Therapeutic Amalgams and Effectiveness   22
Psychotherapy Is Behavioral   25
Psychotherapy Is Cognitive   27
Psychotherapy Is Psychodynamic   30
Psychotherapy Is Strategic   32
Psychotherapy Is Humanistic   35
Psychotherapy Is Also Psychopharmacology   37

3 **The Anatomy of Psychotherapy**   **41**

   Psychotherapy Is Not Paid Compassion   41
   Psychotherapy Is Not Protracted   43
   Psychotherapy Is Not Just Insight   45
   Psychotherapy Is Not Catharsis   46
   Key Ingredient 1: Psychotherapy Is a Corrective Emotional
      Experience   47
   Key Ingredient 2: Psychotherapy is Conducive to
      Growth and Change   51
   Key Ingredient 3: Psychotherapy Is an Understanding
      of the Transference Relationship   56
   Key Ingredient 4: Understanding the Patient's Modus
      Operandi—the Parataxic Distortions   64
   Key Ingredient 5: Understanding the Patient's Inner Conflicts   66
   Key Ingredient 6: Symptom Reduction   73
   All the Key Ingredients at Work: An Illustration   77

4 **Effective Psychotherapy as Focused, Intermittent**
   Psychotherapy Throughout the Life Cycle   **81**

   Elements Shared by All Effective Psychotherapies   82
   Technique Is Dependent Upon Theory   86
   Focused Psychotherapy Transcends Any Single Theory,
      But It Is Not Eclectic   87
   The Ideal First Session   88
   Onion and Garlic Psychodynamics   91
   Taking Cognizance of the Landscape   94
   Powerful Ways to Facilitate Psychotherapy   97

5 **Intermittent, Focused Psychotherapy Throughout**
   the Life Cycle   **101**

   Denise: Forty Years of Intermittent Focused Psychotherapy,
      1959 to 1999   103

6 **Psychotherapy's New Horizons**   **123**

   The Future: One House, One Patient, One System   125
   The Populations and Settings   127
   Elements of Targeted Programs   130
   Characteristics and Utility of Targeted Group Models   132

Prevention versus Cost-Containment   136
Two Examples of Targeted Group Models   137
A Vision of the Future   142

7 New Notes on Old Masters   145

Siegfried Bernfeld, Ph.D., and Sigmund Freud, M.D.   148
Frieda Fromm-Reichmann, M.D.   149
Erik H. Erikson   152
Eric Berne, M.D.   153
Franz Alexander, M.D.   155
Paul Watzlawick, Ph.D.   156
Florence Mateer, Ph.D.   158
Milton H. Erickson, M.D.   160

8 A Sampling of Current Masters   167

The Case of Gene: Simon H. Budman, Ph.D.   168
The Case of Barbara: Elizabeth and James F.T. Bugental, Ph.D. 173
Medicare—The Case of Sonya: Paula Hartman-Stein, Ph.D. 181
Danny—A Case of Panic Disorder: Steven C. Hayes, Ph.D. 188
John—The Present is a Gift: Michael F. Hoyt, Ph.D.   193
The Case of Gilda—Shotgun Therapy:
    Arnold A. Lazarus, Ph.D.   209
Lorraine—Breaking Through Defenses to Grief:
    Leigh McCullough, Ph.D.   216
Emma—Hyperconstriction and Complexity:
    Kirk J. Schneider, Ph.D.   230
The Case of Bob—Family Therapy with a Problem Child:
    Jeffrey K. Zeig, Ph.D.   234
A Final Comment   239

9 Extreme Therapy: The Power of Psychotherapy   241

Dan's Date with Death   243

10 Epilogue   249

References   255
Index   261

CHAPTER 1

What Are "Best Practices," Anyway?

In an editorial addressed to a behavioral healthcare industry that is rushing almost blindly into the promulgation of treatment models that work, and then arbitrarily labeling them as "best practices," Oss (1998) injected this timely question: "What are so-called best practices, anyway?" (p. 3). She points out that every managed care company and provider group has its own committee feverishly writing "guidelines" that actually are intended to help them manage risk (capitation or case rate), while giving the impression their particular treatment model reflects quality rather than mere cost containment. Oss astutely concludes that the answer to her question is simple: There are currently no best practices. However, we are beginning to see what might be called, for lack of a better term, best available practices.

The drive toward protocols and guidelines is relentless, fueled by managed care companies desperate to differentiate themselves in an otherwise cookie-cutter industry. Close behind them are the beleaguered practitioners who are anxious to recapture control of the treatment process through their own brand of manuals. All of this is occurring within an awesome potential to conduct unprecedented research through our organized systems of behavioral healthcare. Where once we numbered experimental subjects in scores, or at best hundreds, the managed care industry can provide hundreds of thousands of patients with millions of episodes, and in all manner of settings from coast to coast. This power, misdirected or poorly conducted, can have the force of a cyclone, leveling everything in its path. We are off to a bad start, driven by business needs or by practitioner politics, each pitted against the other and both ignoring the need for data. In such a race, psychotherapy will surely be trampled.

The need for evidence in formulating future psychotherapies that are both effective and efficient is apparent, but not always appreciated. Yet where once psychotherapy was regarded mostly as an art (Reik, 1949), the current emphasis on data is threatening the art of practice that often differentiates the master therapist from the mediocre one. An example of the advantages and limitations of protocols can be found in the highly manualized practice of surgery. There is a formulated technique for every procedure, yet not all surgeons are alike. There is the gifted surgeon who is differentiated from the herd through such things as the smallness of the incision and the precision of the intrusion, and, more important, by low mortality and high success rates. Even in surgery there is unquestionably the art. The manualization of surgery over the past century has raised the level of competence for the field as a whole without stifling the aspect that is art.

The trend toward standardization is necessary and will continue. That work must not, however, lose sight of what comprises the essence of psychotherapy. It is imperative that psychotherapists define, appreciate, and preserve that essence before it is forever lost.

MANUALS, MANUALS EVERYWHERE, FOR EVERY TYPE OF SHRINK

Where once there were a few protocols (manuals) and essentially no guidelines, there has been an explosion in both. As noted, the managed care companies and provider groups have active committees churning out protocols. In addition, practitioners, hoping to make a name and perhaps even market their manuals, are stampeding in the same direction. These efforts might be described as a reverse process, since they resemble a chef looking back on how he or she cooks and then writing a cookbook. Although this might work in the kitchen, the lack of an evidence base renders such questionably derived products arbitrary in the clinic or treatment room. Yank Coble, representing the American Medical Association and addressing the healthcare industry, put forth the mantra for all future efforts when he stated, "In God we trust. All others must have data" (as quoted in *Time,* November 24, 1998, p. 69).

Hayes (1998) concluded that guidelines cannot be formulated by the managed care industry, the professional societies, or the government, although all three are actively trying. Efforts by the government have quickly bogged down in political squabbles as the various constituencies, each having its own ax to grind, attack the process and one another. Guidelines written by the industry unavoidably reflect cost issues, while their claims of quality remain suspect. Finally, those formulated by the practitioners put one profession ahead of the others, inevitably reflecting guild issues. For example, the guidelines published by the American Psychiatric Association (ApA) are rejected as self-serving by both the American Psychological Association (APA) and the National

Association of Social Work (NASW). Hayes further concludes that guidelines can only be written by a consortium of all the relevant players working seriously toward a consensus based on evidence. Accordingly, he and his colleagues have created the Practice Guidelines Coalition (PGC), which has compiled its first model set of guidelines. Panic disorder was chosen because there were considerable data already in existence rendering the prospect of consensus more likely (Hayes, 1998). These guidelines have so impressed the nation's second largest managed behavioral care corporation that its medical director stated his company would cease to micromanage any practitioner who adhered to them (Shaffer, 1999).

GUIDELINES VERSUS STANDARDS

While most protocols are half-baked and most guidelines premature, they are here, while standards are way off into the future. Guidelines are just that; they serve as a guide to the practitioner who may deviate from them with good reason. Standards, on the other hand, are requirements or imperatives of practice. Deviation from a standard has serious consequences, as it may be grounds for malpractice or revocation of the license to practice. A profession must be very mature to have reached the level of defined standards, and only anesthesiology among all the health professions has been able to do so. It is important to note that many psychologists believe the APA Ethical Code to be a standard of practice. Rather, it is a standard of conduct, not practice, and even when it states a psychologist practices within his/her level of competence, the level is not defined.

Standards not only require an enormously accurate body of knowledge, they raise the danger that practice will be locked into a set of requirements and thus stifle innovation and progress. To a lesser extent, even guidelines and protocols may have a similar dampening effect, although intrinsically they should not. We are on the threshold of some beginning forms of standardization because those who pay the bills are demanding it. In its early stages it cannot be called "best practices," but rather "best *available* practices." As Hayes (1998) succinctly stated, these are not coming; they are here. Stated another way, standardization will be a constantly evolving process, upgrading itself as more data are available upon which to make evidence-based decisions.

ADVANTAGES AND DISADVANTAGES OF STANDARDIZATION

Payers, and to a lesser extent consumers, are determined to end the variability in practice among psychotherapists and the commensurate variability in their treatment outcomes. This variability is the greatest among all of the health professions, forcing psychotherapy to constantly defend itself before its many critics. Standardization addresses directly this variability through several advantages that, not surprisingly, bear with them disadvantages.

(1) Standardization elevates the general base of competence for the entire profession, and thus enhances the effectiveness of the poorly trained or mediocre therapist. This becomes even more important in an era where knowledge is pushed downward, with practical nurses doing the work of registered nurses, RNs doing the work of primary care physicians, and PCPs doing the work of specialists. In our profession there is an increasing reliance on masters-level rather than doctoral psychotherapists, making standardization imperative.

Unfortunately, this addresses the problem of the below-average therapist, raising the "floor" without encouraging a commensurate rise in the ceiling. Nonetheless, this is a temporary limitation, as constant elevations in the floor can be expected to have an effect in raising the ceiling or expanding the number of superb therapists at the top. There are also indications that the immediate problem in the profession lies with its less than competent members.

(2) Standardization calls into serious question practice based on political ideology expressed in a therapeutic agenda. The last decade and a half of the twentieth century has seen several issues of pathology determined politically rather than scientifically. For example, some of these changed the entities listed in the Diagnostic and Statistical Manuals (DSMs), and though most psychotherapists would agree with the final changes, the process by which science can be overruled by politics is a slippery slope, indeed. Where does it stop? In the former Soviet Union organized psychiatry met, concluded socialism was the perfect society, and accordingly viewed dissidents as mentally ill individuals who needed hospitalization. In our own back yard the all-important APA Task Force on Repressed Memories was paralyzed for years by political considerations, and the acrimony continues to this day without a definitive that would help the consumer. Consequently, the issue of "false memories" is being resolved by the courts rather than by scientific data.

Seldom is the scientific atmosphere so ideal that all disagreements are settled by data. It can be asked whether certain necessary psychological changes would have occurred without political activism, and the answer is very likely in the negative. For the interests of the consumer, standardization must be structured to be responsive to appropriate change through data, not impede it (Marques, 1998).

(3) Standardization eliminates unverified "syndromes" and their treatment, both of which often reflect pop psychology, victimization, or the latest in political correctness. Often the diagnosis becomes that which the therapist likes to treat, as there are many borderline, dependent, lonely, or attention-hungry patients who unconsciously become whatever will bring the approval or interest of the therapist. In the past these have included many, if not most, cases of multiple personality as well as a definition of

attention deficit disorder (ADD) that encompasses as many as 60% of the boys in elementary school. One only needs to contrast the Food and Drug Administration (FDA) approved medications that have been verified by clinical trials with those in health food stores, where their exemption from FDA regulation permits the most outlandish (and sometimes dangerous) claims. Such a comparison speaks to the importance of verification.

(4) Standardization enables the public to differentiate legitimate (verified) treatment from the fanciful. Whatever the practitioner might perform, as long as both the practitioner and the patient believe it is effective, there will be about a 35% placebo effect, leaving both patient and therapist with the illusion that the treatment is effective (Kemeny, 1996; Cummings & Cummings, 1997). This is true whether the intervention involves holding crystals during therapy or involves the outmoded practice of leeching. It is incumbent upon the practitioner to provide treatment that is therapeutic above and beyond the placebo effect, and that requires verification through data. The objection that the insistence upon clinical trials might inhibit the discovery of useful treatments cannot be taken seriously in an environment where all procedures are subject to verification.

(5) Standardization curtails the abuses of overtreatment and undertreatment by providing an identifiable standard for each case and each condition. This is the arena of most of the contentiousness occurring between payers and practitioners. The payers are suspicious that therapists profit by overtreating, while the practitioners accuse the managed care companies of sacrificing necessary therapy in the interest of cost containment. Although the profession is far from identifying such a standard, there is increasing evidence that time-sensitive psychotherapy is effective for most patients (Cummings, Budman & Thomas, 1998). There is also evidence that psychotherapists tend to perpetuate whatever they were trained to do even in the face of data indicating there are more effective courses of treatment. Quite startling was the inad-

vertent discovery of an unexpected countertransference. From data assembled to ascertain what paradigm shifts would be necessary in retraining psychotherapists for the current marketplace, it was discovered that therapists who underwent their own psychoanalysis firmly believe that long-term therapy is the best treatment for all or most of their patients (Cummings, Pallak & Cummings, 1996). This was also true for substance abuse counselors, most of whom were themselves recovering. Whatever intervention was the one that broke through their personal denial and led to their own abstinence was rigidly espoused as the best approach for all their chemically dependent patients.

This raises a question regarding the highly touted *Consumer Reports* study (Seligman, 1995), which found that patients who underwent long-term therapy were more likely to express high satisfaction than those who experienced short-term therapy. This study is not so much outcomes research as a more sophisticated survey that reflects a gratitude based on attachment (dependency) and reveals the need to justify the time and money expended. This "halo effect" among long-term therapy patients was first reported over two decades ago (Cummings, 1977), and it is not surprising to find it existing as a form of countertransference among psychotherapists.

GARBAGE IN, GARBAGE OUT

This precautionary saying in the field of informatics is applicable to the explosion of research that is about to take place in behavioral health. This saying is a constant reminder that the computer is capable of taking garbage that we feed it and recycling it with lightening speed into more garbage. As noted, the organized behavioral care industry is capable of conducting research that is of a magnitude never before contemplated. In preparing a recent publication involving 1.6 million episodes in a managed care setting, Wiggins and Cummings (1998) were mindful that if the research had been originally structured by trained researchers who were not themselves practitioners possessing the necessary awareness of what really goes on in an extensive clinical setting, the study would have regurgitated a monument of garbage based on 1.6 million pieces of small garbage. University clinical faculty treating healthy students struggling with the transition between adolescence and adulthood, or independent practitioners specializing in the worried well, are not cognizant of the hard work required when working with seriously disturbed patients. This can lead to research that meets the need for easily identifiable and quantifiable variables that can be sadly removed from the real world.

Norcross (1998) has been identified with integration of the various schools of psychotherapy for the past decade. Speaking as the chair of the APA's Committee on Practice, he expressed dismay that 75% of the psychotherapy outcomes research to date has taken the easy way out, dealing with cognitive behavioral variables to the neglect of psychodynamic, strategic, strictly behavioral, or humanistic modalities. These are much more difficult to identify and quantify, and require a greater sophistication in clinical knowledge, acumen, and experience. This startling statistic suggests other concerns of standardization: (1) Psychotherapy can be reduced to protocols that are more mechanistic than artistic; (2) The broad array of techniques and approaches is lost; (3) It can stifle innovation and creativity; (4) It can prematurely freeze practice into limited cookbooks, deviation from which would jeopardize the practitioner in a court of law. As the industry inevitably moves toward standardization, all of these results can and must be avoided if the essence of psychotherapy is to be preserved.

Many research approaches in psychotherapy can be illustrated by a hypothetical medical example. Pneumonia can be due to bacterial or viral infection, as well as inhalation or a number of fungi and other microbes. Let us consider the treatment for the first three, which constitute the majority of pneumonia cases: antibiotics for bacterial pneumonia, antivirals for viral pneumonia, and oxygenation for inhalation pneumonia. Let us also say that medicine is where it was 75 or 100 years ago. Pneumonia was all alike because it manifested the same constellation of symptoms— among other things, cough, fever, chest pain, and lung inflammation. We now want to test which of two treatments (antibiotics or antivirals) is more effective with pneumonia, so we scientifically randomize our patients into four groups: those that receive an antibiotic, those that receive a form of interferon, those that receive both medications, and those given no treatment. We are unaware that our groups are composed of three types of pneumonia. Our results will parallel the numbers of each type of pneumonia sufferers. If our groups are composed of 40% bacterial, 40% viral, and 20% inhalation pneumonia, our erroneous conclusion is that antibiotics and antivirals are equally effective, but each less than 50%. Had we treated a population of only bacterial pneumonia with the antibiotic, our effectiveness would be shown to be much greater, as would the specific treatment of viral pneumonia. But the more likely conclusion under our original scenario would be that by using both antibiotic and antiviral medications, our success rate is 80%.

Psychological research is almost at this primitive level. For example, depression is often regarded as a unitary entity because all depressions manifest low self-esteem, pessimism, poor appetite, diminished sexual interest, and low energy. The fact is that there are five types of depression, each requiring a specific treatment (Cummings & Sayama, 1995). Some types of mood disorders are biological (e.g., bipolar disorder) while others are psychological (e.g., reactive depression). Our carefully randomized groups will reveal results paralleling the numbers of biological versus psychological depressions in each so that antidepressants and psychotherapy are equally effective, with the combination of the two being the most effective. We have missed the specifics. Specific treatments for specific conditions make medical care as effective as it is, and this must be the future goal of psychological treatment.

Seligman makes an important distinction between *efficacy* studies performed under near laboratory conditions, and *effectiveness* studies conducted in the real world (Morgenson, Seligman, Sternberg, Taylor & Manning, 1999). This is an important distinction, and the federal government's funding agencies are beginning to show serious interest in effectiveness research. Unfortunately, Seligman touts the *Consumer Reports* study on long-term therapy as an example of the latter, even though it is really a very sophisticated patient survey and not effectiveness research at all. In doing so he startlingly overlooks the Hawaii Project (Pallak, Cummings, Dorken & Henke, 1994) and the Fort Bragg Study (Bickman, 1996), both longitudinal, comprehensive research in the real world. Research "cherry picking" (i.e., the deliberate citation of only research that one agrees with, to the neglect of all others) is typical in the politicized psychotherapy environment of today. This has led to the question of whether the field is devoted to dogma or data (Sechrest & Walsh, 1997), and whether psychologists collectively are willing to accept unpopular findings (DeLeon & Williams, 1997). If we are to preserve the essence of psychotherapy, research must be open, replicable, non-political, and empirical, and must be conducted in the real world.

NOT ALL PSYCHOLOGICAL PROCEDURES ARE PSYCHOTHERAPY

There is a difference between what constitutes a procedure, as distinct from therapy. This distinction was obvious in medicine, but it was first introduced into psychology by Manaster and Corsini (1982). A lot of things are therapeutic, such as taking pills, making love, reading a book, getting a job, or going out with friends. But these are not what constitutes a procedure, which must fit certain criteria. Not all procedures are therapeutic. Applying leeches to remove "bad blood" was a past procedure, but it was never therapeutic. Prayer has been shown to be therapeutic (Cooper, 1995; Cummings & Cummings, 1997), but it is not a procedure even though a surprising number of physicians pray with their patients. Consider the spectacle of seeking reimbursement from a third-party payer for prayer! Holding crystals or wearing a copper bracelet during therapy is neither a procedure nor therapeutic, anecdotes from advocates not withstanding.

There are many things psychologists do that are not psychotherapy. Prescribing exercise for depression is therapeutic, but it is not a procedure or psychotherapy. Biofeedback is a therapeutic procedure, but it is not psychotherapy. Eye Movement Desensitization Response (EMDR) is a procedure, and research may well determine it is therapeutic, but, again, it is not psychotherapy. In defining and preserving the essence of psychotherapy, it is important to recognize there are psychological treatments (procedures) that may or may not be reimbursable and that are part of the endeavor called behavioral healthcare, but they may not be psychotherapy. In general, psychotherapy is talk therapy; but not all talk is psychotherapy, even though a good outpouring with a friend may be therapeutic. The essential elements necessary to differentiate psychotherapy from psychological treatment in general will be delineated in a later chapter.

Psychologists are very prone to say, after confiding in a colleague who is also a friend, "Thanks for the hour of psychotherapy." Most of this is tongue in cheek, but not always so, especially when we listen with empathy to a non-colleague friend in a social situation. Manaster and Corsini (1982) give an example of the difference that is true, poignant, and shockingly blunt:

> Psychology instructor to student: "I called you in because I set the passing mark on the test at 70% and you scored below that. You were the only one to fail the test." Student: "I know that." Instructor: "To what do you attribute your poor grade?" Student: "I have not read the text." Instructor: "Also, I don't think you have ever listened to my lec-

tures." Student: "I try not to, but sometimes I hear some of it." Instructor: "At this rate you will probably fail the course." Student: "Well, that is what I want." Instructor: "Why would you want to fail?" Student: "Well, my father wants me to go to this school, while I want to write the great American play." Instructor: "So if you fail this course, this will prove to your father that you can't make it here? Are you aware you may get kicked out of the school entirely?" Student: "As a matter of fact, I was expelled last year." Instructor: "How did you get back in?" Student: "Two reasons. First, my father is on the Board of Governors of this school, and second, I am a genius. I have an I.Q. in the 200 range." Instructor: "What can I do for you?" Student: "Nothing." Instructor: "Well, I'll try to be of help by giving honest examinations and giving you an honest grade." Student: "What do you think of psychotherapy for me?" Instructor: "What for?" Student: "My father suggests it to straighten out my thinking." Instructor: "I'm not sure it would help." Two weeks later the student came by and started a conversation. Student: "I'd like to have a conference with you." Instructor: "What about?" Student: "What we were talking about two weeks ago." Instructor: "No, I'm sorry. And I'm too busy, and cannot give you more time." Student: "Can I talk with you?" Instructor: "Okay, I'm going to my car, and if you want you can talk until I get to the parking lot." Student: "I've decided to go into psychoanalysis." Instructor: "That so? Why?" Student: "To straighten out my head." Instructor: "Is that why you want to go?" Student: "Yes, I am going wrong." Instructor: "And so you think you need psychotherapy?" Student: "What do you think of my going into psychotherapy?" Instructor: "I think I can do psychotherapy for you right now before we get to the parking lot." Student: "What do you mean?" Instructor: (silence). Student: "I don't understand." Instructor: (silence). Student: "We're here. What do you mean?" Instructor: "Grow up, you stupid son of a bitch!" (Manaster & Corsini, 1982, pp. 149–151)

As shocking as this may seem, it is a success story. At the midterm this student got a good grade. At the end of the term he got straight As in all his courses. He did not go into psychotherapy. If he had gone into formal psychotherapy, he might have played the same game he was playing in school—wasting his father's money and his own time. The final remark to him was therapeutic, but it was not psychotherapy.

In order for an activity to be called psychotherapy it must meet seven basic criteria: (1) there must be a relationship, (2) with good communication having been established, (3) in a setting based on theory, (4) which operates in accordance with that theory, (5) with the aim of improving the total person, (6) by a practitioner trained to help and committed to doing no harm, and (7) while the practitioner is a professional remunerated in payment or in kind. The first five criteria are from Manaster and Corsini (1982), and the last two are added from Hippocrates.

WILL MEDICATION REPLACE PSYCHOTHERAPY?

In his celebrated novel *1984*, Aldous Huxley described a future society that would go through life tranquilized by medication. He further predicted that it would not be necessary for a totalitarian government to emerge that would force the "soma" on the individuals, as the populace would clamor for it. In the last decade there has not only been a rapid proliferation of new types of psychotropic drugs, but the number of persons taking them has mushroomed. Shaffer (1999), speaking as a previous chair of the American Managed Behavioral Healthcare Association, disclosed that managed behavioral care, an industry that covers 75% of all insured Americans, is now spending more money on psychotropics than on all other behavioral care services combined. Such medications are intended for seriously disturbed, anxious, or depressed individuals, and, it is hoped, on a temporary basis. Unfortunately we have so broadened the definition of who might be in need that psychotropics are being given in near perpetuity to individuals who do not want to be bothered with the vicissitudes of life. Over 70% of psychotropic medications are prescribed by primary care physicians who, apparently, do not wish to be bothered by their patients' real problems either (Beardsley, Gardocki, Larson, & Hildago, 1988). Persons who are "prozacked" or "zolofted" consider themselves mellowed out, when in actuality they are lacking passion for anything and come across as shallow.

It may well be that their children are being cheated out of having real, fully engaged parents. They gravitate to other overly tranquilized persons, but friends who have not been tranquilized over long periods begin to find them boring.

The real tragedy, however, is that the problems are not being resolved. A person subject to stress headaches who takes aspirin each time has no incentive to address the stress as long as the pain is masked. Similarly, patients who perpetually avoid life never are ready to discontinue their "soma." Meanwhile the managed behavioral care companies' pharmacy costs have reached astronomical levels. Where once it was the cheap way out, it has now become a financial drain.

Psychotherapy, directed at helping these people grapple with the problems of living, is a viable alternative. In a national study on the four-year experience of psychotherapists with psychotropic medications, Wiggins and Cummings (1998) found that on entering psychotherapy 68% of their patients were taking psychotropic medications prescribed mostly by their primary care physicians, and less often by psychiatrists. At the end of the course of treatment only 13% remained on medication, and these were largely persons for whom the medications were deemed necessary: chronic psychosis (8%), bipolar disorder (3%), children with ADD (1%), and all others combined (1%). This study involved 1.6 million episodes, defined as one patient in one course of treatment (variable from 1 to N sessions, with an average of 6.6 sessions). The cost of the psychotherapy was much less than the perpetual dispensing of psychotropic medications, the newer of which are expensive.

WILL OTHER PSYCHOLOGICAL TREATMENTS REPLACE PSYCHOTHERAPY?

In a controversial and polemic paper, L'Abate (1999) all but delivered the funeral oration for psychotherapy. His thesis is simple and straightforward: "Talk therapy" as the predominant psychological intervention has not lived up to expectations; in the future what constitutes psychological intervention will be determined by empirically derived data; a number of different interventions currently available are as or more effective than one-on-one psychotherapy. L'Abate is correct in his argument that psychologists must expand their therapeutic repertoire to include verified treatments that are not strictly psychotherapy (or "talk therapy" in his parlance), but to declare psychotherapy to be forever ineffective is premature.

Psychotherapy is about to experience a resurgence based on data. In citing the research indicating that "talk therapy" has not been as effective as promoted, and implying that it will never become more effective or efficient than it is now, L'Abate fails to take into account several factors: (1) All psychotherapy is not alike since there are various conflicting schools; (2) all psychotherapists are not alike in their competencies or in their approaches, yet in research they are treated as such; (3) psychotherapy integration is in its infancy; (4) specific psychotherapies for specific conditions are just now coming to the fore as a research interest.

THE DEATH AND RESURRECTION OF CLINICAL ROMANTICISM

William James was not only the father of American psychology, he was also the leading proponent of spirituality, consciousness, meaning, and other existential topics as the appropriate subject matter of psychology. Subsequently, the psychophysicists in Germany, and the early behaviorists in America, quickly eviscerated these concerns from psychology. As the nation progressed into the age of rocket science, the romantic side of psychology all but disappeared. It had a spectacular resurgence during the 1960s and 1970s during the human potential movement, but it was surfeited by its excesses and eventually imploded from its own narcissism. Most proponents retreated to "respectability," with even the professional school changing its name from the Humanistic Institute to Saybrook, although many persist today as part of the humanistic psychology movement.

The humanistic psychologist complains that mainstream psychology has essentially abandoned romanticism, with the result that existential therapy has been excluded from reimbursement. Payers refuse to reimburse for endless sessions of not very sick patients grappling with the philosophical question of meaning. The truth is that humanistic psychology has failed to identify its place in the health system, or to justify third-party payment for its services. This is unfortunate because existential issues can be a necessary part of psychotherapy, and can be the primary issues in many instances. Researchers have despaired while attempting to perform studies with the usual fuzzy variables, but with a little ingenuity such research is possible. Change seems on the horizon.

Schneider (1998b) has developed an approach to testing outcomes in this type of therapy that seems promising. However, he not only must confront the skepticism of the behavioral researchers, he must overcome the flakiness of many in his own camp who believe that even William James was far too pragmatic. As this struggle begins to take shape, there is accelerating interest from a completely unexpected source: primary medical care. Cooper (1995) cites a number of well-controlled scientific studies which demonstrate the benefits of spiritual beliefs on health, some of which are part of ongoing research at Harvard and Cornell medical schools. The benefits of spiritual belief include such diverse responses as decreased depression, less smoking, less alcohol abuse, fewer medical complications in maternity patients and their newborns, decreased incidence of colon and rectal cancer, improved coping with breast cancer, higher self-esteem and emotional maturity, reduced levels of stress, lower blood pressure, increased survival following heart attack, and greater ability to maintain healthy eating habits and overcome obesity. All of these investigations are encouraging, since the essence of psychotherapy must include other than just sterile behavioral variables and concepts.

THE BEST A PROFESSION CAN BE

The first recorded conceptualization of professional ethical principles in western civilization is embodied in the Hippocratic Oath, named after the celebrated Greek physician who was born about 460 B.C. Hippocrates did not have at his disposal a formal professional society to enforce appropriate physician conduct, so he relied on the concept of *ethos,* a Greek word that can be equated with character. To the Ancient Greek philosophers, character was moralistically defined as doing the right thing even if no one else is looking. Therefore, Hippocrates saw *ethos* as the best a profession can be, whereas our modern legalistic codes of ethics and licensing laws define the lowest common denominator in terms of their sanctions. Everything above that line is permissible, but not necessarily desirable, while conduct seen as falling below the least common denominator is punishable.

The Hippocratic Oath was taken by students as they entered training with their mentors. It was surprisingly simple compared to our overly complex codes of today. The first admonition was *do no harm,* and from this followed the prohibition against all forms of exploitation—whether sexual, financial, or otherwise. The physician was thereby exhorted to constantly improve treatment, and in turn had the right to be paid. A little-noted feature of the Hippocratic conceptualization was that the patient also had a set of obligations, which included compliance with treatment, respecting one's own health, and responsibility for payment of the bill.

The remarkable aspect of this moral imperative to do no harm, with its unceasing striving that the profession be the best it can be, is that it lasted over 2,000 years as a voluntary exhortation. This was a reflection of the dynamic balance between the responsibilities of the practitioner and those of the patient. In defining and preserving the essence of psychotherapy, we must include the patient as a partner in the patient's own well-being.

CHAPTER 2

Psychotherapy Is an Amalgam of All Techniques and Competencies

Almost as if on cue, the 100th anniversary in 1992 of the founding of the American Psychological Association became the occasion for a clamor to integrate the various "schools" of psychotherapy. Not only did many of the psychotherapy leadership jump on the bandwagon (Albee, 1992; Beck & Haaga, 1992; Coyne & Liddle, 1992; Goldfried & Gastonquay, 1992; Lazarus, Beutler & Norcross, 1992; Mahrer, 1992; Strupp, 1992), an entire issue that same year of the journal *Psychotherapy* (*29*, 1) was devoted to the subject. It appeared at last that the wars among the theoretical factions would come to an end, giving way to the impending era of outcomes research in which data would transcend dogma.

Indeed, the era of data and guidelines has arrived. However, it is characterized by parochial manuals and guidelines, each

reflecting the theoretical position of its author(s), as well as outcomes research based not on integrated systems but on a determination to establish the efficacy of each of the existing factions.
The pundits of integration disappeared with the end of the cen-
tennial celebration, and when the first integrated system was
published just three years later (Cummings & Sayama, 1995), it
was not even recognized as such. In presenting their numerous
cases, these authors carefully delineated what approach predom-
inated in each (behavioral, cognitive, existential, psychodynamic,
or strategic), and stated why one technique was used over
another. Nonetheless, the critics recognized only their own orientation and regarded other points of view as contaminants. An
internationally renowned behavior therapist asked in an open
meeting, "Why is Nick so psychodynamic?" A highly respected
training analyst in New York wrote after reading the book, "You
have abandoned your psychoanalytic training and have become a
narrow behaviorist." Still another psychoanalytic therapist
exclaimed, "Your theoretical orientation is easy to spot; you are a
strategic therapist." At the same time a well-known Ericksonian
decried the position that "psychodynamics is the road map to the
treatment plan," and further lamented that the book was too existential. It is not surprising, therefore, that the humanists asked
Cummings to represent the standardization (negative) point of
view in the published debate on the importance of clinical
romanticism (Cummings, 1999). All of this would be amusing
were it not a sad reflection of psychotherapy's formidable distance
from real integration.

THERAPEUTIC AMALGAMS AND
EFFECTIVENESS

All of the theoretical orientations of psychotherapy have truth,
but none has *the* truth. If one regards these "schools" as a set of

techniques bound together by an overriding approach to the problems of the patients, it will be seen that each addresses a different part of the universe, so that each is maximally effective with some problems and not as effective with others. By joining these techniques into a whole, using one approach or another as appropriate, we can begin developing specific treatments for specific conditions, so that the overall effectiveness of psychotherapy is enhanced beyond any level possible within the confinement of each parochial system. This integration may be regarded as an amalgam, inasmuch as the parameters of each approach remain identifiable within the comprehensive, effective whole. In chemistry an amalgam is a mixture of different substances for the creation of a new outcome, with each of the original ingredients still identifiable. An example would be the many alloys. On the other hand, in a compound the original ingredients are lost since they result in a totally different substance with no apparent similarity to the originals. An example would be the action of sodium with chlorine, resulting in salt (sodium chloride), a compound that is so different from its original two chemicals that only a chemist would be aware of its origins. Combining the various psychotherapy orientations, using each as appropriately effective based on outcomes research, resembles an amalgam in that each approach remains individually identifiable as it creates a new, more effective total system. Nonetheless, the lines of demarcation from one approach to another are blurred as the determining feature is that of data-derived effectiveness.

The senior author and his colleagues spent three decades developing such a set of amalgams, beginning in 1959 at Kaiser Permanente, then at the Mental Research Institute (Palo Alto), through the Hawaii Project, and finally at American Biodyne. All of this was based on years of outcomes research, and the experimental methodology as well as the resultant amalgams have been fully described (Cummings & Sayama, 1995). The result was a clinical system so effective that it enabled a nationally organized behavioral health delivery system to cover 14.5 million eligible lives through hundreds of psychotherapists trained in the amalgams in a therapeutically effective and cost-efficient manner without the use of such nonclinical cost-containment strictures as utilization review, therapist profiling, preauthorization/certification, case management, and other forms of micromanaging the practitioners. Furthermore, in spite of many millions of patient episodes, because of the system's clinical integrity, there was not a single malpractice suit filed in the seven years the amalgams were operative. It might be useful to work backward, dissecting the system into each of its amalgams, and illustrating the specific usefulness of each and with what kind of patient problem. These are behavioral, cognitive, strategic, humanistic, psychodynamic, and psychopharmacological. Psychopharmacological does not refer to prescribing medication, for under our current system this is done by a psychiatrist, a nonpsychiatric physician, or a nurse practitioner. Rather, it refers to the psychotherapeutic techniques and approaches that both precede medication and contribute to its management and compliance.

Seligman (1998) strongly advocated that psychotherapy should include behavioral, cognitive, humanistic, and psychodynamic models, to which we add strategic and psychopharmacological models of psychotherapy. Seligman missed the importance of amalgams of these models within the whole of psychotherapy; presenting them here is an effort to begin to address the kinds of circumstances that suggest and necessitate the use of one over the other. Heretofore the approach employed has been determined by the therapist's orientation, not the patient's need. In fact, psychotherapy has been the only health endeavor where every psychological condition, regardless of its specificity, received the general approach in which the therapist was trained.

The following discussion of amalgams will lay the groundwork for the specifics to be addressed in later chapters.

PSYCHOTHERAPY IS BEHAVIORAL

Some psychopathology involves maladaptive habits, and behavioral therapy is well suited to address these. In actual therapy as practiced today, there is relatively little psychotherapy that is only behavioral or strictly cognitive. Cognitive/behavioral therapy is common and used for a wide variety of problems, as well as exclusively by some therapists for all problems. What has been regarded as radical (noncognitive) behavioral treatment has been steadily declining, and may be found in its pure form in only a few systems (e.g., Robinson & Hayes, 1997; O'Donohue, 1998). Cognitive therapy, on the other hand, has been rapidly gaining the ascendant position (Garfield, 1998). Nevertheless, pure behavioral approaches persist as valuable interventions, among them relaxation techniques, guided imagery, skills training, and desensitization.

The Case of Elise: Never on Time

The patient was a 28-year-old single woman who had been late for work for as long as she had been employed, beginning at age 18. Her failure to alter this behavior had cost her several jobs in her relatively young career. She entered therapy because a benevolent yet determined boss admonished her to get treatment for this problem or be fired. Her supervisor, a maternal woman 20 years older than Elise, had been overly indulgent and forgiving, repeatedly accepting the patient's contrition, only to be disappointed when the tardiness persisted. Once treatment began, Elise's prominent, psychodynamically trained psychologist viewed her tardiness as both hostility and an attempt to control those around her, beginning with her mother. In grammar school Elise consistently was late to school, resulting in frequent parent/teacher conferences in which her mother was highly embarrassed toward the teacher, and increasingly furious with her daughter. Yet she always accepted Elise's expressed guilt and her promise to do better. This was a recurring theme throughout Elise's school years, giving fuel to the therapist's comparison of the obsequious mother with the equally ineffective female boss.

Elise was late for the first and every succeeding session with the psychologist, and he made the usual negative transference interpretations. As these interpretations were proffered, her tardiness increased, until she arrived for the final session with only five minutes remaining. Seeing no progress after 23 sessions, the boss recommended a psychologist who had helped another employee in the past. The new therapist took a behavioral approach, set up a schedule of increments leading toward timeliness, and arranged with the boss for the appropriate and properly spaced reinforcements. Within 10 weekly sessions the patient was arriving to work either on time, or a few minutes early. Her therapy was terminated after two biweekly follow-up sessions, and the patient indefinitely continued her on-time behavior, not only at work but with other obligations in her life. It was learned that two years later, during which her on-time behavior continued, she resumed treatment to address other issues in her life.

The presence of tantalizing psychodynamics is not sufficient justification to pursue these in the face of repeated failure. In such instances it is not unusual for the sincere psychoanalytically trained psychologist to ascribe the lack of progress to the patient's resistance and then persist in the course of treatment. Even if the resistance were real, the determiner of the technique employed should be effectiveness under the present circumstances, not the stubborn behavior of either patient or therapist. Such resiliency would not brand the therapist as eclectic, which to Lazarus, Beutler, and Norcross (1992) means wishy-washy, poorly trained, or uncommitted. Rather, the psychotherapist needs to be clear on the reasons why one method is preferred over another. Elise was action-oriented, below average in intelligence, and not prone to self-reflection. These are common characteristics in the general population, and although they may not contribute to free-association and subsequent insight, a patient's eligibility for psychotherapy should not be predicated upon any particular dogma's definition of psychological-mindedness. Elise's tardiness, which began with her entry into school at age 5, remained pervasive over two decades. By age 28 it was severely characterological and not likely to be altered by insight therapy.

PSYCHOTHERAPY IS COGNITIVE

Psychopathology can involve maladaptive conscious thinking for which cognitive therapy is ideal. Not infrequently such maladaptive conscious thinking can result in depression or anxiety, and in the overall approach to treating the patient there are times when these should be regarded as secondary diagnoses. Most often, however, the depression and anxiety are treated without touching the underlying faulty thinking which may have achieved lifestyle proportions. Instead, the cognitive aspects of the low self-esteem and the lack of self-confidence are successfully, but not fully, addressed. The depression is alleviated but the cognitive causation is untouched.

The next case will illustrate that merely choosing the appropriate cognitive modality may not be enough. Within such a choice comes the need for skillful decision as to the specific intervention. The second case introduces the concept of an amalgam in the treatment of a recurring agoraphobic.

The Case of Loni: The Perfect Way to Be Perfect

The patient was a 38-year-old married woman with three children. Her husband was a highly paid vice-president for a large corporation, while she ran a successful financial planning business out of her home. She delighted in her three beautiful children who were excelling in school, her attentive executive husband, and a business that allowed her to set her own hours. Her large home in exurbia reflected a high degree of success and her excellent taste. She could not understand why every one-and-a-half to two years she would be unable to cope and would need psychotherapy.

The first breakdown came in college when Loni was unable to turn in her term papers and other homework assignments because she saw her work as inadequate. She became suicidal and was successfully treated in the university counseling center. Since that time, she experienced eleven more episodes, necessitating treatment which was always effective within two to four months. These episodes were typically bouts of severe depression, or involved disabling obsessive-compulsive symptoms. Twice she became agoraphobic and had to struggle to leave the house.

Loni was a perfectionist, the perfect daughter of a perfectionistic father. When she became dysfunctional again at age 38, instead of being treated for depression she was referred to a cognitive perfectionistic lifestyle group program. Highly resistant at first, by the fifteenth and last session, she had drastically altered her thinking and her lifestyle. She no longer subjected herself to unattainable standards, and her husband's perfectionistic demands, which sometimes seemed to replicate those of her deceased father, no longer bothered her. She became more relaxed with her three children, especially toward the daughter she heretofore was certain "would turn out neurotic like me." As of this writing, it has been over seven years since her last recurring episode (adapted from Cummings & Cummings, 1997, p. 335).

The Case of Dedre: Marriage Is for Never

A 53-year-old married woman with two children, Dedre had suffered four previous episodes of agoraphobia during which she was unable to leave the house unless she was accompanied by her husband. The spouse was a highly regarded principal in a national consulting firm who had been called upon four times to relocate to a distant city in order to create and manage a new branch office for the firm. Dedre hated to move and her agoraphobia recurred after each relocation. She was treated with densensitization and an address of the cognitive fear she had of straying too far from home. This thought was always with her in subdued form, but it was exacerbated into panic attacks which rendered her house-bound after each move. Cognitive therapy was successful in treating all four previous episodes, so on the fifth relocation, when she found herself agoraphobic again, Dedre asked and received a referral to a new psychotherapist from her previous psychologist in the city she had just left.

In her fifth treatment, along with the cognitive aspects, her new psychologist became very aware of a persistent, underlying hostility toward her husband that seemed to be apart from her anger at having to move again. He discerned that Dedre was unconsciously angry at her husband all of the time, and this only flared into consciousness when forced to leave her last house and the new friends she had finally made and repeat the process again. The psychologist treated this hostility psychodynamically, and uncovered that Dedre was dissatisfied in her marriage and had wanted to leave her husband for over 25 years. This desire would come to a head each time she was called upon to move, and she prevented herself from leaving her spouse by immobilizing herself with agoraphobia. It was as if she unconsciously was saying to herself, "How can I leave Roger when I can't even leave the house without him." With the resolution of the ambivalence toward the dependent relationship, Dedre became happy in her marriage for the first time in years, lost her previously ever-present fear of straying too far from home, and encouraged her husband to accept an offer to become executive vice-president of a different firm, even though this meant another relocation fresh on the heels of the fifth one.

Had not Dedre's new psychotherapist been skilled in both cognitive and psychodynamic (uncovering) interventions, the patient would have once again experienced temporary relief only to repeat the dysfunctional state in the future. It might be speculated that eventually her repressed unhappiness with her husband would have surfaced into agoraphobia even without having to relocate. As she became older, there would have been more pressure to leave before becoming too old to form a new relationship with another man. The important point is that an amalgam of both cognitive and psychodynamic therapies was needed to fully treat this case, and that such patients may well be the majority of the persons psychologists treat.

PSYCHOTHERAPY IS PSYCHODYNAMIC

The patient's psychopathology may involve unrecognized inner conflicts, and for these psychodynamic approaches are often ideally suited. The more the conflict reflects the failure of repression, the more likely uncovering therapy can reconfigure the conflict toward the restoration of a healthy, workable repression. Here psychoanalytically oriented interventions may well be the treatment of choice. Stated another way, psychodynamic approaches work well with patients on the neurotic, rather than on the personality-disordered, spectrum. Character (personality) disorders are more common today as an outgrowth of the increasingly common dysfunctional family, but pure neuroses still exist.

The Case of Martin and His Pastoral Pornography

A 49-year-old evangelical pastor suffered increasingly poor vision which he attributed to macular degeneration. Several thorough ophthalmology examinations found no pathology of the retina or its macula in either eye, yet the patient's vision continued to deteriorate bilaterally. Functionally, he was almost blind, and needed help in preparing his sermons as he no longer could research and record Biblical and other religious references. He resisted efforts by his ophthalmologists to label his condition psychological, but eventually he agreed to seek psychotherapy for the depression resulting from his "blindness."

Uncovering therapy revealed that Martin had briefly and frantically immersed himself in pornography accompanied by masturbation. His discovery of the "adult bookstore" was preceded by over six months of impotence during which his wife was very understanding, but his performance anxiety became pervasive. Pornography made him potent and temporarily relieved the anxiety. This relief would quickly abate and he would have to seek more pornography, always fearful he would be seen entering the shop by someone who knew him. Therapy was able to connect his "blindness" to his pornographic behavior, first as a perceived punishment from God, and then to his guilt feelings, which identified the visual problem as self-imposed. With this insight Martin's vision returned intact, and he continued treatment for his impotence, which improved steadily.

Although they would not necessarily profit from uncovering therapy, there are patients whose behavior, viewed through their psychodynamic defense mechanisms, reveals a road map to the treatment plan. The subsequent psychotherapy may not be psychoanalytic in nature, but psychodynamic training divorced from the "psychoreligion" can determine the most appropriate intervention.

The Case of Nongrieving Arnold

A widower of 72 was placed in a bereavement program on the basis of his wife's recent death and his subsequent sad behavior. Once he began to participate in the group he did not manifest the typical grief response: missing the deceased and expecting a sudden reappearance, engaging in much affectionate reminiscing accompanied by tears, adopting the deceased's habits or behaviors, frequently calling out the name of the deceased, wanting to be alone with one's thoughts. Rather, Arnold was self-depreciating and tearful, and instead of feeling the expected sadness at the loss, he berated himself for not having been nicer to his deceased wife before she died. He manifested introjection, in which his rage at himself disguised his rage at her. He was rediagnosed as reactive (rage) depression and removed from the bereavement group in favor of individual treatment for his depression.

It became apparent that Arnold had severe unresolved issues with his wife, which had begun fifteen years before when he became impotent after surgical removal of his prostate gland. He later discovered his wife was having an affair with his business partner. Arnold had repressed rage at his deceased wife (not an uncommon defense after the death of a spouse) and had also hidden his own suicidal plan from himself. Arnold was on what suicidologists call "automatic pilot," rushing toward suicide without conscious awareness. With appropriate referral for depression therapy, based on his psychodynamic defense mechanism of introjection, Arnold's life was spared (adapted from Cummings, 1997, pp. 6–7).

PSYCHOTHERAPY IS STRATEGIC

Much of psychopathology defies change in the interest of perpetuating the patient's faulty, inappropriate, or ineffective lifestyles within a larger system. With the increase in the incidence of personality disorders, characterized primarily with the defense mechanisms of denial and projective identification, strategic interventions are required if the psychotherapist is to impact the patient's problems. Many of these personality-disordered patients have been in therapy a number of times, during which they learned to play the game and to derive marginal or secondary benefit without effecting any real change in their lifestyle.

The Case of Raymond: Nor Any Drop to Drink

A 44-year-old man asked for help in quitting drinking after his fourth drunk driving arrest. Raymond was facing a jail sentence for his repeated behavior, and he was referred by his lawyer, who wanted his client in treatment for alcoholism while awaiting trial, ostensibly with the hope of convincing a judge with an overly crowded court calendar of the patient's sincerity and rehabilitation. This ploy had worked twice before and the patient got off with a suspended sentence. On the last drunk driving arrest the patient had hit a twelve-year-old boy on a bicycle, seriously injuring him. Raymond's manipulative lawyer won the case for his client because it was dark and the boy did not have the required lights and reflectors on his bicycle. However, all three arrests were on his record, and the court was not likely to be indulgent on this fourth violation.

A prominent psychologist highly respected by the court was necessary to the lawyer's scheme, and this gave the psychotherapist the leverage to refuse treatment in favor of other psychologists who might more easily be manipulated. The psychotherapist scoffed at the patient's determination to remain sober, pointing to his past behavior as indicative of continued drinking. He offered to make a referral, but lamented that none of the prospective therapists would have the same credibility with the court. "But you can look so contrite, and your lawyer is very clever. I'm sure you'll overcome that small drawback."

Speaking out loud the inner thoughts and schemes of oppositional patients, especially if the therapist can use their own language, often results in the patients assuming the doctor's role. Raymond, indeed, began to talk as if he were the therapist. He insisted he was sincere, that he needed to become sober before his life was ruined, and agreed to a series of treatment steps in which continued abstinence would be the criterion that would convince the ever-skeptical psychologist of the patient's sincerity. Eventually the patient not only remained sober, but at his belated trial date, and in accordance with discussions in his therapy, he agreed to a 90-day jail term to reinforce his successful one-year abstinence. Once out of jail, he made restitution to the family of the boy he had hit with his car. Six years later the patient has remained sober and is an active member of Alcoholics Anonymous. Everyone is pleased, with the possible exception of the criminal defense attorney who had hoped he had a client for life.

With personality disorders adept at splitting the environment, the psychotherapist is often called upon to treat the patient's community along with the patient. An experienced psychotherapist must never be surprised at such patients' inventiveness, or the vulnerability of the well-meaning helpers surrounding them.

The Case of Sharon and Her *Passel* of Pastoral Counselors

A 31-year-old single woman was undergoing religious counseling prior to her being rebaptized as a born-again Christian. Suddenly, during a session with her pastoral counselor, she revealed a second personality who was not only skeptical of the religious process but was possibly even an atheist. The baptism could not take place in the face of this absence of religious conversion, and after it was postponed, the new personality demanded and got her own pastoral counselor. Eventually eight different personalities emerged, each with its own serious religious conflict, and each requiring her own pastoral counselor. Now that Sharon was being seen by every pastoral counselor on the church staff, new "personalities" began emerging on a daily basis. Soon there were over sixty "personalities," and the pastoral counselors were overwhelmed. Finally the exasperated head pastor of the church intervened and a referral was made to a psychologist.

On initial evaluation Sharon was found to be a borderline personality disorder with several previous therapies. The psychologist challenged the nine pastoral counselors to point to one source of scripture in which Jesus Christ addressed any individual as having more than one soul needing salvation. In amazement, they agreed and backed away, allowing the psychologist to treat the patient. Sharon was informed that individual psychotherapy is a treatment limited to the patient and her therapist, and the presence of any other persons violates that confidential relationship. The first time one of the multiple personalities emerged, the psychologist terminated and rescheduled the session. Thereafter Sharon kept out the so-called other personalities, and eventually reported they did not exist. She was baptized and she began a life in a new religious atmosphere where new friends could help her curtail many of her borderline impulses. However, Sharon could not have been treated until her many well-meaning but bungling pastoral counselors were successfully removed from the treatment.

PSYCHOTHERAPY IS HUMANISTIC

Many patients manifest problems of will and responsibility for which humanistic or existential psychotherapy is indicated. The reevaluation of meaning in one's life is not an uncommon experience in mid-life, after a jolting event, or following a heart-rending tragedy. Jungian therapists in the past have addressed problems and reevaluations surfacing in mid-life, but the majority of such work, along with spiritual issues, is the province of the humanistic psychologist. The difficulty has been that by not focusing on what might strictly be regarded as psychopathology, reimbursement for the psychotherapist's services—no matter how important the treatment is to the patient's well-being—has not been forthcoming. There is a limit to the number of potential patients willing to pay out of pocket, and it is not surprising that many of these have been top business executives who could not only afford it financially but whose success accords them the luxury to reexamine their future lives.

The Case of Richard, the Narcissistic Lawyer

This 52-year-old lawyer would seem the last to enter any kind of psychotherapy. Successful, articulate, and flamboyant, he became the lawyer for a celebrity that was the focus of a media frenzy. He relished the national prominence into which he had been suddenly thrust. He played to the cameras, making certain he uttered clever soundbites that would be part of the evening news, and he enjoyed making a splash at the socialite parties to which he now found himself regularly invited. He enjoyed seeing himself on the talk-show circuit and he eagerly accepted every invitation. He had several short-lived affairs with the kind of women who characteristically throw themselves at celebrities. In time, however, his client was no longer the media darling and he faded from view.

Richard refused to accept this reality. He pouted, neglecting his work and his family while he tried to find ways to regain media attention. His wife and children became estranged and his partners, now that he was bringing no money into the firm, demanded more "billable" hours from him. At first he was angry, then he became depressed. His new-found flamboyance disappeared and he lost confidence in himself as he became lonely and isolated. He stopped going to work entirely. He began to reassess his life and entered psychotherapy. His psychologist was impressed that the existential crisis was more important than the consequent depression, and did little to make him more comfortable. Instead he encouraged the patient's struggle.

In time the patient regained his family and he rediscovered his Jewish roots. He became active in his temple and in two Jewish charities, and he restructured his law practice into more meaningful, albeit less lucrative channels. For the first time in his life he felt that life was tranquil, and that he was neither running away from something he did not understand nor chasing something elusive. His health plan, however, paid for only the first eight sessions of a year and a half of semi-weekly treatments.

PSYCHOTHERAPY IS ALSO PSYCHOPHARMACOLOGY

Increasingly psychologists are treating patients whose psychopathology involves a disordered brain or neurochemistry. These patients are receiving medication in conjunction with psychotherapy, which a number of studies reveal to be the optimal arrangement. For some the psychotherapy increases compliance with the medical regimen; for others it provides the psychotherapy which, without the medication, would not have been possible; for still others it completes the treatment necessary for the patient to function effectively. There are very few psychotic and organic conditions for which accompanying psychotherapy is not a desirable, and perhaps necessary, component.

The Case of Sarah and the Wrong Treatment

A 31-year-old single woman had seen three different psychologists over a nine-year period. The change in therapists was the result of relocation—originally from New York to Chicago, and finally to San Francisco. The first psychologist had treated Sarah for a borderline personality disorder, and because of her constant turmoil, poor social relationships, and disastrous employment history, the next two psychotherapists saw no reason to alter the diagnosis. That is, until Sarah suffered the first full-fledged bipolar episode, beginning with mania and culminating in a depression that required hospitalization. During her mania she became very sexually promiscuous, was almost arrested for disorderly conduct, and was apprehended twice for shoplifting. She was placed on lithium, and because she was angry at her psychotherapists for having misdiagnosed her, she did not return to psychotherapy until she required a second hospitalization. It was then discovered that Sarah could feel her emotions even behind the lithium, and although the medication kept her in control, she enjoyed the potential hypomania. At such times she stopped taking her medication so as to experience the "high," and on this occasion she stayed off too long and relapsed. Upon release from her second hospitalization she reentered psychotherapy, which kept her in compliance with her medication and helped her understand and better cope with the fluctuating emotions that were apparent even with the lithium. Sarah not only regained control of her life, but was able to sustain interpersonal relations and even marry. She continued her lithium and her psychotherapy, eventually at a very effective one session per month.

Where in the case of Sarah the initial psychologists interfered with the need for medication, in the following case the medication and subsequent stabilization of the psychosis were the work of a skilled psychologist.

The Case of Gary: I'm Not Crazy

A 34-year-old single paranoid schizophrenic refused to take his antipsychotic medication because he "was not crazy, and only crazy people take that medicine." He was seen by a psychologist upon his discharge from the latest of several hospitalizations, and in his first session he intimated that the medication they gave him in the hospital helped, but he was not crazy. The psychologist, without challenging Gary's belief, used the words the patient had used to describe himself. He was asked whether, indeed, he suffered not from a psychosis, but from "raw, jangled nerves."

The patient enthusiastically jumped on this and complimented the psychologist on her perceptiveness. She then informed him that from her own studies in psychopharmacology the particular medication was very effective with raw, jangled nerves. She lamented that the psychiatrist did not know this and believed that the medication was only for psychosis. Unfortunately, he would not prescribe it unless he believed the patient was crazy, and even more unfortunately this particular psychiatrist insisted on telling his schizophrenic patients they were psychotic. Why not let the psychiatrist believe that Gary was crazy so he could receive free of charge through the health plan the medicine that was so successful for raw, jangled nerves. The patient liked this game, inasmuch as the elements of conspiracy suited his paranoia. He agreed to the plan, and soon he was receiving and taking his medication. Shortly thereafter his psychosis was stabilized and he was able to maintain independent living without hospitalization. Gary delighted in informing his psychotherapist that the plan was an excellent one, that the psychiatrist still thought he was "schizo," and that his raw jangled nerves were gone. The twinkle in his eye and his enormous smile indicated he was wise, but he enjoyed the game and the sense of well-being, and he continued both his medication and his monthly sessions with the psychologist.

CHAPTER 3

The Anatomy of Psychotherapy

There are certain key ingredients common to all psychotherapies, whether behavioral, cognitive, humanistic, psychodynamic, strategic, or pharmacological. It is the presence of these defining characteristics that ultimately will lead to one psychotherapy—empirically derived, and artfully delivered. Before discussing these key ingredients, it is important to look at common misperceptions. Let us first address the things that psychotherapy is not, in spite of the profession's widely held beliefs to the contrary.

PSYCHOTHERAPY IS NOT PAID COMPASSION

Psychotherapists are by necessity compassionate people, but psychotherapy is far more than compassion—which is available through family, friends, the clergy, charities, and the many persons of goodwill in our environment. There are limitations to compassion, and the love of humankind alone does not qualify one to tamper with another person's psyche. The prestige and respect accorded our profession vests a great deal of responsibility in the hands of the practitioner. A never-ending series of critical judgments and decisions, all intended for the healing of the patient, is the ongoing work of the trained, dedicated psychotherapist. There is no place for either an amateur or the unscrupulous.

A psychotherapist obtains years of education and training to do far more than just replicate what is readily available through one's church or temple, the Red Cross, or the Salvation Army, or one of the many do-gooder institutions that are important in and integral to a civilized society. Yet many practitioners see nothing wrong with providing nothing more than weekly solace for a lonely patient who otherwise would have no outside intimate contact. This has been referred to by some cynics as "paid friendship." There are those who would regard the fostering of such dependency as unethical (Austad, 1996). Therapy is the place to achieve understanding, not a safe place to obtain gratification at the expense of the employer, the government, or the taxpayer. Therapy is intended to enable the patient to live a meaningful life in the real world, not to establish residency in the treatment room.

Sometimes the critical decision of the therapist is to provide tough love, challenging the patient's rationalization or denial. Sympathy rather than empathy can be destructive. Sympathy excuses the patient from having any responsibility for his or her own behavior; empathy on the other hand takes cognizance of the unfortunate circumstances having buffeted the patient, and helps the patient achieve a life in spite of them. Sensitivity to victimization is an important part of psychotherapy, while over-victimization ultimately cripples the patient. The therapist's misguided compassion and sympathetic countertransference can be seductive to the patient, fostering dependency and causing the patient to settle for a lot less in life than otherwise might be possible. Often the most compassionate course the therapist can take is to help the patient accept responsibility. This was illustrated in the case of Raymond (Chapter 2), who was helped to take responsibility for his drinking, sparing him from a pattern of alcoholism in which repeatedly driving while drunk might eventually kill or maim someone, destroying his own life in the process.

PSYCHOTHERAPY IS NOT PROTRACTED

Psychotherapy is neither long term nor short term; it is the right length to treat the patient's condition. As such it is both long term and short term, and everything else in between. It should be dictated by effectiveness and efficiency, not psychotherapist bias, narrow training, and incompetence, or, on the other side of the equation, an overly cost-conscious managed care company.

Garfield (1998) has traced the transition during this century of long-term therapy to brief therapy, which has occurred in spite of massive resistance from most privately practicing psychotherapists. Yet before 1937 psychoanalysis was usually concluded in six months and rarely exceeded one year. With the death of Freud, psychoanalysis rapidly became more and more protracted, eventually lasting five, ten, and even fifteen years. At the same time there were concerted and largely successful efforts to restrict psychoanalytic training to persons holding an M.D. degree. When Alexander and French (1946) attempted to return psychoanalysis to its pre-World War II length, their efforts were rebuffed with a surprising degree of hostility. Yet in the last half-century books and training seminars on brief therapy have proliferated to the point that it is difficult to keep up with the field, while books on long-term therapy have dwindled to nothing. Either, as Garfield points out, most patients are now getting brief therapy, or all practitioners already know how to do long-term therapy and need no further training or instruction.

It is easier to see seven patients four times a week over seven years, than to see thirty patients a week for an average of six sessions, with a tremendous turnover resulting in seeing several hundred patients in the same seven years. This enormously hard work, coupled with the scarcity of referrals in an era of psychotherapist glut, results in practitioners not only welcoming long-term therapy, but also fiercely defending it, an attitude Cummings (1995) has attributed in part to "unconscious fiscal convenience."

There is a growing body of evidence that time-sensitive psychotherapies are effective with a large number of patients, perhaps as many as 85% of all those seen in the usual practice (Austad, 1996; Budman & Steenbarger, 1997; Cummings, Pallak & Cummings, 1996; Hoyt, 1995), but it is not advocated that *all* psychotherapy be brief psychotherapy. Even Miller (1996), an outspoken critic of short-term therapy, grudgingly concedes there is a place for time-sensitive psychotherapies and that psychotherapists of the future must be trained in both short-term and long-term interventions to know when to use one or the other.

As early as two decades ago Cummings (1977) found in his research on brief psychotherapy that at least 10% of patients need and should receive long-term therapy, while another 5% are interminable and efficient schedules must be devised which will treat them for life. The clinician of the future will be trained to use short- or long-term therapy as appropriate. When that has been accomplished, the profession will have *clinically determined psychotherapy* rather than the current *clinician-determined psychotherapy.*

There are conditions which unnecessarily prolong therapy, and there are economic pressures that curtail treatment prematurely. In avoiding both of these, there is no substitute for the training and skill of the psychotherapist. Effective psychotherapy embodies certain key ingredients which are present whether the treatment is of long or brief duration. Allowing these elements to flourish will enable the psychotherapist to heal the patient more effectively, as well as more rapidly; patients not only want help, they want it sooner rather than later. Viewed from the perspective of the key ingredients, the arguments revolving around long-term versus short-term psychotherapy become tedious and obsolete.

PSYCHOTHERAPY IS NOT JUST INSIGHT

Insight can be an important accompaniment to therapy, and can often precede change, but it is not in itself therapeutic. Improvement in treatment is reflected in behavioral change, not in insight alone. It is surprising that many therapists espouse insight as a sign of progress, so much so that both the therapist and the patient stack insight upon insight, prolonging therapy and avoiding the awareness that little or no change in behavior is occurring. In fact, so-called insight becomes an end in itself, indulging the patient's narcissism and assuaging the therapist's guilt that the treatment is unnecessarily protracted. The ongoing joke, of course, is Woody Allen, who after twenty-four years of psychoanalysis is a fountain of insight, translating it into entertaining and engaging motion pictures but seldom reflecting it in the way he conducts his personal life. It is parodied in the motion picture *Analyze This,* where the gangster patient (portrayed by Robert De Niro) first denies he was going to kill his psychoanalyst (portrayed by Billy Crystal), but then admits, "Well, yes, I was going to whack you, but I was conflicted about it." The insight into the conflict, though not sufficient to alter murderous behavior, is proffered as progress!

In effective psychotherapy, therapeutic progress must always be measured in demonstrable improvement in behavior. Ideally, the changes in behavior can be quantified and objectively measured. In psychoanalytic training, as well as other forms of psychodynamic training, however, an early cynicism develops regarding the limitations of insight as a precursor to behavioral change. The following question has survived at least six decades of analytic candidates: "If Van Gogh had been psychoanalyzed, would he have cut off his ear?" The answer is, "Yes, but he would have known why." In spite of this almost universal and seemingly ineffectual therapist insight, both patient and analytic trainee then continue to avidly pursue patient insight as if it were an effective goal in itself.

PSYCHOTHERAPY IS NOT CATHARSIS

Defined as the release of anxiety by emotionally reliving the events of the past (Rosenhan & London, 1968), catharsis as an effective therapeutic tool was abandoned by Freud early in his career. This does not refer to the relief a patient characteristically experiences in therapy when his or her problems have finally been admitted and discussed in an accepting atmosphere, but rather to the encouraged dumping of emotions as an end in itself. Catharsis had a national resurgence during the so-called human potential movement of the 1960s and 1970s where it became popular to "let it all hang out." The senior author witnessed time and time again the same individuals at Esalen and other centers catharting week after week as an end unto itself. It resembled chronic diarrhea, where each bowel movement made the person feel only temporarily better, with another and inevitable bowel movement already on the way. It was narcissism personified, and it eventually imploded. Yet an emphasis on catharsis persists with many therapists, and it is the hallmark of pop psychology that to get one's emotions out is healthy.

To the contrary, the work of Williams & Williams (1994) and others has demonstrated that those who are always expressing their anger suffer more high blood pressure and cardiovascular disease than those who control their emotions. Articles, books, and therapists who recommend catharsis as a way of dealing with anger may actually foster aggression in an increasing spiral of discharge-need-discharge-need (Williams & Williams, 1994). Yet ask any citizen on the street whether expressing anger is therapeutic, and the answer will be a resounding yes. No wonder when the analyst (Billie Crystal) in *Analyze This* recommends to the gangster/patient (Robert De Niro) to "hit a pillow when angry," and De Niro empties his pistol into a nearby pillow, the audience resonates approvingly.

Such pop psychology would be irrelevant were it not that many practicing psychotherapists today strongly believe that catharsis is therapeutic, and employ it in their daily work with patients.

KEY INGREDIENT 1: PSYCHOTHERAPY IS A CORRECTIVE EMOTIONAL EXPERIENCE

Our patients either come from a dysfunctional background or they have created an environment for themselves that is dysfunctional. In most of our patients both are true, for we learn to be adults and derive our parenting skills from the adults who parented us. Thus any dysfunction is passed from generation to generation, guaranteeing that psychotherapists will never run out of patients. However, there are exceptions to this sequence. Many individuals who grew up in pathogenic families or in conditions of poverty or abuse seem to overcome their backgrounds and interrupt the cycle. Even some previously dysfunctional families undergo a "purification" process and become successful.

In providing a corrective emotional experience, the psychotherapist, as a parent figure, must offer an emotional atmosphere that is much different than the one in which the patient grew up and probably continues to reside. This does not mean, however, that it is incumbent upon the therapist to make up for the unfortunate things that have happened to the patient or to excuse the patient for the self-imposed misfortunes. The therapist is a professional, not a substitute parent, whose job it is to understand and impart resiliency to the patient.

RESILIENCY

The profession of psychology has just recently begun to study the concept of resiliency. In the past we have been so intent on studying and understanding pathology that we have overlooked the fact that most persons subjected to psychological pathogens do not grow up to be neurotic, personality-disordered, or psychotic, just as most people who are exposed to a virus do not succumb to it. Nature by definition *is* resiliency, but in our patients this psychological "immune system" did not protect them. Now, however, just as medicine is discovering ways to bolster the physiological immune system, psychologists are on the threshold of discovering the components of psychological resiliency. One extensive study, the Lilly Family Depression Project (Budman & Butler, 1997), seeks to discover the factors that enable some children growing up with depressed parents to escape becoming depressives themselves, and is experimenting with ways to teach this resilience to those who lack it.

This has been called the building of buffering strengths by Seligman (1998), who urges psychotherapists to impart to their patients such strengths as courage, interpersonal skill, rationality, insight, optimism, honesty, perseverance, realism, capacity for pleasure, putting troubles into perspective, future-mindedness and finding purpose. In his promoting a "positive psychotherapy," Seligman acknowledges that much of the benefit may be ascribed to a placebo effect.

Independently viewing the problem of placebo and arriving at a similar conclusion, Salzinger (1998) insists it is time psychologists stop lamenting the placebo effect and start using it therapeutically. Medicine has known for some time that the placebo effect has an impact on strengthening the immune system (Cooper, 1995; Kemeny, 1996), and the best predictor of the strength of the placebo effect has been the provider of the treatment (Shapiro & Morris, 1978). Accordingly, medical students have long been taught to present a treatment positively and with optimism.

Acceptance of the Patient

Empathy is what enables the psychotherapist to accept and understand the patient. This understanding provides the psychotherapist with a critical judgment upon which therapeutic decisions can be made, all in the best interest of the patient. Without empathy the therapist is unable to step into the patient's shoes or respect and understand the patient's often fierce resistance to change. Resistance is not the enemy of psychotherapy; it underscores the patient's terror at leaving something familiar, even if unworkable, to adopt something scary and unknown. It reminds the therapist that the solution to the patient's conflict has not yet been made apparent, and that he/she must work harder to help the patient through the barriers of fear.

It is empathy that prevents the therapist from behaving like the detached parent, who, not understanding the patient, is either punitive or indulgent. For most therapists the imperative not to be judgmental is so overblown that the mistakes made will invariably be made on the side of indulgence. Examples are guilt-reduction interventions in sociopaths and personality disorders, particularly borderline patients who are so adept at feigning remorse. This is absolutely antithetical to productive psychotherapy, and is akin to a firefighter trying to extinguish a fire by pouring gasoline on it.

Prohibiting self-destructive behavior, and the provision of needed boundaries, in impulse-ridden patients requires a great deal of empathy, and therapists who lack it shy away from doing the difficult therapeutic endeavor.

The presence of empathy prevents the psychotherapist from losing distance from the patient, resulting in the loss of objectivity. Without empathy the therapist may overly identify with the patient, responding in the manner with which such a practitioner would like to be indulged under similar circumstances. These therapists hide behind cries of authoritarianism when, on behalf of the patient, they are required to be authoritative. They take the cheap approach. Excellent examples of this are the therapist who obtains the adolescent's approval by joining with him or her against the parents, or the therapist who sides with the patient against the spouse, both in defiance of reality or beneficial treatment.

THE SQUEAMISH PSYCHOTHERAPIST

Perhaps the greatest liability for the therapist who lacks empathy is the compulsion to be overly accepting. Although this may be appropriate for many neurotically guilt-ridden patients, it is fodder for the personality-disordered patient. Consider the typical sequence in the treatment of the borderline patient whose main mechanism is that of projective identification. The patient becomes more and more demanding, threatening suicide as an excuse for calling at all hours. The therapist struggles to be accepting and responds to the patient's demands, only to find them increasing. The therapist begins to feel anger, an emotion not permitted for the all-accepting practitioner, so this is quickly covered by more accepting behavior. As this sequence escalates, the therapist is suppressing more and more anger, all the while the typically adroit borderline, realizing the therapist's trap, takes the process beyond the therapist's control. Eventually the psychotherapist is exasperated, but without admitting rage, confesses a lack of ability to treat such a complex case and refers the patient on. The patient gloats, having "proven" the projective identification (it is not I but those around me who are no damn good), and goes after the next therapist's scalp.

Consider a far more therapeutic approach to such a patient, remembering that patients do not expect us to be accepting of their obnoxious behaviors, but that they do expect us to be nonpunitive and not to abandon them. The aforementioned overly accepting therapist did, indeed, abandon the patient in spite of all the probable therapeutic rationalizations. A skillful therapist would not hesitate to say to a patient in a firm, but nonpunitive manner, "What is going on today? You are even more obnoxious than usual." Such a statement is far more reassuring to a patient who realizes the therapist is cognizant of the obnoxious behavior and still works with him/her, versus the patient who worries that any day now the therapist will realize "how awful I am and will dismiss me". It is appropriate to place limits on after-hours phone calls and all other acting-out behaviors that could jeopardize the success of therapy.

In training sessions with the squeamish therapist, the authors ask the following question: "Would you go to a surgeon who is afraid of the sight of blood? How could such a surgeon do the difficult incisions, especially if they involved saving your life? Then why should you expect a patient to see a psychotherapist who is afraid of psychic blood? How could that therapist do the incisive intervention?"

KEY INGREDIENT 2: PSYCHOTHERAPY IS CONDUCIVE TO GROWTH AND CHANGE

Growth is the striving of all living organisms, and psychological growth is unique to human beings. Psychological growth requires achieving a deeper and broader identity through overcoming developmental crises throughout life. These crises arise out of developmental tasks such as entering school, the advent of adulthood, marriage, parenthood, divorce, mid-life changes, adapting to old age, and facing death. A more mature identity is both the result and means of fulfilling these developmental tasks.

PSYCHOTHERAPY IS ALWAYS THE LAST RESORT

Although growth is inevitable, in our patients the growth process has gone awry. It is the function of the psychotherapist to restore healthy growth by helping the patient remove the impediments. The patient cannot move forward until the anxiety inherent in the magnitude of the changes necessary is overcome. In the face of this anxiety the patient continues the behavior that is nonworkable. Typically, the patient has tried every permutation of the dysfunctional behavior, and entering psychotherapy is the final resort. Almost never is it the first response. But because the patient has ostensibly entered psychotherapy, it does not follow that the patient is eager for change and will not sabotage the progress. One needs to be especially vigilant with the patient that is in and out of therapy as a way of life. Being a psychotherapy patient is often an excellent way to avoid change!

RESISTANCE AND THE REPETITION COMPULSION

As previously stated, it is the psychotherapist's responsibility to allay anxiety so that the patient can accept change, but it is also important to skillfully accentuate the anxiety when it is the best way to propel the patient forward. For example, a spouse-abusing husband will quickly lose any motivation to change and will bolt therapy if the wife prematurely forgives him and lets him back into the house. Continuing the separation can be a source of tension that keeps the patient in therapy.

For years psychotherapists have been unable to explain the repetition compulsion. Why does a behavior that is not successful and results in even more pain persist? Why is it not subject to extinction? To account for it Freud devised the death wish, a metapsychological concept that falls far short of explanation. Probably the best explanation is found in B.F. Skinner (1952), who determined that behavior learned at critical developmental windows was difficult, if not impossible, to extinguish. Extrapolating this to the clinical phenomenon of the repetition compulsion, the first successful response to a trauma becomes the modus operandi for life. The learning curve is instantaneous and the extinction curve is zero. The following examples illustrate how repetition compulsion begins.

A baby can learn panic attacks as a modus operandi in the following way. On her way home a mother remembers she needs a loaf of bread and a quart of milk, and she pulls into the parking lot of a convenience store. The baby, who is at a critical point in its development, is asleep in the car seat. The mother decides to run in quickly without awakening the baby, but, conscious of predators, she carefully locks the car. As is often the case, the purchase takes longer than expected, the baby awakens, and not seeing the mother begins to cry. Well-meaning strangers try to comfort the baby through the locked windows, which only adds to the infant's anxiety. Panic mounts, and just when the baby is at the top of the panic scale, the mother arrives and scoops the child up in her arms. The baby has learned that any time you are abandoned, have a panic attack! Despite its never working again throughout that person's life, a panic attack is the response to everything from threat of divorce to failing a class in school.

In a second example, a mother gets sick and goes to the hospital during the critical age of an infant. She is away several days. The infant gets increasingly depressed, refuses to eat, sleeps all day, cries all night, and refuses comfort. The baby becomes severely clinically depressed, and at the height of the depression, mother comes home from the hospital. The infant learns that the solution is to have a depression! Thereafter, that patient, during every trauma—whether it is divorce, childbirth, loss of a job—will react with depression, even though it is never rewarded again.

Eradicating that first successful response to trauma that happened at a critical age is impossible. If this is the goal, therapy is interminable. The more realistic goal is to enlarge the patient's repertoire to frustration and anxiety so that he or she does not reflexively fall back on the response that was successful in infancy.

THE THERAPIST AS CATALYST

While the first successful response to trauma is imprinted on everyone, not all people need psychotherapy. Children growing up in a normal, healthy environment will develop many other adaptive alternatives in the course of living. In the absence of this adaptive development, psychotherapy provides the corrective emotional experience.

There is another dynamic that drives the repetition compulsion. Not only anxiety, but the striving for growth compels us to repeat scenarios or scripts that are symbolic equivalents of early traumas upon which we are fixated. This repetition is an attempt to achieve mastery. To the extent that our energies are fixated on early trauma, they are not available for growth. Therefore, we are compelled to repeat the experience of the original trauma in order to free our energies to grow. When this repetition occurs in relation to the therapist, the skillful practitioner will respond in a way to bring insight and closure, thus freeing the patient for the next step in growth. Often it is surprising how a lifetime of repeating a scenario can be telescoped into one catalytic event with the therapist, resulting in rapid understanding and progress.

The Case of Lester, the Limpid Librarian

A 28-year-old single man came into treatment because he was unable to finish his doctoral dissertation in mathematics. He was an obsessional man whose very high intelligence was being crippled by ruminative thinking that never arrived at a conclusion. During his course work he excelled, probably because mathematics has a definite answer on either side of an equation. Now faced with a dissertation in which he was required to engage in speculative thinking, his behavior was one of paralysis; he was unable to move ahead and equally unable to walk away from the task. This had been going on for over two years, during which time he took a job in the local library for which he was markedly overqualified. In the first three sessions he was stilted in his speech, grossly overintellectualizing trivia revolving around his flunky job, and unable to discuss anything of importance. Emotional tone was nonexistent.

During these sessions the therapist learned that Lester's father was a controlling man who hid his own emotions in overintellectualization. The home resembled a library. Each of the children were regularly assigned books to read that were chosen by the father, who began each dinner with, "In accordance with your assigned reading, the topic for discussion at the table tonight is Homeric scholarship as seen through the differing eyes of the English versus German classicists" (or some other such utterly esoteric subject that was far removed from anything in this family's real life). Lester complained bitterly about his father's controlling intellectualizations, but he continued living his life according to the "library" rules in which he was brought up. At the end of the third session the therapist assigned three books, one each on Freud, Jung, and Adler. As he removed them from his bookcase he asked that the patient read these before the next session. The patient brightened up, as here was something he could easily do. The therapist began the fourth session by stating, "Our topic for today pertains to who was the better therapist, Freud, Jung, or

Adler." Lester was startled but he complied. When he asked for feedback on his discussion, he seemed perplexed to hear the therapist mouth a series of platitudes. This was repeated for two more sessions, with books on Carl Rogers, Milton Erickson, Erik Erikson, Karen Horney, Frieda Fromm-Reichman, and Jay Haley. In session five when Lester asked what the relevance of all this was to his inability to complete his dissertation, the therapist's response mimicked the father's usual cryptic coldness: "I'll be the judge of that."

Half way through session six, during which the therapist asked the patient to compare Erikson's life stages to Freud's psychosexual development, Lester broke. He began to yell and shake as can only an obsessional who has lost his isolation. He screamed, "I don't have to do this shit!" The therapist screamed back with equal volubility, "I know you don't have to do this shit, but do you *really* know it? Your whole life is shit!" Lester sank back into his chair stunned. His behavior was remarkably different from then on. Gone was the stilted, overintellectualized and emotionless Lester. There emerged a new Lester who did not know exactly how to walk, talk, or think, but who was no longer terrified of leaving both libraries—one the place of employment and the other the place of emotional paralysis. He finished his dissertation with unprecedented rapidity, and he continued in therapy to complete other unfinished aspects of his life.

KEY INGREDIENT 3: PSYCHOTHERAPY IS AN UNDERSTANDING OF THE TRANSFERENCE RELATIONSHIP

By its very nature, the psychotherapist-patient relationship will more or less, depending on the intensity of the treatment, resemble the parent–child relationship. It is fertile ground for all manner of childhood and adolescent emotions, ranging from differentiation through dependency. The term transference applies strictly to the therapist's becoming, in the eyes of the patient, the embodiment of the parent or other significant persons in the patient's life. Therapist anonymity is the backdrop upon which transference feelings flourish, since the absence of information allows the patient to see in the therapist that which he or she expects to see.

Freud regarded transference as pivotal in psychoanalysis, for it was the fulcrum upon which the neurosis would begin to unravel. Through interpretation of the transference, the patient attains an understanding of the unconscious conflicts that determine how the environment is viewed and subsequently engaged. To Freud the neurosis was easily understood, but to treat it there must be substituted the "transference neurosis," which, once established, is persistent and requires long-term intervention before it will yield. As psychoanalysis became longer and longer, Freud regarded the transference neurosis as perhaps stubborn, or even intransigent. Yet he defended free association and its resulting lengthy treatment by stating, "The application of our therapy to numbers will compel us to alloy the pure gold of analysis plentifully with the copper of direct suggestion" (Freud, 1933, p. 402). There are two well-known stories that contradict Freud's own words. He reputedly cured Gustav Mahler of impotence during a three-hour walk in Lyden, Holland. This occurred in about 1909, just before Mahler came to America to take over the New York Philharmonic Orchestra. Furthermore, in three sessions he cured the pain in Bruno Walter's conducting arm, enabling his return to work.

The transference neurosis may be positive or negative, but it does not necessarily follow that a positive transference always facilitates therapy while a negative one impedes treatment. A positive transference can reflect dependency and can even become erotic, thus crossing over into a negative transference inasmuch as the realization of the patient's love fantasies would disarm the therapist as an effective practitioner. The transference neurosis is fraught with dependency, prolonging therapy. Such undue dependency is invariably accompanied by anger at the situation. The transference neurosis is, therefore, intense and ambivalent.

It must be appreciated that Freud was a pioneer and a genius. In nineteenth century Vienna it was unthinkable that anyone would confide innermost thoughts to another, and especially if these involved sexual fantasies or conflicts. In response to this cultural inhibition, Freud devised the couch, which was the antithesis of conversational posture and by its novelty enhanced talking. He further facilitated free association by sitting behind the couch and out of view. In the present era, however, when people appear on television to deluge us with their innermost "secrets," while off television pestering anyone who will listen to their litany of complaints, the couch is no longer a useful therapeutic instrument. Constipation has been replaced by diarrhea, with no demonstrable improvement in the treatment process or its accompanying neuroses. The personality disorder has proliferated, replacing inhibition with the need to learn civility, restraint, delayed gratification, and the propriety of when to shut up. There are many facets in the way transference neurosis is conceptualized that are as obsolete as the couch. Effective, efficient psychotherapy demands that the intensity of the transference relationship be maintained while eliminating, or at least modulating, the transference neurosis.

Intensifying the Transference Relationship While Minimizing Dependency

Effective psychotherapy, by its very nature and especially if it is focused, is intense. It is corrective, active, strategic, direct, interpretive, modifying, and restrictive (Cummings & Sayama, 1995). Built into effective psychotherapy, however, are a number of techniques which continue the intensity of the relationship while reducing drastically the potential dependency. Ultimately this combination enhances therapy, and includes the following techniques.

THE THERAPEUTIC CONTRACT: PARTNERING WITH THE PATIENT

From the beginning of therapy it is important to involve the patient as a partner in her or his own treatment. At the first session the therapeutic contract makes clear that the therapist is there to serve as a catalyst, but the patient is the one who will do the growing. This contract is stated: "I will never abandon you as long as you need me, and I will never ask you to do something until you are ready. In return for this I ask you to join me in a partnership to make me obsolete as soon as possible" (Cummings, 1988, p. 312–313).

This contract is based on a simple but pervasive principle which has been called the intrinsic Patient Bill of Rights: "The patient is entitled to relief from pain, anxiety and depression in the shortest time possible and with the least intrusive intervention" (Cummings, 1988, p. 312).

This therapeutic contract not only makes clear the therapist-patient partnership, but also indicates that as soon as the patient is ready, he or she will be asked to do something important in his or her own behalf. This sets the stage for the homework.

HOMEWORK

More than anything else, it is the assignment of homework that convinces the patient that she or he is, indeed, a therapeutic partner. It intensifies the relationship in that it keeps active the therapeutic situation throughout the intervening period while the patient is performing the homework. It fosters independence because the therapeutic process is not defined by two, three, or even four sessions a week. It further promotes independence because the patient is actually accomplishing something behaviorally.

There is no available "cookbook" of homework assignments. Rather, the homework is tailored to the needs of each patient. It must be in keeping with the therapeutic contract in that it is something the patient can do, yet it must be difficult enough so the patient returns with a sense of accomplishment. It should always be in the direction of the next step in change or improvement for each particular patient. The homework is assigned for the intervening period with the patient's understanding and consent. Again, in keeping with the thrust of therapeutic partnership, failure to complete the homework requires that the patient come in, acknowledge the failure, and then forfeit the session.

In all of this the therapist must be in tune with the patient so that the homework is doable, and then be able to draw "psychic blood" and send the patient home if the doable homework has not been completed. When this technique is properly and skillfully executed, the therapist will be amazed at how much the appropriate assignment and enforcement of homework will increase the intensity of the therapeutic alliance without a corresponding increase in dependency. Instead of the negative transference of anger, the patient displays pride in and satisfaction with demonstrable benchmarks of accomplishment.

SYNCHRONIZING THERAPEUTIC GOALS

There is enough understandable resistance to change without burdening the treatment with a wrestling match between a therapist and a patient because they are inadvertently pursuing antagonistically different goals. Patients come to us wanting to be good patients, so they will mouth lofty goals (the *explicit* contract proffered by the patient), all the while hiding the true, or *implicit* contract. The result is that therapist and patient are working toward different goals, frustrating both of them.

In every case somewhere in the first session the patient will reveal the true goal, but usually in such a way that it is most likely overlooked by a therapist who latches onto that goal which most likely coincides with a standard therapeutic mission. For example, a patient comes to therapy ostensibly to save his marriage. Sometime during the first session he will drop the real reason: "I'm afraid no matter how hard I try, my marriage will end in divorce." Setting aside the explicit contract (save my marriage), the implicit contract and real goal is to divorce yet be able to say, "I did everything to save my marriage, including going into psychotherapy." The transference in this relationship in every sense can be described as a wrestling match, with the therapist baffled because the patient frustrates every attempt to save the marriage, while the patient feels betrayed because the therapist does not discern what he really wants. Watzlawick (personal communication, May 1980) laments that these wrestling matches occur in thousands of psychotherapy sessions with an equal number of practitioners every day, all the while the therapist is ascribing the lack of progress to patient resistance.

THE OPERATING ROOM IS NOT A HOTEL ROOM

It would never occur to a surgeon to allow a patient to see the operating room as anything other than a necessary but artificial chamber that must be vacated as soon as the surgery is performed. After a brief period in the recovery room, the patient is encouraged to become ambulatory as soon as possible and undertake doable exercises, such as walking to the bathroom or down the hospital corridor. Yet when the senior author was in psychoanalytic training, he was taught to require the patient to promise he or she would make no life decisions until his or her analysis was completed. The patient was exhorted to regard the therapy as the most important event in her or his life. Not only do these attitudes foster dependency, but how can one make the kinds of decisions which will eventually enable the termination of therapy?

In effective psychotherapy the patient is discouraged from making premature or impulsive decisions, but is, nonetheless, encouraged to make appropriate decisions at regular intervals. The homework is frequently the vehicle for these decisions, but equally often the changes in behavior are initiated by the patient. In all aspects the patient must regard the treatment room as a temporary, necessary, and artificial situation, with life being in the real world. To the extent the emotionally troubled patient must be in a therapeutic cocoon in the beginning, this cocoon is the vehicle through which the patient undergoes a metamorphosis and flies away from therapy and into life.

The therapist must guard against any form of gratification occurring in the therapy rather than in the real world. Allowing dependency, whether it is found in a therapeutic drift that enables the patient to avoid the uncertainty of change or a cozy relationship that for the lonely patient is a substitute for real friendships and interpersonal commitments, is counter to productive therapy. The therapy can be pleasant at times, but enjoyment, accomplishment, fulfillment, and satisfaction take place in the patient's real world, not in the safety of the therapist's office. Denying the patient gratification again raises the intensity of the relationship without a commensurate increase in dependency. Rather, it has the effect of propelling the patient toward freedom.

SIMULATING THE TRANSFERENCE

According to Chapman (1978), Harry Stack Sullivan was a master at emulating the patient's transference as a therapeutic tool to greatly intensify the relationship while catapulting the patient toward independence. For example, a young man that was ostensibly mourning the premature death of his father was unconsciously masking his rage at the man he regarded as an indifferent, rejecting parent. His therapist discerned that the patient also hated his sister, who was blatantly favored by the father. Yet the patient could not come to grips with his hostility for either. In time the patient could be edged closer to his feelings, but the therapist chose to hasten the process for the sake of the patient, who was suffering a profound reactive depression. In a session in which the patient was mouthing how much he missed his father, the therapist first walked to the window and lamented that the rainstorm had the potential to ruin his golf game scheduled for later that day. It should be noted the father had missed the patient's high school graduation with the excuse he had an imperative business meeting when, as the patient years later learned, he was actually playing golf. The patient seemed baffled and fell into silence, during which time the therapist began reviewing another patient's chart. Annoyed, the patient asked the therapist what he was doing. The therapist replied that this woman was a very difficult case and one who needed his most profound attention, much more than did the patient. The patient erupted into fury, accusing the therapist of being no better than his golf-addicted father, who cared only for the sister. The therapist allowed the patient to vent his rage for half an hour while flailing about the room, after which he yelled, "I'm not your father!" The patient was stunned, fell back into his chair, thought long and hard, and finally broke his own silence: "That is what this is all about, isn't it?" The patient was literally catapulted out of his depression and in subsequent sessions began grappling with his real conflicts, having been spared weeks, and perhaps months, of therapy that would have been necessary without this technique.

Simulating the patient's transference is an extremely effective technique, but one which should be undertaken after careful deliberation and only by a very skilled psychotherapist. Will it intensify the relationship? Yes. Will it decrease the dependency? Absolutely.

Finally, it goes without saying that the gender of the therapist has impact on the transference only at the beginning of treatment, and even then minimally in most cases. The exceptions include such untoward situations as a woman who has been raped or was molested by her father, and who has an understandable difficulty relating to a male therapist. Once the therapeutic process is in full bloom, mother and father transferences occur with regularity toward both female and male therapists.

COUNTERTRANSFERENCE

All therapists are cautioned against, and trained to refrain from, countertransference behavior, defined as a loss of objectivity in which the patient is seen in terms of the therapist's own needs. However, Harry Stack Sullivan (Chapman, 1978) has conceptualized countertransference as a therapeutic tool. For example, instead of acting on his or her own response to the patient, the therapist who finds an anger toward the patient welling up might ask, "I wonder if this patient is trying to make me angry?" This provides the therapist with cues that otherwise would not be present if the therapist were attempting to suppress and hide the feeling. In some well-thought-out instances, it would even be appropriate for the therapist to ask the patient, "I find myself getting somewhat annoyed. I wonder why you might be purposely trying to make me angry." Such cues can be valuable in treating not only the angry patient, but also seductive, manipulative, and elusive patients. This useful technique requires not only a great deal of skill, but also even more understanding of the countertransference and its usually destructive force.

KEY INGREDIENT 4: UNDERSTANDING THE PATIENT'S MODUS OPERANDI—THE PARATAXIC DISTORTIONS

There are authorities who equate transference and parataxic distortions, but it is useful to separate the two. Transference per se can be regarded as the characteristics the patient imbues in the therapist because of past experiences with significant persons. The therapist is seen as having the attitudes, responses and behaviors toward the patient that these close figures once had in early life. On the other hand, a parataxic distortion is the characteristic manner in which a patient deals with those in her or his life, especially if they represent close, dependent, or otherwise important relationships. It is the patient's modus operandi in dealing with life. It is no longer the reliving of past emotional events, but rather a daily reaction to everything in life.

In the treatment room, according to Sullivan, there are three persons: "(1) the parataxically distorted imaginary therapist, (2) the patient who is interacting with this illusory therapist, and (3) the actual participant-observing therapist who is seeking to identify whom the parataxically distorted therapist represents. The therapeutic task is also to discover what the parataxic distortion is seeking to accomplish. Unmasking a parataxic distortion often precipitates anxiety. It is one thing to talk about a traumatic interpersonal association in one's past life (transference) and another to discuss a painful relationship with the involved person sitting a few feet away" (Chapman, 1978, pp. 121–122).

This differentiation is important in understanding the patient so as to enable that patient to understand one's own behavior. Consider the statement, "That's a dull necktie you have on today, doctor." This may reflect the patient's feeling that he or she is being rejected by the therapist in a manner similar to that of his or her conservatively dressed, rejecting father (i.e., transference). Or it may represent the patient's guilt and fear of reprisal for being angry with the therapist for having to be in a dependent, unavoidably one-down relationship (i.e., projection of one's own anger). In the first instance the patient may be reacting angrily to an interpretation the therapist made at the last session, which the patient sees as "typical of my rejecting father." In the second instance the patient is responding with characteristic hostility to any situation perceived as having some power over her or him.

The parataxic distortion is an attempt to communicate and respond to interpersonal situations in a warped manner. To Sullivan, as with Erik Erikson (1963), there is the assumption of an underlying tendency to health to the former, and growth to the latter. In this view the therapist's task is to help the patient remove the obstructions so that the tendency to health can resume. In the words of Sullivan, "The problem in the garden is not the flowers, but the weeds; if the weeds are eliminated, the flowers grow in a healthy way" (Chapman, 1978, p. 132).

KEY INGREDIENT 5: UNDERSTANDING THE PATIENT'S INNER CONFLICTS

It may seem curious to the reader that this key ingredient is listed following the initial four since it would seem that inner conflicts are the very core and definition of the patient's difficulties. Yet in most instances the preceding key ingredients are the vehicles for the resolution of the patient's inner conflicts, especially so because most conflicts we encounter in our patients eventually are revealed as interpersonal problems. A listing of all the possible inner conflicts is impossible because they are infinite. However, if one looks at the most common conflicts confronting the therapist, a group of conflicts that would describe as many as three-fourths of our patients becomes apparent.

PROBLEMS WITH INTERPERSONAL CLOSENESS

Fear of closeness has been present long before there was psychotherapy of any kind. However, there has never been a generation in the last 150 years in which alienation and fear of closeness have been so paramount. As many as half of the so-called baby-boomers are single when one defines the term to include couples living together but not married.

A very common syndrome is the inability to get along with a love object once a serious commitment has been made to that relationship (marriage, parenthood). In the treatment room it is common to see men and women who have had as many as three divorces, yet have been living successfully with someone without marriage for the past several years. Often this "living together" exceeds in length all of the defunct marriages. In keeping with the limitations of insight, a person who cannot handle commitment eagerly responds: "I don't do marriage well. If I married John (or Jane) we would be divorced in no time." Other ways of avoiding closeness are various marriages of convenience, open marriages, or consistently marrying someone who is certain to be incompatible, as well as frequently ending a relationship only to begin another brief one, all the while declaring this is the one! By consistently choosing someone who has an even greater commitment problem, the individual can lament, "It is not I but my partner who fears commitment."

Growing older is terrifying to the baby-boomer because there is a gnawing awareness that "when I am old there will be no one looking out for me." Most of the current elderly generation is blessed with a plethora of family caretakers, who out of love and closeness will see to it that the older adult, with or without Alzheimer's, will not be neglected. It is no wonder that the aging baby-boomer generation, finding itself without this safety net, is buying unverified herbal products at an unprecedented rate in a desperate but losing effort to stave off the aging process. These fears of closeness probably involve more than half of our patients today if one regards drug abuse as just another manifestation of the same problem. The psychotherapist of the future will have to contend in psychotherapy with an entirely different array of problems that will be the consequences of a lifelong fear of closeness in the next Medicare population.

APPROACH-AVOIDANCE CONFLICTS

It is not unusual to want something and fear it or reject it at the same time. The person that wants to become a professional may hate college because it requires studying, and thus be thwarted in the desire to achieve. A compromise is to attend college for as long as possible before being thrown out or until parents stop paying for it. This is a familiar problem in student counseling centers. There are indulgent, tuition-oriented colleges that will play the game up to a point, allowing the student to take a light load of Mickey Mouse courses. But eventually there is a day of reckoning even here.

The variety of approach-avoidance problems is all but infinite, and the therapist has to be wary of the patient's motivation. Is it to find a way of continuing the compromise, or is it a serious concern with the problem?

A typical approach-avoidance problem is one that represents a continuance into adulthood of the adolescent problem of the dependency-autonomy conflict. Stated simply, it demands that the individual be relieved of responsibility while being allowed to indulge in anything he or she desires. There are benchmarks along the way in which the approach-avoidance conflict can be manifested: high school, college, a job, courtship. Some individuals get through closeness and marriage only to have their stability derailed by the responsibility of parenthood. Approach-avoidance conflicts can be encountered at every stage of life, often without any apparent warning. It is not unusual to trace these back to stages in life in which their own parents failed.

GUILT REACTIONS

These include guilt feelings resulting from a multitude of behaviors that violate the individual's religion, morality, acknowledged responsibility, social view, ethics, sense of empathy, or correctness.

Guilt reactions also include a failure of repression in individuals who are aware of incompatible desires but who have not actually acted upon them. These are neurotic reactions, rather than personality disorders, where the feelings of guilt are difficult to ignore or push aside. There may be compensatory behaviors, such as making a financial contribution to a children's advocacy organization after having emotionally neglected or physically abused one's own children. But usually the perpetrator does not completely escape the gnawing feeling of being wrong or inadequate.

In these cases the therapist must skillfully separate actual guilt from neurotic guilt without condemning the patient or being punitive. Certainly abusing a child should invoke guilt, and that is a healthy emotion. That guilt-ridden parent is eager to overcome the short fuse that results in the unacceptable (and illegal) behavior. On the other hand, there are guilt-ridden individuals who have not hurt anyone but who neurotically imagine they have or will. For these individuals guilt-reduction therapy is in order, such as in the following example.

The Case of Elmira

Married with two children, this 33-year-old woman kept having the obsession that her six-month-old daughter would suffocate from sudden infant death syndrome (SIDS). This fear was particularly strong when Elmira was emotionally upset. During such times she would spend sleepless nights going into the baby's room every twenty minutes to make certain she was still breathing. She had read that a child should not be placed in a certain position in the crib, but she could never remember which was the potentially lethal position, face down or face up. All night long she would change the baby's position back and forth, and after each change she would be convinced the opposite position was the right one.

She came to treatment crying, having condemned herself as a monster who must hate her baby so much she did not know how to care properly for her. Convinced that any night her baby would die of SIDS, Elmira wondered if she needed psychiatric hospitalization. This woman was so *neurotically* guilt-ridden that the ostensible obsession did not fit this woman's personality. Far from it, as she was an excellent mother. The therapist discerned this glaring contradiction and skillfully guided the discussion to her husband. It became apparent that Elmira had explosive feelings toward a spouse who drank himself to sleep every night after dinner, neglecting her and the children. She had begun to develop murderous thoughts of suffocating him with a pillow while he was in a drunken stupor. She quickly repressed these thoughts, which emerged in the obsessions toward the child. This was a safe displacement: while she could possibly suffocate the husband, she would never allow this to happen to the baby. Her psyche had temporarily resolved the conflict, but she was increasingly stuck with the guilt feelings concerning her daughter. The psychotherapy appropriately focused on her marriage, not her motherhood.

Non-Guilt Reaction

With the proliferation of personality disorders, the patient who lacks or feigns guilt when such would be appropriate is filling our treatment rooms. These persons see themselves as victims, but may initially present a façade of guilt. They frequently enter therapy to escape the consequences of their behavior, and will usually gravitate to therapists who have a reputation of seeing victimization where none exists. Their initial response is usually complicated by anxiety over their plight, which often can resemble remorse. Guilt-reduction therapy with these patients is contraindicated since it is like pouring gasoline on a fire. The moment their discomfort is lifted they usually bolt therapy. The key to an impacting treatment is the perpetuation of their discomfort in the interest of therapy.

The Case of Rick

A 38-year-old married father of three children had been remanded to the court system for physical child abuse on three occasions, twice by the school authorities and once by the children's pediatrics nurse. In each case Rick was "sentenced" to seek therapy until the psychotherapist could attest to his rehabilitation. The combination of an overworked child protective services, a crowded court calendar, an overly forgiving wife, and an ineffectual psychotherapist resulted in this man's recalcitrant, unremorseful behavior. Each time the psychotherapist prematurely reported him rehabilitated, something that was eagerly accepted by his forgiving wife and an overworked judge.

On the fourth occasion Rick was remanded to the court, a different juvenile judge was presiding, and she barred the previous therapist from participating. She assigned Rick to a psychotherapist with whom she had successfully worked before. The new therapist demanded the patient agree to weekly progress reports to the court, which would respect the confidentiality of the therapeutic content but would disclose any manipulation or foot dragging by the patient. After an early session, the therapist did, indeed, send a negative report to the court, which brought down on Rick the wrath of the judge who, realizing she could not rely upon the wishy-washy mother, was committed to protecting the children even if she had to impose a stiff jail sentence. Thereafter the patient cooperated in his treatment and even became committed to it. The therapist was eventually able to render a true report of rehabilitation. Rick never beat his children again.

IATROGENIC REACTIONS

The list would not be complete without touching on the many cases that are therapist-induced. There are therapists who see in every patient that one syndrome they like to treat, and there are patients, such as borderline personality disorders and suggestible hysterics, that are eager to derive the therapist's interest and attention by becoming "just what the doctor ordered." Favored syndromes come and go, but some fad or fads are always with us at any given time.

Tourney (1967) wrote a revealing history of therapeutic fashions in psychotherapy from 1800 to 1966. In retrospect, many seem absurd, as surely some of our current fads will seem ridiculous to future practitioners. One of the earliest in our modern era was the overdiagnosis of schizophrenia in World War II by young physicians just out of school who were asked to perform the work of front-line psychiatrists. They were assigned without having completed internship, much less psychiatric training. Confronted with the serious and baffling symptoms of "battle fatigue," these young doctors concluded these soldiers were schizophrenic. Any professional who has worked at the Veterans Administration is aware that the V.A. has tried for years to rediagnose these men, but the veterans' organizations besiege the Congress since this would result in the loss of disability pensions. Although many truly are schizophrenic or have other serious mental illnesses, most are personality disorders with a low frustration tolerance that broke under conditions of military service. By the time of the Vietnam War the overdiagnosis of schizophrenia had ceased, and posttraumatic stress disorder was in vogue. To be certain, there is PTSD, just as there is schizophrenia, but it has been grossly overblown. In civilian life it has been stretched to include the slightest stress, trivializing the severity and seriousness of true PTSD.

Not too long ago borderline personalities simulated agoraphobia, the "darling diagnosis" of the period, leading the National Institute for Mental Health to erroneously speculate that 11% of the population was suffering from crippling phobias. Now these have given way to a succession of other diagnoses: multiple personality disorder, victims of incest disorder, repressed memory disorder, and a host of other disorders emerging from the overly used concept of victimization. Again, certainly these disorders exist but not in the frequency some therapists believe, even though it is to the delight of our borderline patients who can simulate whatever the doctor orders. The senior author had a therapist working for him as a center director in a rural midwestern town. Seven out of every eight patients seen by this psychologist suffered from multiple personality disorder. He justified this by describing the backwoods, uneducated, and hysteroid nature of the community. But when this psychologist was promoted and transferred to a metropolitan community, its more sophisticated citizens were suddenly found to be suffering the same frequency of multiple personality disorder as had the rural population.

No one knows how many thousands of psychotherapeutic hours are expended treating not the patient's actual condition but that which is in the eye of the beholder.

KEY INGREDIENT 6: SYMPTOM REDUCTION

That symptom reduction could be a basic goal in psychotherapy is probably the most controversial of the six key ingredients of psychotherapy. For decades the terms *transfer of equivalence* (psychodynamic) and *symptom substitution* (behavioral) were sufficient to strike terror and inhibit therapists from directly attempting to alleviate the patient's symptoms. They imply that removing a symptom before correcting its root cause will result in the appearance of an even worse symptom. Yet, as previously stated, in effective psychotherapy the patient has the right to freedom from pain, anxiety, and depression in the shortest time possible. How does a therapist fulfill this Patient Bill of Rights without making the patient's condition worse through the appearance of a more serious and even more debilitating symptom?

In reviewing 35 years of medical cost offset research—in which the treatment was targeted to reducing the patient's somatization (defined as the translation of psychological problems into physical symptoms), thus reducing the patient's overutilization of inappropriate healthcare—the finding was dramatic. In over two hundred research studies there was not a single instance of symptom substitution reported. Since the transfer of equivalence is most likely to occur when therapy that alleviated the symptom is very brief, Cummings and Follette (1976) did an eight-year follow-up on a group of patients who had reduced their medical utilization by 65% after only one session of psychotherapy. This is the condition under which symptom substitution is said to most likely to occur. The eight-year follow-up revealed that not only had the patients stopped somaticizing, they had corrected in their lives the causes of their somatization, although they never connected the two. Yet no transfer of equivalence took place and somatization behavior never reccurred, even in another patient cohort that was followed for eighteen years.

It is interesting, that transfer of equivalence and symptom substitution are common terms in the psychotherapeutic literature, but there is not much documentation that they are frequent occurrences. Often invoked is the well-known sequence in which alcoholics who have refrained from drinking for several weeks substitute compulsive overeating, compulsive gambling, or other chemicals in the same generic class as alcohol (barbiturates, benzodiazapines). This is not an arguable example, inasmuch as alcoholism is not just a symptom but a complex set of behaviors as well as measurable physiological (tissue) changes. When a rapid disappearance of a complex behavioral system occurs, the psychotherapeutic literature has often labeled this as a *flight into health*. Again, the supposition is that only intensive therapy with deep characterological changes can significantly alter one's lifestyle.

Symptom substitution and flight into health have been passed from one generation of psychotherapists to another, with the waving of a precautionary flag but without sound research documentation. If anything, the research indicates that it is only an occasional outcome and is most likely to occur when a symptom has been wrenched from the patient by posthypnotic suggestion or some other technique that circumvents the patient's direct, active participation in the process (Levis, 1985; Tourney, 1967). Even Freud became less concerned with the alleged phenomenon once he discontinued his own use of hypnosis (Freud, 1957). The impressive literature on brief therapy further dispels the notion that only long-term therapy with deep characterological changes can truly effect behavior (Bloom, 1992).

On the Importance of Being Ernest Once Every Quarter Century

Ernest was a 28-year-old single man who came in complaining that alcohol was ruining his life, but he did not know what to do about it. He had lost a series of jobs and girlfriends, and every time he vowed to cut down on his drinking his resolve would disappear within a few days. In keeping with the therapist's experience that an alcoholic needs to take the first step toward commitment, the patient was asked as homework to decide whether or not he was ready to embark on a program dedicated to a life of abstinence. If he decided in the affirmative, he was to call for an appointment. The patient did not call and the case was closed as a failure.

Out of the blue 23 years later the patient called to make another appointment, stating, "I saw you 23 years ago and I've never had a drink since. Now I'm going through a messy divorce and I am afraid I might start drinking again. I guess I need another appointment to take me through the next 23 years." Once Ernest, now 51, was back in the office, the therapist asked him what was said that had made such an impression. Ernest replied, "Oh, I remember it well. You said that your grandmother always said if you are doing something that won't work, you may not know what else to do, but at least you can stop whatever you have been doing. How about just quitting drinking until you find out what else you might do? That was just the right thing to say, and I left your office and haven't had a drink since."

The therapist could not help but think, "If this is a flight into health, how can I get tickets on the same airplane for all my other patients?"

Officer Rafferty: They're My Fingernails

When the senior author was still in supervision he had the first appointment with a motorcycle police officer, who came into treatment for the purpose of quitting biting his fingernails, something he had done off and on since childhood. He was embarrassed about this behavior and regarded it as childish. In response to probing, he stated, "That motorcycle isn't going to kill me; I'll let the speeder get away first." Both supervisor and therapist were impressed with the terror this man had of "dumping" his motorcycle while pursuing a speeding car. He was afraid to admit it, and the nail-biting both reflected and deflected this anxiety. The supervisor strongly cautioned against removing this symptom prematurely as there could be disastrous consequences, the worst of which might be an anxiety-induced fatal accident.

The therapist did not need to be reminded; he stayed as far away from the symptom as possible. For weeks they talked about the officer's concepts of manliness, derived from his immigrant Irish father, and how admitting fear was in keeping with neither manhood nor police work. He liked the extra pay the motorcycle force was given, but that was not the main reason he continued. These discussions went on for several weeks when one day the patient mentioned how much he was enjoying for the first time in his life having his nails manicured whenever he got a haircut. When did he stop biting his nails? "Oh, I thought you noticed. I haven't bitten my nails since the first time I saw you." Then, proudly holding up his hands to display his long nails, he smiled, "See!" Thereafter, the therapist tried to discuss the concept of transfer of equivalence with his psychoanalytic supervisor, but the latter always seemed to have other matters that needed attending.

ALL THE KEY INGREDIENTS AT WORK: AN ILLUSTRATION

Stephanie was a 47-year-old married woman with three grown children living away from home. She was referred for intractable headaches, which she called her "migraines" and which her physicians had diagnosed as psychosomatic because they did not fit the pattern for migraine or any other physical illness. For several years she was given demerol for the debilitating pain, and fearing she was becoming dependent on it, her physician switched her medication to codeine. She complained bitterly that the new medication was not as effective, which led to a tug of war between her and her doctors, eventually generating an unwelcome referral for psychotherapy.

The patient was an irritatingly aggressive woman who had been giving her doctors, as well as everyone else around her, a very bad time. Her father was a critical man who never gave Stephanie approval of anything she did. The mother was passive and although she recoiled at her husband's criticism of her, she did nothing about it. On the other hand, whereas Stephanie adopted her mother's attitude of fear and passivity toward her father, she rejected her mother's otherwise total passivity and became controlling and demanding with everyone else. At an early age she began badgering her four younger siblings, then spread her behavior to include her friends. Finally she was abusive to her own mother. However, she never confronted her father.

At the first session Stephanie confessed to being difficult and speculated it would not be long before the therapist would become so annoyed with her that he would refer her on. She was passive and fearful toward the therapist when she saw him as her critical father (transference), but she was demanding and controlling when she was operating within her modus operandi (parataxic distortion). At the end of the first session the therapist gave her the homework (a growth opportunity) to list all of the annoyances she would heap on the therapist that she believed would result in his abandoning her as all of her friends had done. Instantaneously she stopped being annoying, became passive, and developed a severe headache. The therapist had preceded the homework by assuring her there was nothing she could say that would result in her being abandoned in therapy (providing a corrective emotional experience), but her parataxic distortions and her life experiences caused her to doubt the veracity of the statement. It was also apparent to the therapist that the patient would rather be known as an irritating person than to be regarded as fearful of her father or passive like her mother (inner conflict). In actuality, she was fearful, and by denying it with aggressive behavior paid the price of intractable headaches (symptom). It was as if the entire struggle (her conflict) was colliding within her pained skull.

During the next three sessions Stephanie did her homework, complaining loudly and inappropriately about having to do it. But whenever the therapist commented on it, she fell into silence and developed a severe headache. At the fifth session the therapist announced he was going to say a series of critical things, using the same words that her father was prone to use, and they would see how long it would take for the headache to appear. The intent of the paradox worked; the headache did not appear and Stephanie never had another one (symptom reduction).

The next several sessions involved the working through of her obnoxious behavior. At first the therapist verbally reported her irritation scale, but then an opportunity presented itself. The therapist had bought a small, one-scale toy xylophone for his infant daughter, and it was sitting on the desk. At that session he spontaneously hit a high note, musically telegraphing Stephanie's irritation level. She smiled, and thereafter he would hit the note at the height of the scale that would best reflect the degree of her obnoxious behavior. This would cause her to stop her ranting and reflect on what she was doing. During one session, when Stephanie was particularly obnoxious, the therapist mistakenly struck the lowest note. She stopped, looked quizzical, and asked, "I thought I was at my worst. No?" The therapist responded that he struck the wrong note, but the mistake probably reflected that he had become immune to her crap. She asked, "Is my obnoxious ranting and raving just crap?" The therapist replied, "Yes. Both your fearful passivity and your obnoxious façade are both crap. You don't need either anymore, just as you don't need those painful headaches. You can be your real self, something in between, like both assertive *and* civil." She progressed very rapidly after that and therapy was terminated at the nineteenth session. She came in about two years later to express her gratitude, and to proudly tell the therapist the past two years had been the happiest of her life.

CHAPTER 4

Effective Psychotherapy as Focused, Intermittent Psychotherapy Throughout the Life Cycle

Focused psychotherapy is a partnership between therapist and patient that directly addresses the problem and seeks its solution, concentrating on the here and now and what has to be done next. Although "solution-focused" therapy is a form of focused psychotherapy, the strict term applies more to the approaches developed by de Shazer and his associates (de Shazer, 1982, 1985; de Shazer & Berg, 1992). Solution-focused therapy can best be understood as a constructivist, postmodern, and poststructural approach that has much in common with other focused therapies (Hoyt, 2000). However, its emphasis on the relativity of reality and its other somewhat nihilistic preoccupations is not necessary for treatment to qualify as focused therapy under a broader definition. In fact, under strict contructivist thinking, even the word treatment is taboo and should be replaced with the term facilitate.

All of this reminds us of Aldous Huxley's novel *1984,* in which society has invented "double speak," different words for the same thing, as a clever way of diluting the existence of real problems and the lack of genuine change. Feeling good about something becomes a substitute for real change. If one were to follow the postmodernist trend, even the term therapy in solution-focused therapy implies pathology and should be changed to a more trendy term, such as reeducation, reorientation, or perhaps even the ultimate absurdity, rebelief. It may be more productive, however, to look at the elements shared by all effective (focused) psychotherapies.

Before doing so, it should be stated that focused psychotherapy strongly believes that even though psychotherapy is a partnership with the patient, there is a special place for the psychotherapist as the doctor. This parallels current medicine, in which the physician, recognizing that most disease stems from faulty lifestyles, seeks a partnership with the patient toward health. The patient's participation is necessary, but there are points at which the role of the doctor is special, important, and even paramount. Similarly, the partnership with the patient in psychotherapy is invaluable; the patient comes to a psychotherapist because he or she needs the doctor. As such, we offer more than the pastor, rabbi, priest, or counselor; otherwise why should someone seek *our* services? Whether in medicine or psychotherapy, the doctor's role ultimately is to treat. For these reasons focused therapy does not shy away from the honesty of the terms doctor, treatment, or patient. The latter term is of importance even beyond these considerations, as will be seen in Chapter 5.

ELEMENTS SHARED BY ALL EFFECTIVE PSYCHOTHERAPIES

As previously stated, the distinction between brief and long-term therapy is no longer relevant if the therapist applies certain elements that increase effectiveness. Therapy then becomes the right length required for an individual patient within his or her particular circumstances. There is general agreement that effective psychotherapy has the following seven essential characteristics (Budman, Hoyt & Friedman, 1992; Cummings & Sayama, 1995; Hoyt, 1995).

Rapid and Positive Alliance

Skilled psychotherapists have at their disposal a variety of techniques and approaches that facilitate bonding between patient and therapist, which is known as the therapeutic alliance. These are particularly useful with those persons who have never bonded, or who have been so traumatized that they are reluctant to bond. The effective therapist, however, will skillfully accelerate the formation of a positive therapeutic alliance rather than passively wait and hope for its development.

A Focus on Specific, Achievable Goals

For decades it was popular to state the goal of therapy to be "self-actualization." In the era of reimbursement for timelessness, it was considered appropriate to meander throughout as much of the therapeutic landscape as the patient was willing to traverse. Yet after decades of self-actualizing therapy, no one ever came up with an adequate definition of where it was going and an evaluation of what had been accomplished. With the current focus on clearly understood and achievable goals, both therapist and patient are aware when there is either meandering from the goal or a therapeutic drift when the wind is out of the sails.

A Clear Definition of Patient and Therapist Responsibilities and Activities

This makes the therapeutic alliance a true partnership. The responsibilities are clearly spelled out and agreed to in a therapeutic contract in which the therapist will not abandon the patient or ask her or him to do something until able to do so. In return, the patient agrees to a partnership designed to make the therapist obsolete as soon as possible. Within this framework there are explicit patient responsibilities, among which is that the patient will be asked to take the next step when it is determined he or she is ready and able, although reluctant.

An Emphasis on Patient Strengths and Competencies with an Expectation of Change

Effective psychotherapy is optimistic psychotherapy, encouraging and empowering the best a patient can be. This is not a new concept, but effective therapists have rediscovered the optimistic therapy that was the hallmark of such therapists as Alfred Adler who, seventy years ago, would say to his patients who were faltering, "Whatever you do is hard in the beginning, but after a while you succeed" (Adler, 1930, p. 86). He frequently admonished his patients that "many individuals prefer to be influenced by their defeats rather than by their successes" (p. 77). If a patient balked, insisting it was beyond her or his ability, Adler reassured them that he would never "beseech a lame man not to limp" (p. 263). In his writings he frequently alluded to the phenomenon that our patients want to be pampered and coddled only when we make these more available and attractive than the hard work of therapy. What Adler called "creative power" is very similar to what Erikson (1963) saw as nature's inevitable drive toward growth that in our patients has gone awry and needs to be released again.

An Active Assisting of the Patient Toward New Perceptions and Behaviors

These changes inevitably result in a more effective, responsible, and fulfilling lifestyle. These are within the patient's own context. In contrast to postmodernist thinking, there are some things that are immutably wrong regardless of the so-called "knowing as being dependent on the knower." Among these are such obvious behaviors as self-destructiveness, destruction of others, abuse of children, rape, and exploitation of any kind. A patient's redefinition of divorce as a marvelous and fulfilling experience does not address the devastation felt by the victimized child, often for life. Effective psychotherapy still addresses rationalization for what it is.

An Emphasis on the Here and Now and What Needs to Be Done Next

The importance of the past in shaping the individual is indisputable, but its importance to psychotherapy is only relevant to the extent the unresolved past is causing problems in the present. For example, if everyone who at age eight stole a quarter from mother's purse had to go into psychotherapy, this would include almost all of us. If what happened at eight was mishandled, leaving a lesson unlearned, the adult may now steal from friends' purses in the college dormitory, shoplift whenever in a store, or do some other dishonest equivalent. The problems this causes in the patient's current life renders the event at age eight significant to the present, leaving something that must be addressed in psychotherapy. The emphasis is on what comes next, in this case a lesson finally learned and a behavior positively altered.

Therapy That Is Sensitive to Time

Inasmuch as the patient wants to get on with life, the scheduling should be flexible and tailored to a patient's needs. There is nothing sacred about the weekly fifty-minute hour. A patient who is struggling to avoid hospitalization for crippling anxiety may be seen daily and even twice daily for the first week. A schizophrenic who is staying out of the hospital in an independent living program may need a reality check with a psychotherapist only once a month. A session may be fifteen minutes or two hours. Spacing and duration are determined by what will move therapy in the most effective and efficient manner, not what is most convenient for the therapist. Furthermore, the session may take place outside the office (hospital, medical clinic, home visit, nursing home, or in the work of a military psychologist, on the battlefield). The inflexible psychotherapist who works only with 50-minute weekly office visits is disqualified from doing focused therapy.

TECHNIQUE IS DEPENDENT UPON THEORY

Effective psychotherapy is more than a bag of tricks. It is dispensed in accordance with research and clinical findings, for theory organizes what we do into a comprehensive and meaningful endeavor. Without the cohesiveness of theory, the outcome is a crapshoot. Not only would the therapist not know what to do at any critical point, the effects would be unpredictable. The senior author recalls the many occasions at Esalen Institute watching Fritz (Frederick) Perls working before a group. The "patient" was most often a colleague or a student. On one memorable occasion it was Carl Rogers. Because of the almost effortless manner in which Perls worked, most observers saw only a series of techniques. They overlooked the fact that Perls had 24 years of training and a solid theoretical orientation. This was not always true of his followers, many of whom sought to emulate the master by the seat of their pants. The prevalence of these "wild" therapists may, in part, explain the fading away of Gestalt therapy after the death of its founder.

Hoyt (2000) insists that his approach is that of espousing anything that works. However, one needs only to read his latest book to realize his erudition, grasp of theory, and his many years of training and experience. He is capable of discerning what works, rather than guessing that something might work.

In our retraining of hundreds and even thousands of psychotherapists in a system of focused psychotherapy employed during the existence of American Biodyne, known as the Biodyne Model, it was found that only two variables were predictive of success. The first was the willingness on the part of the trainee to learn a new model employing 68 empirically derived focused and targeted interventions; the second was a grounding and intensive/extensive training in any systematized school of psychotherapy. Even though the focused therapy was a form of brief therapy, even long-term psychotherapists who demonstrated both criteria did well. Those who were eclectic, less intensively trained, or not grounded in theory did poorly in the retraining, even if they already claimed to be brief therapists.

Psychotherapeutic art is the culmination of theory, training, experience, and technique, all woven into a successful, intuitive whole by one who has mastered all of these and is able to implement them with patients a step beyond that possible for most therapists. We call this person a Master Therapist. We know of none deserving that appellation who has not earned it by being grounded in theory, intensively trained, vastly experienced, and technically brilliant.

FOCUSED PSYCHOTHERAPY TRANSCENDS ANY SINGLE THEORY, BUT IT IS NOT ECLECTIC

The skilled therapist knows when to use one technique rather than another, even if these cross theoretical boundaries. This does not reflect a smorgasbord available to any therapist to pick and choose at random; rather, it is the product of understanding the theoretical frameworks supporting each technique, resulting in a knowledgeable choice that is purposeful and almost surgically specific. The focused therapist cannot be content to be well grounded in only one theory, but must understand all theories to employ interventions skillfully.

For those psychotherapists invested in only one theoretical way of thinking, the broadening of skills will be difficult. In the early development of a theoretical position, it is imperative to guard its purity, but as knowledge accumulates and theories are subjected to research the boundaries blur. There is much overlap, with often differing technical vocabularies saying the same thing. However, there are also enough differences that the psychotherapist must learn and appreciate the differing theoretical positions. The following is a list of frequently used therapeutic techniques or interventions, classified by whether they are behavioral, psychodynamic, or strategic.

Behavioral Interventions

Relaxation, systematic desensitization, schedules of reinforcement, exposure treatment, homework assignments, cognitive restructuring, role playing.

Psychodynamic Interventions

Free association, interpretation of the transference, interpretation of the inner conflicts, interpretation of the projections, mimicking the transference, joining the delusion.

Strategic Interventions

Reframing, paradoxical intention, double bind, prescribing the symptoms, prescribing the resistance, humoring the resistance, overwhelming the resistance, doing the unexpected (novel), denial of treatment.

THE IDEAL FIRST SESSION

If treatment is to be focused, a number of goals ideally should be accomplished the first session (Cummings & Sayama, 1995). This is not always possible. But if the goals are always before the therapist, whether they all get done during the first, second, or third sessions is not as important as the realization that the treatment is not off to a gallop until they are reached.

1. *Hit the ground running.* The first session must be therapeutic. The concept that the first session is primarily devoted to taking a history is nonsense. An experienced therapist skillfully obtains information as the sessions progress, but always knows when not to move forward until certain historical facts are in evidence.

2. *Perform an operational diagnosis.* The operational diagnosis asks one thing: "Why is the patient here today instead of last week, last month, last year, or next year?" When you answer that, you know what the patient is there for. The operational diagnosis is absolutely essential before the treatment plan is formulated.

3. *Elicit the implicit contract.* This is also essential before the treatment plan can be formulated. The explicit contract is the reason the patient gives for being there; the implicit contract is the real reason for being there. For example, a patient who states he is there to save his marriage but opines, "I'm afraid no matter what I do my marriage will end in divorce," is really there to justify divorcing his wife.

4. *Formulate the therapeutic contract.* A therapist proceeding without a treatment plan is like a pilot taking off without a flight plan. Without an adequate treatment plan therapy will be unnecessarily protracted, at best meandering or faltering and at worst unsuccessful. Unfortunately most therapists do not know how to formulate such a treatment plan which is guided by the operational diagnosis and the implicit contract. If these are not apparent in the first session, the therapist delays the treatment plan. Further, if a treatment plan has been formulated on an operational diagnosis or implicit contract that proves in a subsequent session to be in error, the treatment plan is reformulated.

5. *Create a therapeutic contract.* Every patient makes a therapeutic contract with every therapist in the first session, every time. But in 99% of the first sessions the therapist misses it because it is usually thrown out by the patient as an aside. Be wary of the patient who appreciates your pleasant office or the comfortable chair "because I'm going to be here a while." Anything resembling such an aside is a disguised contract for long-term therapy. The therapeutic contract that is important was stated earlier: "I shall never abandon you as long as you need me, and I shall never ask you to do something until you are ready. In return for this I ask that you join me in a partnership to make me obsolete as soon as possible." The exact words can be modified in accordance with the patient's education and socioeconomic status, but it must be certain that the patient has understood and agreed. It also means that when the patient is ready, the therapist will encourage the next step and require completion of homework.

6. *Create running hypotheses in your mind* as to what the patient is doing, saying and wanting, but always revise these into new hypotheses as the facts accumulate. Formulating hypotheses guides the therapist's inquiry and direction, and keeps the therapy operating at an efficient pace.

7. *Do something novel in the first session.* Find something novel or unexpected to do in the first session. This will cut through the expectations of the "trained" patient and will create instead an expectation that problems are to be immediately addressed.

8. *Give hope in the first session.* This is not done through the usual "reassurance," which is of limited value. Rather, achieve a small therapeutic gain in the first session. If this is not possible, give an example of a successful therapy of a patient with the same problem. But make certain the patient can identify with the example in terms of age, gender, ethnicity, and socioeconomic status.

9. *Be honest without being blaming.* Patients bring in all kinds of maladjusted, unfortunate, illegal, and unacceptable behavior.

They also test whether we will be judgmental. Many therapists, in an attempt to avoid anything that sounds like blame, fall into a state of less than honesty. When patients catch us in that posture, at worst they will have contempt, and at best will doubt anything we say genuinely in the future. For example, if a patient says, "You must think I'm terrible the way I beat my children," the answer should be, "It is always terrible for a child to be physically abused. But you are apparently here because you want to stop doing that terrible thing. If that is true, then we shall schedule our next session well within the time period you can control that behavior. How long can you go before the impulse to beat your children overwhelms you?" If the patient says three days or just twenty-four hours, the next session is scheduled for three days or twenty-four hours hence.

10. *Give homework in the first session and every session thereafter.* It is not possible to have a "cookbook" full of homework that is arbitrarily assigned. Tailor the homework to be meaningful for the patient's goal and therapeutic contract. In accordance with that therapeutic contract, it must be something the patient is capable of completing. Ideally the homework represents the next increment of improvement toward the goal. Enforce the homework as a condition of continuing treatment.

ONION AND GARLIC PSYCHODYNAMICS

More than four decades of experience with focused psychotherapy have demonstrated that the therapists most adept at formulating a treatment plan are those who have an understanding of psychodynamics. When knowledge of psychodynamics is not used merely to induce patient insight, but is used instead to understand the patient sufficiently to formulate a treatment plan, it becomes the most valuable tool available for that purpose. Unfortunately, current trainees are not sufficiently prepared to do this, and for that reason we have constructed the Onion/Garlic Chart (see Figure 1).

	Onion (Repression)	Garlic (Denial)

ANALYZABLE	Anxiety
	Phobias
	Depression
	Hysteria/
	  conversion
	Obsessive-
	  compulsive
	  personality
		Additions
		Personality styles
		Personality
		  disorders
		Impulse neuroses
		Hypomania
		Narcissistic
		  personality

		Borderline personality

**NON-
ANALYZABLE**
	Onion
	(Withdrawal)
	Schizophrenias
	  controlled by
	  individual
	  suffering
		Garlic
		(Withdrawal)
		Schizophrenias
		  controlled by
		  attacking the
		  environoment
		Impulse
		  schizophrenia

FIGURE 1.   The Onion–Garlic Chart

The four-part figure begins with the premise that all of our
patients can initially be divided into those who suffer (intrapunitive) and those whose style is to make others suffer (extrapunitive). The name of the chart comes from the simple fact that if you
have onions for lunch, all afternoon you will unpleasantly taste
those onions. On the other hand, if you eat garlic for lunch you
will taste nothing, but all afternoon others will be avoiding your
garlic breath. The onion patient is guilt-ridden and suffering. The
garlic patient does not feel guilt, makes everyone else suffer, and
cannot understand why everyone is bothered by his or her behavior. The former are neurotic; the latter are personality disorders.
This differentiation is important because guilt-reduction therapy

with personality disorders—unfortunately, a very frequent thera-peutic mistake—justifies the behavior in the patient's mind and increases it. Psychotherapists tend to be intrapunitive individuals and are easily conned by character (personality) disorders. These patients essentially suffer the unavoidable consequences of their behavior, not the guilt feelings stemming from their behavior.

The main psychological defense mechanism found in neuroses (onion) is that of repression, while the main defense mechanism of personality disorders (garlic) is denial. The approach to the repressed patient is to deal with the guilt feelings that necessitate the repression, thus freeing the corrective behavior. The approach to the personality disorder is the constructive confrontation of the denial, thus correcting the behavior. Most therapeutic failures will be avoided if garlic overlay is treated before one tackles any under-lying onion. Even the most onion patient will at times manifest garlic behavior. When that occurs, stop the onion treatment and address the garlic. Furthermore, even though the garlic patient will eventually manifest onion, especially if therapy is successful, the therapist should be very careful in treating that onion. It is fre-quently short-lived as garlic quickly returns.

In addition to guilt reduction (onion) and constructive con-frontation (garlic), our patients can be further divided into those who are capable of self-understanding of their behavior (i.e., ana-lyzable), and those who only understand their behavior by learn-ing to anticipate its consequences (i.e., nonanalyzable). In addi-tion to the constructive confrontation of denial, many patients require the painstaking construction of limits and boundaries. Finally, psychotics should never be opened up; rather, the patient must be helped to develop methods in which the uncontrolled psychotic ideation and behavior are contained.

The Onion/Garlic Chart also denotes the best entry points for each of the diagnostic entities. It will be noted that these entities do not conform to the usual DSM or ICD nomenclatures, but rather to treatment-oriented "diagnoses." These entry points enable the focused psychotherapist to implement the treatment plan with the efficiency promised in the Patients' Bill of Rights. These considerations are beyond the scope of this discussion, and for greater detail the reader should investigate the procedures of focused or problem-solving psychotherapy (e.g., Cummings & Sayama, 1995, pp. 109–224) and applications to family therapy (e.g., Haley, 1977).

TAKING COGNIZANCE OF THE LANDSCAPE

Within all of the foregoing is the context that the patient brings to treatment. We call this the landscape, or the ground that is to be weeded. Cactus will not bloom on Long Island and an orchid will not flourish in the desert. We watched with amusement a Scottsdale neighbor who was transplanted from Belgium attempting to grow African violets year after year without any success. She disregarded all advice, insisting she had left Brussels because her favorite flowers would not grow in the cold, damp weather. In coming to warm Arizona she refused to accept the fact that the desert sun may be too hot for many flowers that otherwise welcome warmth. Further, the ignorant gardener cannot differentiate a flower that is yet to blossom from a weed that is blooming. Another neighbor hired several teenagers to weed the area around the growing ground cover he had recently planted. As is often the case, the weeds were growing faster than the ground cover. The teenagers, not knowing the difference, pulled up most of the ground cover and left almost all the weeds.

Psychology has taken the lead in promoting sensitivity to age, ethnicity, gender, religion, sexual orientation, and other cultural issues and differences. Such sensitivity is now fortunately taught as part of the curriculum in every APA-approved psychology training program. This has not always been so. As early as the 1960s the lesbian and gay male community in San Francisco demanded of the Kaiser Permanente Health Plan that gay therapists be available. As the chief psychologist, the senior author had been sensitive to this issue and had a number of gay male and lesbian psychologists on the staff. The problem was that they were not openly gay, preferring to keep one foot in the closet. Administratively respecting this privacy was not a sufficient answer for gay patients, and rightly so. An openly gay psychologist was recruited, and the other gay psychologists then came out of the closet, after which the lesbian and gay community no longer routinely demanded gay or lesbian therapists. Once the community was satisfied that the health plan was sensitive to such issues, the gender or sexual preference of the psychotherapist ceased to be a primary concern, although it continued to remain as a specific concern with certain kinds of problems.

A similar experience occurred with the African American community in San Francisco during the 1960s. The mental health service had a significant number of African American psychotherapists, but until the health plan increased its number of such ethnic minority physicians, there were frequent misunderstandings and confrontations. Fortunately the African American community had confidence in the health plan psychologists, who were able to address and conclude satisfactorily most of these misunderstandings.

Without knowing the patient's cultural context, the therapist is unable to differentiate a proper concern from a rationalization. In this case, therapists tend to err in the opposite direction, insulting the patient by requiring less than would be required of other patients who are not members of a minority cultural group. Being cognizant of the landscape means knowing that all gardens have weeds. However, in weeding a particular garden the gardener must know what in that landscape is a weed and what is a flower. Furthermore, the climatic and soil conditions of that landscape determine the choice of flowers that will flourish. We do not choose the patient's flowers. Ultimately it is the patient, not the psychotherapist, who determines what flowers to plant in the garden.

It must be remembered that the patient, ignoring reality, may wish for flowers that are inappropriate in that landscape. Again, the therapist must possess both sensitivity and the reality principle, something that is not possible without being cognizant of the landscape. Overvictimization, a common mistake by well-meaning majority therapists working with cultural minority patients, can be seductive. All patients look for excuses; pandering to the patient's wishes in this regard is to have far less than appropriate expectations for that patient. When this occurs, the patient, though seduced into premature comfort or even smugness, is ultimately short-changed. She or he does not attain the behavioral and lifestyle changes that would have been possible.

We have seen this overvictimization attitude even when the therapist is a minority and the patient is not. We recall a young woman who became suicidal following the break up of a second turbulent marriage. Her lesbian therapist advised her that all men victimize women, and at first she enjoyed feeling totally vindicated for her lousy choice of husbands. But when the therapist suggested the patient live for a while in a lesbian commune, the patient balked, stating, "I have enough trouble with men without my therapist doing the rationalizing for me." She quit, found another therapist, and today she is a happily married mother.

A skillful psychotherapist can be so aware of the patient's context that the patient's own language can be employed therapeutically. It is important to know what the parents called the patient when angry, how peers taunted the patient in childhood, or, most important, what current names the patient uses when angry at himself. These are never used to mimic or mock a patient, but when used appropriately and with exquisite timing, the effect can be profoundly positive. A skillful therapist would never just mimic a patient's regional or ethnic accent, but being able to say a word or phrase at the opportune moment just as the patient would say it to his or herself increases the effectiveness exponentially. We recall a patient whose inner name when blaming herself was "asshole." When she was berating herself unmercifully for 20 minutes during a session, it was particularly effective for the therapist to ask in her own Georgia accent if it wouldn't just be simpler to call herself an "ah-ice-hole" and go on?

Speaking in the patient's language is a must with schizophrenics who may seem to be communicating in our language but actually remain guarded and secretive. We recall one schizophrenic who would revert to speaking without using any prepositions or conjunctions. The therapist learned to speak exactly the same way, and the result was absolute baring of the patient's innermost thoughts. Another schizophrenic revealed one day that he only trusted persons who used the "P.A.C. approach." The therapist painstakingly worked with the patient until he learned this meant using a lot of words which began with those letters of the alphabet; they did not have to make sense. By the therapist starting every session with something like, "How are you this perambulating, pyramidal, prolific, patterned p.m.?" the patient and therapist began the session with instant rapport. With the schizophrenic particularly, and with all patients to a lesser extent, the therapist's knowing the patient's context sufficiently to use the same language remarkably propels treatment forward.

POWERFUL WAYS TO FACILITATE PSYCHOTHERAPY

Two additional techniques not yet mentioned have the ability to propel psychotherapy forward toward positive outcomes. Much has been written about these techniques, yet most psychotherapists are unaware of them, or if they are aware they seldom use them.

Change Behavior First, Not Feelings or Attitudes

Patients can muck around with feelings ad infinitum, with little or no resultant change. When the senior author began his career half a century ago patients rarely talked of feelings. When asked how they felt about something, they would respond with what they would think about it. The therapist would have to urge them to pay attention to how they felt, not how they thought. The opposite is true now: patients respond according to feelings and without really thinking of the consequences. And where feelings are endless, attitudes are very resistant to change. In fact, it is nearly impossible to change a patient's attitude by addressing it directly.

On the other hand, change the behavior positively and new, realistic feelings and attitudes will emerge shortly thereafter. The lesson is that feelings are self-perpetuating, attitudes are enduringly resistant, while behavior is easily altered by the techniques available to the psychotherapist. It is a well-known fact, for example, that alcoholic feelings and attitudes persist as long as the patient is drinking. After only two weeks of choosing to be abstinent, feelings change and attitudes are altered toward the rewards of sobriety. After six months of abstinent behavior the feelings and attitudes are remarkably altered, and after one year they are profoundly different, with the most compelling feeling, that of the craving, now gone.

The Case of Beatrice and Her Veggie Burger

Bea was a 22-year-old woman who had been a vegetarian since age 14, the typical age when idealistic adolescents first confront their horror of killing and devouring animals. Her dilemma was that she had fallen in love with what is commonly known as a steak-and-potatoes-man who abhorred vegetables. He insisted that she grill steaks for him, an act that would completely gross her out. The wedding date had been set, and Bea's attitude was that if he really loved her he would give up meat. His response was expected: if she loved him she would cook meat for him. When asked to imagine the next 25 years of marriage to a meat eater, she simply could not even think about it "because I love him so much and I cannot live without him." It made no difference that the world has many available vegetarian males, Bea loved Rod and "that's all that matters."

Under the guise of her doing something loving, even though gross, her homework was to cook a steak for Rod and watch him eat while they dined together, for each of the 12 days before the next appointment. The paradoxical intent was for Bea to show Rod how much she loved him, so that he, then, would give up meat for her. At the next session Bea stated she had called off the wedding because she and Rod had broken up. The therapist learned that it was on the sixth straight night of cooking steaks that the ostensibly overwhelming feeling of love disappeared, and the attitude that she could not live without Rod was gone.

Do Not Strong-arm the Resistance

Patients have a right to their resistance, for even though their behavior is not working it is familiar and comfortable, whereas change is scary. Attacking the resistance, or even addressing it directly, has the unwanted propensity of strengthening it. The patient comes to treatment guarding the resistance and leaning heavily in its direction, even though the verbalizations may seem to the contrary. Patients want to be seen as good patients, so they do not admit their fear of change. The psychotherapist can very effectively move therapy forward by taking advantage of the direction of the resistance and going with it. This is similar to using the opponent's momentum in judo. Psychologically strong-arming the resistance is as difficult as physically strong-arming a much larger opponent in judo. With persistence, the therapist can go along with the resistance and then slowly turn the patient around much like one would an ocean liner rather than turn abruptly as if the patient were maneuverable like a motorcycle. It might even be regarded as axiomatic: strong-arming the resistance is never effective. This technique is demonstrated in Chapter 5 in the case of Denise, who also illustrates focused psychotherapy over a span of 40 years.

Intermittent Focused Psychotherapy Throughout the Life Cycle

Over two decades ago "The General Practice of Psychology" (Cummings & VandenBos, 1979), later named "Brief, Intermittent Psychotherapy Throughout the Life Cycle" (Cummings, 1990, 1991), defined the practice of psychotherapy as being similar to what the physician does in primary care. The original authors wrote:

> Psychology has developed a variety of specific techniques which are applicable to specific emotional problems, thus enabling brief psychotherapy to be particularly effective. In the past it was said that the therapist and patient had only one chance to solve present and future emotional distress, a criterion applied to no other form of intervention. By combining dynamic and behavioral therapies into interventions designed to ameliorate the presenting life problem ... this general practice of psychology postulates that throughout the life span the client has available brief, effective interventions

designed to meet specific conditions as these may or may not arise
(Cummings & VandenBos, 1979, p. 430).

They went on to state that psychotherapy had to abandon the
concept of cure that prevailed during that era in favor of recognizing there are life stages in which the patient might do well,
while in other life stages there may be difficulty. These include,
but are not limited to, infancy, childhood, puberty, adolescence,
young adulthood, courtship, marriage, divorce, parenthood,
middle age, loss of parents, independence of children, old age,
disability or chronic illness, death of spouse, and one's own
death. It was Erikson (1950) who first extended psychosexual
development and other growth far beyond the first several years
of infancy and early childhood into stages throughout the life
span. He postulated that growth is the propensity of all living
organisms, but in our patients the growth process has gone awry.
The job of the psychotherapist is to restore the inevitable growth
process, and then get out of the patient's way until (if and when)
we are needed again.

Cummings and VandenBos saw the psychotherapist functioning more as a psychological primary care physician, as a replacement for that valued healer who has long since disappeared—the
general practitioner. This physician never refused a housecall,
knew all the children because he or she had delivered them, and
was not too proud to examine the family dog if one of the children
complained that "Fido" was ill. With the fractionation of our
health system, in which one specialist may not be aware of what
another specialist is doing and with most disease being the result
of faulty lifestyles, Cummings and VandenBos (1979) saw the psychological general practitioner as the focal point around which the
patient's care and prevention were evaluated and coordinated.

What is now regarded as "intermittent focused psychotherapy
throughout the life cycle" began in the 1950s when the senior
author became the chief psychologist at the Kaiser Permanente
Health Plan. There now exist over four decades of clinical experi-

ence with a large number of patients, their children, as well as their grandchildren and great grandchildren. The following case is a good illustration.

DENISE: FORTY YEARS OF INTERMITTENT FOCUSED PSYCHOTHERAPY, 1959 TO 1999 (NARRATED BY NICK CUMMINGS, WITH COMMENTS BY JANET CUMMINGS)

One day in February of 1959 I was spending the noon hour at my desk eating a sandwich while I was catching up on entries into my patients' charts. Everyone else, including the receptionist, had left the building, which was kept open so that the waiting room was available for any patient that arrived early for a one o'clock appointment. Suddenly I was aware that a very attractive blond, blue-eyed young woman was standing in my doorway. She apologized for wandering down the hall, stating, "I'm thinking of going into psychotherapy, and I'm just looking you over." I stood and walked into the hall with her, where we both stood talking for a few minutes. She asked what kind of psychotherapists were on staff, and I replied straightforwardly that we were all very good psychologists, psychiatrists, or social workers, and added facetiously that none of us had horns and a tail. She laughed, concluded she wanted an appointment, and asked if it could be with me. We walked to the reception desk and I personally arranged an appointment for early the following week.

1959: EPISODE 1

Session 1-A

Denise arrived early for her appointment and was very stylishly and expensively dressed. She was 23 years of age, and married to

44-year-old Jeff, a certified public accountant in independent practice. There were three children: 3-year-old Lynn, 2-year-old Paula,
and 6-month-old Connie. Denise was a stay-at-home mother, made
possible by Jeff's upper middle class income. She was born in a
farm community of immigrant parents. Her mother favored her
older brother, who could do no wrong, while the patient was
regarded as never being able to do anything right. The father was
ineffectual. Denise attended a civic luncheon where Jeff was the
speaker, and listening to this suave, handsome man she decided
she was going to marry him. She followed him to the parking lot,
seduced him into a date, and several months later, after a whirl-
wind courtship, they were married in a fashionable wedding. They
now lived in an expensive house in a prestigious neighborhood.
Once married she discovered that Jeff was a "turnip," as in that
which you can't get blood out of. This was her way of saying Jeff
was incapable of displaying any affection, to her or the children.

Her presenting symptom was the recurring obsession that she
would stab 6-month-old Connie. This was especially strong when
she was diapering the infant and a rack of kitchen knives was
nearby. In desperation she got rid of all sharp knives, but the obsession persisted. She was crying in the session, condemning herself as
being a terrible mother. The fact is that Denise was a very affectionate and caring mother, and the symptom did not fit. This was displaced hostility. Although Denise would never stab her child, she
was angry enough at turnip Jeff that she harbored unrecognized
murderous thoughts. A treatment plan was formulated in my mind,
and after she understood and accepted the therapeutic contract, a
return appointment was made for the next week.

Denise was seen as an obsessional hysteric, and the treatment
called for being in the space opposite where she was at any given
moment. When she was being obsessional, the therapist would
interpret the hysteria, and vice versa. The treatment plan was as
follows:

(1) The entry point was to go in the direction of the patient's
    resistance.

(2) When she was being hysterical (seductive) the therapist would address the obsession, and vice versa.

(3) Goal was for her to see the parataxic distortions: husband as father, not as the brother she now saw, and later to see that she equated Jeff as rejecting, both as mother and brother, toward both of whom she harbored unconscious murderous thoughts.

(4) Expect the following transference situations: young therapist as older brother most of the time, but also alternating as good and bad father, as well as good and bad mother.

(5) Watch out for the erotic transference, and limit the acting out.

The patient had shown the therapist a picture of the bassinet she had made for Connie. It was very beautifully lined in satin, and the therapist commented it looked like a coffin. Although the patient was taken aback, she was even more startled when she was given her homework: replace Jeff's bedding with satin sheets and retrieve the rack of kitchen knives, which she should place next to the baby's bed.

Janet's Comment

The therapist is using the appropriate entry point for an obsessional hysteric: be in the opposite place of where she is. When Denise was obsessing about the stabbing (hysterical displacement), Dr. Cummings talked of death (i.e., the coffin). In a subtle way there is a linking of husband and baby via the coffin (bed) without directly confronting the resistance. It would be strongarming the resistance to openly link the husband with the stabbing. The resistance was honored while at the same time the stage is set through the homework assignment for future connections.

Session 2-A

The following week Denise proudly brought a photograph to prove she had, indeed, completed the homework of putting satin sheets on Jeff's bed. Almost immediately she plunged into two stories. The first was of a sexy party she and Jeff attended during which there was a contest to see which woman present could most walk like a "French whore." Denise won easily, and she briefly illustrated the winning walk for the therapist, cutting the demonstration short when she observed no response from him. Then she told a second story. A moving van was delivering furniture to her new neighbors next door. The movers had constructed a narrow ramp so they could get a large refrigerator up an incline. Denise donned the skimpiest bikini she owned and at the moment the moving men were balancing on the ramp, she emerged from the house with the three girls. As she related the story she laughed profusely, describing how the two men almost fell from the ramp, refrigerator and all. "The fools; it's only a piece of skin!"

As she looked for the therapist to join in the laughter with her, he, instead, continued to look at the photograph, commenting that Jeff's bed looked like a coffin. This was in keeping with the treatment plan to refer to the obsessional side whenever the patient was seductively acting as a hysteric. She reacted with fury: "Do you think I want my husband dead? What kind of a wife do you think I am? Do I? Answer me. Do I?" Ignoring this, the therapist asked, "Why do you display yourself so pathetically, because you are not really an ugly duckling." Denise fell into stunned silence. In time she began to talk about her childhood during which her mother told her she was ugly. Then at age 16 she grew big breasts and discovered sex and seductiveness. As it was the end of the hour, she was assigned the homework of making a satin comforter.

Janet's Comment

When Denise talked about sex through the two stories, Dr. Cummings talked about death (the obsessional side). When she asked about her husband's death, the therapist talked about sex—that is, her ugly duckling childhood. How did he know she felt ugly in childhood? It was apparent from her overcompensatory behavior of sex and seductiveness.

Session 3-A

The patient came in admitting she had not done the homework because her symptom was worse. The thought of stabbing Connie was constant. The patient was advised that in accordance with the initial agreement she would forfeit the session. At first she refused to leave, protesting that she needed help more than ever. "I need help; how heartless can you be?" The therapist replied that she should do her homework so she could get the necessary help. The patient departed, grumbling all the way down the hall.

Janet's Comment

This illustrates the value of denying treatment. Many therapists would fear that the patient would not return. Quite the contrary, Dr. Cummings knew she would return as this would strengthen the transference bond. Remember, this woman had an ineffectual father and she always longed for a father strong enough to protect her from the rejecting mother.

Session 4-A

The patient swept in, announcing that she had completed the homework. She did not bring in a photograph of the satin comforter, and as she described it at length, her behavior was seductive and grossly exhibitionistic. She sat with her legs parted, revealing the absence of underwear. The therapist stated blandly, "I am not a gynecologist; I am a psychologist." The patient cried profusely the remainder of the hour, using almost an entire box of Kleenex. The therapist said nothing. At the end of the hour I called time and assigned the homework. She was to write a term paper on how she would get along without Jeff.

Janet's Comment

Although the therapist addressed the hysteria (seductiveness) directly, the flagrancy of the behavior warranted an exception. It is for the patient's own self-respect and part of the treatment plan to limit the acting out and curtail the erotic transference. After interpreting the seductiveness directly and letting the patient be hysterical (crying) for most of the hour, the homework is strongly on the side of the obsession (Jeff's death). The homework subtly deals with death without linking it to the baby-stabbing obsession. Dr. Cummings is aware of the patient's anger toward him, probably stemming from having been sent home the last session. But Denise is not ready to face her inward anger, which is of murderous proportions.

Session 5-A

Denise arrived in a bubbly manner, waving her homework paper in the air. She began reading in a mocking voice, "Why I can't get along without Jeff." Her manner was disdainful as she listed a number of nonreasons, such as "who would play the turnip if Jeff weren't here?" Then she became quite animated as she talked of enrolling in modeling classes. The point of the story was to tell her therapist that during the past week she seduced the director and several of his associates. Some of them were filming a Suzuki motorcycle commercial (a Japanese product was being introduced to the American market that very month). Denise was filmed half clothed, making a mock commercial in which she seductively said, "The boys all like me ever since I let them play with my

Suzuki." She finally seemed to wind down, at which point I asked, "Why are you pathetically throwing your body around? You are neither ugly nor helpless."

Then Denise was told she was forfeiting another session because she had not really done her homework. She was given two assignments: (1) Do your homework right, not mockingly, and (2) choose between promiscuity and Jeff. If you wish to sleep around, leave Jeff. If you wish to stay with Jeff, stop sleeping around.

Janet's Comment

Denise is getting even with her therapist. Feeling rejected when her seductiveness in the previous session did not work, she seduced several men in one week. Again Dr. Cummings seeks to serve her self-respect by limiting her acting out and sparing her from later embarrassment. This is the second time treatment was denied because the homework was not done.

Session 6-A

Denise swaggered into the office wearing her riding habit, complete with boots. She was carrying a riding crop. She announced that she realized how much she could not get along without Jeff after she had mistakenly pulled into a self-service gas station and realized she did not know how to pump gas. It should be noted that self-service gasoline was just then coming into vogue. She enumerated a number of things Jeff had to do for her. After reciting a rather long list, she matter of factly stated, "Oh, yes. I stopped sleeping around." I acknowledged that she had, indeed, completed her homework and then fell silent.

After about 15 or 20 minutes Denise broke the silence and asked, "Why don't you like me?" I quickly replied, "Because I'm a horse's ass that needs to be whipped." The patient was taken aback. "How did you know I was thinking something like that?"

She went into a long apology, repeating over and over again, "I really didn't mean it." I maintained a stony silence. I spoke only at the end of the session to give her the homework for the ensuing week. This was to learn to pump gas.

Janet's Comment

It is not atypical for hysterics to dress according to a role that reflects their attitude at the moment, and not be aware of its meaning or that they are telegraphing their real feelings. Dr. Cummings identified her anger at him without being punitive. But neither did he leave her off the hook. Denise had to live with her suddenly acknowledged wish to whip her therapist. From the way she swaggered seductively in her riding habit, whipping the therapist was both hostile and sexual. Then Dr. Cummings did something novel: he assigned the task of learning to pump gas. This is not a frivolous assignment as it subtly nudges the patient toward the idea of self-sufficiency by using the patient's own language.

Session 7-A

The patient was very proud of herself as she described how she learned to pump gas. The therapist obviously looked pleased but did not praise her unduly, implying that this was only the first of many things she would be learning.

Denise talked nonstop for the entire session. She described her childhood growing up with a rejecting mother, a hateful brother, and an ineffectual father. When her father did something nice for her she would dream that he would become strong and protect her from brother Bill and mother. She told a story from the time she was age 12. The family was eating dinner when Bill announced that he had proof Denise had been "pedaling her ass all over town." She felt mortified, pleaded it was not so, lost her appetite, and cried all through dinner. It was only at the end of dinner that Bill laughed and said, "I meant on her bicycle!"

The homework assigned was to determine how she would get along without Jeff and without pedaling her ass all over town.

Janet's Comment

The therapist is again using the homework to conceptually nudge Denise toward self-sufficiency and away from dependency on Jeff's money. Her needing Jeff's money to feel secure is a great deal of her desire to see him dead. But it is too early to link the baby-stabbing symptom to murderous feelings toward her husband. To do so would be strong-arming the resistance. Dr. Cummings also incorporated the patient's own language (as derived from her brother) for promiscuity: pedaling her ass all over town.

Session 8-A

The patient completed her homework by way of a detailed fantasy in which she would marry a successful, attentive man after leaving Jeff. In her fantasies she and her new husband would have a set of his–her Mercedes Benz automobiles. He would be very successful, very loving, and *widowed*. (Note: I owned a Mercedes Benz which was parked in a space with my name on it. Denise would have to pass this as she entered the building.) As she continued with a prolonged description of her imagined second husband, he began to look more and more like the therapist. As she ran down, I asked, "Should I stab my wife?" Denise was stunned into silence. After 10 minutes or more, she whimpered, "Of course not."

The homework assigned was direct: List 10 reasons why you should not stab your husband.

Janet's Comment

For the first time the therapist connects the stabbing to independence. If the therapist stabs his wife, then he is free to become the patient's second husband. It took eight sessions before it was possible to do this without strong-arming the resistance. This is particularly important when working with hysterics. A premature connecting of the obvious with an hysteric will cause her to bolt therapy. It should be noted that what might seem to be aloofness, coldness, or unresponsiveness by Dr. Cummings is none of these. His approach strengthened the positive transference while keeping the erotic transference to a minimum.

Session 9-A

This was a remarkable session. The homework was the vehicle for a complete breakthrough. Denise realized just last week that her obsession of stabbing the baby had been absent for three weeks. Now the patient is ready for insight and understanding. Important behavior changes can now be expected. She shook her head in dismay as she told me that all along it was Jeff she wanted to stab, not Connie. She looked for me to indicate I was proud of the progress she had made. Instead I asked matter of factly, "Are you still pumping your own gas?" Denise snapped, "Aren't you ever going to say something nice about me?" Therapist: "Not until you say something nice about yourself."

Denise reflected for a time, then asked, "If I'm so beautiful, why did I marry a man 21 years older?" Without waiting for an answer she talked about this at length, describing Jeff as handsome, successful, debonair, but not sexy. I interjected, "Then he is more like your father than your brother." The patient was ready to put it all together. She realized at once that a man could be exciting like brother and at the same time stable like father. It was not either-or. Suddenly she exclaimed, "I *do* love Jeff." At this point the next homework was obvious: Seduce the turnip.

Janet's Comment

Again the therapist concentrates on helping the patient increase her self-esteem and do things that would reduce her learned helplessness. She can show her love and her competence at the same time by bringing sex into the marriage.

Session 10-A

Denise did, indeed, seduce the turnip. She arranged a trip to Carmel, bought sexy lingerie, and arranged the ultimate in a seductive weekend. Jeff responded beyond her expectations. She was ecstatic. Following the second honeymoon weekend she drove to her hometown and visited with her mother and went to her father's grave. She also visited Bill and his family, during which she pulled her brother aside and told him for the first time that he had been a lousy older brother. Finally, Denise asked, "Do you think I did my homework this time?" To which the therapist affably replied, "I think you're getting ready to fire me." The patient laughed contagiously. She was delighted with the new homework: Go on a two-week second honeymoon and return for an appointment in three weeks.

Janet's Comment

The patient is doing well, but instead of complimenting her directly, which she would see as seductive, Dr. Cummings introduces the concept she may be ready to go it on her own. Instead of the therapist pushing the patient out, she has the ability to fire him. This precludes feelings of rejection and again encourages self-sufficiency.

Session 11-A

The patient and her husband had a wonderful time on the assigned two-week second honeymoon. They spent one week in Las Vegas and the second week in Palm Springs. Then Denise added another part to the homework. She and Jeff bought his–her Mercedes Benz automobiles. Eventually the patient got around to asking if she had to continue coming in. I described how she had the privilege of coming in if and when she might need to do so in the future. On leaving she approached me. Then as if realizing she would be overstepping therapeutic boundaries, she shook hands and smilingly said, "Consider yourself hugged."

Janet's Comment

Having gotten permission to interrupt treatment and feeling competent and in control of her life and marriage, the patient leaves therapy. This concludes the first episode of treatment (1959), a total of 11 sessions.

EPISODE 2: 1968

Session 1-B

Denise returned to therapy nine years later because Jeff died of pancreatic cancer. It had been only a few short months from the diagnosis to his death. She was depressed, crying, and out of control in spite of the antidepressant that had been prescribed by her primary care physician. Her daughters were now ages 12, 11, and 9.

The treatment plan that was formulated was to first free up the mourning that was being hampered by the use of antidepressants and the reactive depression which was flooding her feelings in lieu of mourning. Then it would be possible to facilitate the mourning process.

The matter of the antidepressants was discussed and Denise agreed to go until the next session (one week) without them. The strategy was for me to behave as the now-deceased turnip. When she was crying her heart out, I would occasionally interrupt to ask, "Is something bothering you, Denise?" I also pointed out the ways she was fortunate. Jeff left substantial life insurance as well as mortgage insurance. She had money and the house was paid for. Besides, she could now marry a successful, exciting widower.

Her homework was to list all the ways in which she was fortunate to have been married to Jeff.

Janet's Comment

Since reactive depression is introjected rage, in this case at the husband for dying just when all was going well, the therapist is using the technique of mobilizing rage in the service of health. His acting like Jeff enables Denise to externalize the rage and displace it on Dr. Cummings instead of punishing herself through depression.

Session 2-B

Denise stormed into the office, glared at me, and then read her homework, which was 10 reasons why she is fortunate not to be married to me. She went into a tirade at me, saying I was the worst psychologist in the world because I lacked compassion for my patients. She made a point of saying I was worse than any turnip in the universe. But her depression was completely gone; the anger was directed outward at me, not inward at herself. When she settled down from her tirade, which I had ignored, we discussed her homework, which was to mourn (cry as much as she could, allow herself to miss Jeff and to reminisce about the good times they had together, give herself permission to excuse herself from well-meaning friends whenever she felt like being alone, etc.)

Janet's Comment

The mobilization of rage in the service of health was effective, mainly because the therapist did a good job of imitating the turnip, which is all she was then remembering of Jeff. With the depression gone, the patient is free to do the healing work of mourning.

Sessions 3-B and 4-B

Denise continued the process of bereavement in an accepting, encouraging therapeutic environment, with the continued homework of doing the work of mourning. She was helped to understand that successful bereavement takes about one year. Denise felt strong enough to do the work of mourning on her own, providing she could call on the therapist if she needed help. She was assured this was so.

Janet's Comment

This concludes the second episode of therapy, which was only four sessions. This is typical in intermittent psychotherapy throughout the life cycle. The patient generalizes a strength derived from previous therapy and the knowledge she can return at any time, so return episodes tend to be brief even in a tragedy like the death of a spouse.

EPISODE 3: 1969

Session 1-C

Patient returns after only one year because she met a new Jeff, a successful and handsome engineer who lived and worked in southern Illinois. "I did my homework. I listed 10 reasons why Jeff and I should marry, and I could find only one why I shouldn't." She recounted the 10 positive reasons, among which were that the new Jeff was attentive and sensual, and anything but a turnip. The one negative was that she would have to leave California and would not be able to see me if she needed to do so. My reply was a rhetorical question: "There are no airlines between Illinois and San Francisco?" It did not take Denise long to assign her own homework, which was to marry Jeff.

Janet's Comment

By his one question Dr. Cummings acknowledged her excellent homework and threw the decision back to her. It also reassured her that he was still available in spite of the distance. For the next 13 years the patient wrote one or two times a year. In between she talked to the therapist in her head, again something that is very typical for patients in intermittent therapy throughout the life cycle. Her letters would reveal how she could hear the therapist's reply in her head. She missed California, but her marriage was wonderful and Jeff was a responsible, loving stepfather to her three daughters. She was an avid skier, and having the money to do so, she had constructed a ski "slope" on their several-acre estate. In fact, on one of his visits to a new center in southern Illinois, which Dr. Cummings' company had created, the center director, in extolling the attractions of otherwise flat landscape, said, "We even have a local ski slope." Thus, episode three was comprised of only one session.

EPISODE 4: 1982

Session 1-D

Denise and Jeff had returned to California and she came in to say "hello" and to bring me up to date. All three of her daughters were married and living somewhere in California. The youngest, Connie, who was the object of the stabbing obsession 23 years ago, was close to receiving her CPA status, having followed in her father's footsteps. Denise's mother had died and she handled it okay. She did the mourning as she had learned to do it after Jeff's death. She described how she talked to me in her head for 13 years and got answers. "I knew if I did not get an answer I could hop on an airplane and come out to see you." I welcomed her back, commented on how self-sufficient and happy she had been during her absence, and assured her I was still here.

Janet's Comment

To make such an appointment after so many years and without being in distress is not unusual for patients in intermittent therapy throughout the life cycle. The patient had returned home and was touching base after 13 years out of state. It is frequent that after a decade or more, and with no extant problem, patients come in for a "checkup," which is really an excuse to make certain the therapist is still in practice and available. Episode 4 was also only one session.

EPISODE 5: 1983

Session 1-E

Denise's brother had died of a heart attack while chopping wood. "I am so grateful I gave myself homework to overcome my anger at Bill. The last several years we have become good friends. I finally got to know my sister-in-law, too, and I like her. We became close these last few years."

Janet's Comment

The often surprising thing is how patients in focused psychotherapy have learned to handle trauma and loss. Learning does generalize. Denise, after the first episode of 11 sessions, handled her first husband's death in 4 sessions, and her mother's and brother's deaths on her own. These did involve talking to her therapist in her head, an acquired skill that is not uncommon in focused psychotherapy. It is also not unusual for a patient to come in and report her success.

EPISODE 6: 1993

Session 1-F

The patient returned after 10 years because Jeff is retiring and she is opposed to it. She had a fantasy that Jeff would become a prestigious executive in a Silicon Valley firm and she would graciously entertain important guests. She could not be the gracious hostess if Jeff were not the important executive. She was given the following homework: How do you want to live now that Jeff is retiring? She was to return in one month.

Janet's Comment

In keeping with her therapy throughout, Dr. Cummings, using the homework, points out that she is in charge of her own life only.

Session 2-F

The patient had done her homework. She and Jeff left the condominium they had purchased when they returned to California, and she had bought a large, prestigious home in an excellent neighborhood. She had done all of this in one month! She planned to enjoy decorating the house exquisitely, and she had concluded that she was not dependent upon Jeff to be a gracious hostess. Her second husband was a charming gentleman, and the two of them were a most attractive couple.

Janet's Comment

With very little help (two sessions) Denise once again took control of her life. She had a marvelous time decorating the house, and she subsequently sent Dr. Cummings clippings of the results from *House Beautiful* magazine, where her home was featured.

EPISODE 7: 1996

Session 1-G

Denise is now age 60! However, any difficult feelings she might have had reaching that age were already resolved in her self-assigned homework, which had been completed before she came in. It was difficult to think of Denise as 60, inasmuch as she looked much younger. In her own words, "I look 45. I still have a great figure and I can pass and even look good for 45. But when people find out I'm 60, I am told I look spectacular. So why hide my age? I'm proud of how I look."

She also told me that the $50,000 in life insurance left by her first husband, with excellent investments over the decades, had grown to $1,600,000. She has her husband, her good looks, financial security, and she is enjoying her grandchildren.

Janet's Comment

Denise has acquired a modus operandi of making an appointment in advance to see Dr. Cummings, and seeing this as a deadline. She uses the interim to assign and complete her own homework, and comes in proudly to display her success. Still essentially an hysteric, her exhibitionistic tendencies have been altered so that they serve her maturity and continued self-sufficiency rather than reflect her original self-destructive behavior.

EPISODE 8: 1999

Session 1-H

Denise originally made the appointment because she learned she needed surgery. She was agitated and worried, and decided seeing me before the surgery would help her through it. However, her worsened physical condition necessitated advancing the date of the procedure, and by the time I saw her, it was all over. Removal of bleeding polyps from her colon was successful, and there was no cancer. However, in spite of the fact that all went well, Denise was struggling with the issue of creeping old age. Even though she looked years younger than her age, she was beginning to realize that she cannot stop the clock entirely. She had early signs of the arthritis common in women in their sixties, and was feeling other aches and pains following what earlier would not have been regarded as strenuous activity. She was assigned the homework of finding a way of eliminating these annoying aches and pains. She laughed as she went out the door, saying, "Dr. Cummings, you have a way of making me realize things by asking me to do the impossible that I am insisting should be possible."

Janet's Comment

As most patients who have improved following a paradoxical intervention, Denise is aware of the technique the therapist is using. In this session she had resolved the problem before she left the office and was amused that she still needed the prodding of her therapist.

Session 2-H

As expected, Denise arrived not really needing the appointment. Under her physician's direction she was taking a low-dosage medication mornings and evenings for her arthritic pain, and this was working. She also modified her expectations of herself; she remained very active, but accepted that her activities had to be at the pace of a woman in her sixties.

Janet's Comment

Denise has been seen for 40 years, demonstrating a typical course in intermittent focused psychotherapy throughout the life cycle. A lifetime of problems required a mere total of 23 sessions with her therapist. Dr. Cummings will undoubtedly see her again because he is available to her, and in the interim she will continue to talk with him in her head. After 11 sessions of focused psychotherapy in the initial episode, where she was overwhelmed by an obsession she would stab her 6-month-old baby, Denise needed only 12 more sessions over the next 39 years. Would this outcome have been better if Denise were initially kept in long-term therapy to prevent any future problems? It is doubtful that the outcome would have been better or even as good.

Over half a century of experience with focused psychotherapy, applied intermittently throughout the life span of the patient by my father and the many colleagues he has trained, demonstrates this is an effective and efficient way to practice. It also demonstrates the generalization of the coping mechanisms the patient learns. In addition, it reveals that patients know when to return. They talk with the therapist in their heads, and come in when the answer is not forthcoming. Finally, I and the many psychotherapists who have adopted my father's lead, attest that intermittent focused psychotherapy throughout the life cycle is a rewarding way to practice. Not only does the therapist experience remarkable competence, but the therapy is congenial to the current cost-containment age without in any way depriving the patient of needed treatment.

CHAPTER 6

Psychotherapy's New Horizons

Psychotherapy as we know it, frequently referred to as "talk therapy," is entering a third century. Beginning in Paris and Vienna in the nineteenth century, it flourished once it was exported to America in the twentieth century. It exploded in popularity following World War II, at which time the official psychoanalytic movement sought to restrict training to physicians. This was a mistake which set the stage for the proliferation of non physician psychotherapists, resulting in the more recent decision of the American Psychiatric Association to remedicalize psychiatry and leave psychotherapy to the psychologists and social workers. Psychiatry, through its efforts to restrict psychotherapy as medical practice, created a competition that eventually defeated its purpose. The second half of the twentieth century saw many

advances in psychotherapy, which went beyond psychodynamic
formulations to behavioral, strategic, and systems models. These
were spearheaded mostly by psychology, but certainly not
entirely. As we neared the end of the twentieth century three
trends were apparent: (1) Long-term therapy was declining
sharply, along with the solo practice of psychotherapy; (2) effec-
tive/efficient psychotherapies reflecting considerable integration
and delivered in group practices were gaining the ascendancy; (3)
the failure of official psychology to solve the masters-level issue
and to restrict psychotherapy to a doctoral profession was as big
a blunder as that of psychiatry in its attempts to restrict psychotherapy to medicine. Doctoral psychology had created a com-
petitive monster, with masters-level psychologists and social
workers depressing remuneration to doctoral-level psychologists.
Psychology is a beleaguered profession while psychiatry has
become largely a medicating, hospitalizing, administrative, and
liaison profession. This is the picture as psychotherapy enters the
twenty-first century.

Beginning in the nineteenth century and continuing through
the twentieth century, in spite of efforts to medicalize psychotherapy, medical treatment and psychological treatment remained sep-
arated into two different houses. The house of psychotherapy was
akin to walking into a temple, and confidentiality, secrecy with a
disdain for empirical research, parochial training within psy-
choreligious schools, the certification of adherents, and aloofness
disguised in psychobabble became pariahs that perpetuated a
strict mind-body dualism. As if these were not enough, the
providers' arch-enemy, managed care, carved out behavioral
health from the health care system and put it into entities that
were entirely independent from the healthcare companies that
contracted with them. Added to the mind-body dualism was now
the chasm created by two systems of informatics that did not talk
to each other, a death knell to efficiency and effectiveness in an era
in which information and its rapid transmission are the keys to

success. These factors have fostered not only a separate mental health system, but have promulgated language that promotes dualism. Hence, we have clients instead of patients, issues instead of symptoms or problems, expression and understanding of feelings instead of behavioral change, and facilitation instead of treatment. We shall see all of this change in the twenty-first century.

THE FUTURE: ONE HOUSE, ONE PATIENT, ONE SYSTEM

The first half of the twenty-first century will see behavioral care become an integral and indistinguishable part of primary care. This is where behavioral care rightfully belongs, since 60 to 90% of visits to physicians are either patients who are somatizing or have problems of stress and distress complicating and hampering the treatment of physical disease. Additionally, most disease today can be traced to faulty lifestyles. Clearly, psychotherapists not only belong in the primary care system, but psychological treatment should be at its core just as much as biomedicine is.

In an integrated system the medical and behavioral treatment is seamless. The patient is not aware when he or she has gone from one to the other. If the physicians wear white coats the psychotherapists wear white coats, and if the physicians do not wear white coats neither do the psychotherapists. To the patient they are indistinguishable. With the psychotherapist on site in the primary care system far more patients who need psychological treatment are identified, and 80 to 90% of these enter psychotherapy instead of only 10% in the fractionated system. Since the future of psychotherapy is a part of primary care, we strongly favor a return to the appropriate terminology: We see patients with symptoms and conditions that we treat with interventions for the purpose of improving their health, both physical and psychological. This honesty of language does not preclude the fact that patients must be partners in their own care, physically as well as psychologically, and that the treating physician or psychologist is no longer the authoritarian figure of the past. Diversity does not obviate patients' need for treatment of conditions ranging from high blood pressure to suicidal behavior. Most of our patients, along with treatment of their physical disease, need help in becoming compliant with medical regimen and in altering their faulty life styles.

Although everyone gives lip service to the integration of behavioral health with primary care, the resistance is fierce. There are centuries of medical hierarchies with turf to protect. It has been said it takes 35 years to change the climate in a medical school. Psychotherapists are fearful of losing their identity, something they see as inevitable if they leave the sanctity of their offices. Funding structures tend to solidify the status quo. The pre-eminence of specialties would be replaced by the emphasis on primary care.

Yet, in spite of all this resistance, there are a number of large, prestigious locations where the integration of behavioral health and primary care is not only a stated goal, but in various stages of completion. These include, but are not limited to Allina, Group Health Cooperative (now Kaiser Group Health), HealthPartners, Kaiser Permanente, and probably the most sophisticated endeavor to date, that at HealthCare Partners in the Los Angeles area. The latter is about to publish extensive research and experience that are bound to become the gold standard in the drive toward integration. In addition, several medical schools have become HMOs, or have formed joint ventures with large health insurers, or both. Among these are Duke University, a private institution, and the University of Missouri, Columbia, a public institution, showing that it can be done within either environment. These pioneering efforts will become a wave as they attain results that employers and other payers, as well as the patient/consumers, will want emulated. Early efforts uniformly report unprecedented patient satisfaction with a seamless, integrated healthcare system.

The current manner in which psychotherapy is delivered will continue, with some modification, as a relatively small psychosocial system side by side with the newer system of care. The vast majority of psychotherapy will be delivered within an integrated healthcare system. So much will this be the mainstream that the term "health psychologist" will disappear in favor of behavioral care specialist, working side by side with the primary care physician, the nurse, and other healthcare professionals that will comprise treatment teams. There will be profound changes in psychotherapy. It is important to describe these to show that they embody all of the essential elements and requisites of psychotherapy as we know it now. Its forms, however, will be radically different. We call this psychotherapy's new horizon.

THE POPULATIONS AND SETTINGS

As can be implied from the foregoing, the new psychotherapies will be in organized settings. An integrated program cannot take place in solo practice, and even small group practices cannot achieve the critical mass required to mount these interventions. The integrated psychotherapy of the future will not only be focused, it also will be targeted to specific populations and specific conditions. It has been found that many such targeted therapies are more effective if conducted in a group format rather than in individual therapy (Kent & Gordon, 1997). This is not a surprising finding; it was first apparent several decades ago in the treatment of addictions. With the addict, the peer culture and its pressures toward abstinence enhance sobriety, whereas a cozy relationship with an accepting and forgiving individual therapist seldom yields such positive results. Similar results have been found in chronic illness in which peer support and encouragement are prime ingredients for success, as well as in severe personality disorders where the necessary boundary building is encouraged and enforced by peer pressure rather than by what would be regarded as a parental/authoritarian therapist. The former creates group cohesion, while the latter sparks rebellion.

In a national model with millions of patients, it was found that 50% of the patients showed greater improvement with the targeted group model and another 25% could benefit from time-limited (closed) group therapy; for only 25% patients was individual psychotherapy the most effective treatment (Cummings & Cummings, 1997). It is anticipated that this kind of ratio will prevail in the integrated systems of the future, requiring the psychotherapist to make a drastic paradigm shift from the present preference for conducting individual therapy.

The targeted psychotherapy program will have a large psychoeducational component, since it has been found that even becoming knowledgeable about one's physical or psychological condition in itself results in significant improvement (Budman & Steenbarger, 1997). It employs behavioral, psychodynamic, and strategic interventions melded into programs designed and targeted toward a specific physical or psychological condition, with considerable mixing and matching among the various programs possible. It is beyond the scope of this book to provide an exhaustive list of such programs, but the following are among the most used (for a more extensive review of targeted programs see Cummings, Cummings, & Johnson, 1997):

Agoraphobia, multiple phobias and panic/anxiety disorder including initial house calls for patients who are house-bound

Asthma, with separate programs for adults and children and a special program for the parents of asthmatic children

Bereavement programs for the recently widowed, especially for those with marriages that were of 40-, 50-, or 60-year duration

Borderline personality disorder, which can often include narcissistic personality disorder

Cancer programs, which can be further delineated into breast, prostate, colon, or other cancers for which the patient is undergoing medical treatment and where a large psychological component is almost invariably present

Chronic daily headache program

Chronic fatigue (Epstein-Barr) syndrome, known as the "yuppie syndrome," which remains amazingly prevalent and persistent

Depression, which is the largest single psychological complication confronting the primary care physician

Diabetes, again with separate programs for adults and children and a special program for parents of diabetic children

Eating disorders, especially those which have led to diabetes and other medical complications, as well as those classified as morbid obesity

Fibromyalgia program. This condition is among the most baffling and persistent for the primary care physician, but has been found to be helped by targeted programs.

Hypertension, which is among the deadliest and least compliant of physical conditions, and for which psychological interventions have been shown to significantly increase attention to the medical regimen

Independent living programs for schizophrenics

Low back pain, which is the most commonly somaticized condition, addressed by special teams of physicians, psychologists, nurses, and physiotherapists comprising the new back clinics. It is interesting that these back clinics seldom have an orthopedic surgeon as part of the team but have one available for referral of the infrequent case that is not predominately psychological.

Pain education and management programs

Skills not pills programs designed to reduce the undue reliance on medication

Somaticizer programs, designed to address those patients who develop the latest popular medical condition and are consistently among the highest overutilizers of healthcare

Stress management for individuals with chronic illness, often divided into chronic illnesses in older adults and chronic illnesses in younger individuals

Many of these programs involve psychologists working on teams with physicians. At first they will erroneously be seen by those not intimately involved as supportive therapy. Although peer and therapist support are an integral part of all such programs, they involve much more.

ELEMENTS OF TARGETED PROGRAMS

There are a number of elements that targeted psychotherapy programs have in common (Cummings & Cummings, 1997), although not every protocol will contain each and every one of the following:

Educational component, from which the patient learns a great deal about the medical or psychological condition, as well as the interplay between one's body and emotions

Relaxation techniques, which include meditation and guided imagery

Pain management for those populations suffering from chronic pain. This includes help in reducing undue reliance on pain medication and addressing any problems of iatrogenic addiction

A support system, which includes not only the group milieu but also the presence of "veterans" who have been through the program. A useful modification of the element of support is the pairing of patients into a "buddy system" that allows them to call each other, meet for desensitization or homework, and generally be there for each other in time of need

Stress management, adjusted to meet the needs of specific conditions and populations

Behavioral techniques, including desensitization, schedules of reinforcement, cognitive restructuring, etc

Strategic interventions, designed to cut through resistance, especially with the personality disorders, somatizers, and other conditions that are otherwise likely to impede therapy

Psychodynamic formulations to aid the patient in the understanding of conflicts that are most likely to be displaced into physical symptoms or chronic pain

A self-evaluation component which not only enables the patient to assess how well she or he is doing psychologically, but also teaches the patient to monitor such critical features as blood pressure, diet, insulin, and other signs important to chronic illness

Homework assigned after every session. The homework is never perfunctory; rather, it is carefully designed to move the patient to the next step of self-mastery. It is always relevant to the condition being treated and may include desensitization, behavioral exercises, planned encounters with one's relationships or environment, readings, and other assignments which are critical to the well-being of the patient

Treatment of depression for those patients whose severely altered mood is interfering with their ability to participate in the program

Self-efficacy (after Bandura, 1977), the belief that one can perform a specific action or complete a task. Although this involves self-confidence in general, it is the confidence to perform a specific task. Positive changes can be traced to an increase in self-efficacy brought about by a carefully designed protocol that will advance the sense of self-efficacy

Learned helplessness (after Seligman, 1975), concept that holds helplessness is learned and can be unlearned. Some patients with chronic illnesses or dysfunctional backgrounds fall into a state of feeling helpless in the face of their disease or life's complexities. A well-designed protocol will enable a patient to confront and unlearn helplessness

A sense of coherence (after Antonovsky, 1987), required for a person to make sense out of adversity. Patients with chronic physical or mental illness, or those with severe personality disorders, feel not only that their circumstances do not make sense but that neither does their life. The ability to cope often depends on the presence or absence of this sense of coherence, and the protocol should be designed to enhance this

Exercise, an essential part of every protocol, which should be a highly encouraged activity even in individual psychotherapy. It is a feature most often neglected by patients and overlooked by psychotherapists. Exercise helps ameliorate depression, raises the sense of self-efficacy, and promotes coping behavior. The patient should be encouraged to plan his or her own exercise regimen, and then stick to it

Timing, length, and number of sessions, which vary from protocol to protocol, reflecting the needs of each population or condition, and in accordance with research and experience

Modular formatting enables a protocol to serve different but similar populations and conditions by inserting or substituting condition-specific modules

CHARACTERISTICS AND UTILITY OF TARGETED GROUP MODELS

Targeted group programs serve three functions to varying degrees, depending on the primary function in a specific model: treatment, prevention, and management. This is not unlike the same characteristics found in individual psychotherapy, where the goals of treatment, prevention, and patient management vary according to the presenting condition.

Treatment

The important feature of targeted group models is that they are therapeutic, and for many conditions, more so than individual psychotherapy. The emphasis on psychoeducation, group cohesion, and support—and the grounding in the primary care setting—all combine to enhance the focus of the psychotherapy. Preliminary results indicate that the greatest therapeutic effect is most likely to be not only with disease populations, but also with lifestyles which reflect the patient's overscrupulousness: agoraphobia, adult children of alcoholics, perfectionist personalities, and other conditions in which the patient suffers from overbearing neurotic guilt. These patients keep their appointments, engage themselves attentively, respect the authority of the professional, and always do their homework.

For many of these conditions the therapeutic effect of the targeted group model may be considerably superior to individual psychotherapy. The one notable exception may be depression sufficient to render group participation difficult or impossible. But even with depressed patients seen individually, there is an enhanced outcome when the treatment is in a primary care setting where the primary care physician remains integral to the treatment. The collaboration between physician and psychologist results in appropriate use of antidepressants, with proper dosages throughout and titration taking place as early as the psychotherapist sees warranted. This close a collaboration is hardly possible in the traditional setting.

This does not mean that patients without these characteristics do not benefit from targeted group models. Quite the contrary, they do benefit; but the therapeutic effect is less in comparison to the improvements stemming from patient management. These include personality disorders such as borderline personalities, addicts, and other patients who are rebellious, challenge authority, are likely to thwart appointments, and avoid homework assignments. These are the patients who do not suffer direct feelings of guilt, and their main distress is the result of their own chaotic lifestyles.

A note of caution is indicated. It is important that personality disorders not be placed in groups where the patients are neurotically guilt-ridden, as they will literally wreck the group and drive the other program participants to despair. The mistake of mixing these two types of patients occurs frequently because personality disorders can become depressed, anxious, or phobic, while borderline patients in distress can mimic just about any psychological condition. We have seen instances where in an asthmatic or agoraphobic group a borderline patient that should not have been included suddenly begins to reveal multiple personalities, which begin to capture undue attention and divert the group from its therapeutic purpose. In assigning patients, the primary diagnosis of personality disorder must prevail over the dual diagnosis reflecting the secondary condition.

With chronic physical conditions such as asthma, diabetes, emphysema, essential hypertension, rheumatoid arthritis, and other diseases, the goal is not to cure that which cannot be cured. This does not mean that reduction in pain and morbidity are not in themselves therapeutic; the emphasis, however, is in disease management.

Management

It is precisely with these kinds of intractable conditions, both medical and psychological, that patient management is important. The enduring personality disorders, including borderline personality, are an ongoing problem for the primary care physician who experiences their constant demands and complaints, their misuse of the medications prescribed, their lack of compliance, and their susceptibility to various diseases because of their faulty lifestyles. The primary care physician is aware of the overwhelming psychological component and needs the collaboration of an onsite behavioral care specialist as part of the team to help reign in their acting-out behavior. In a targeted group model the responsibility for monitoring acting-out behavior is vested in the group, which is much more savvy and strict than the physician or psychotherapist could possibly be. Consequently, these patients become manageable and less vulnerable to the consequences of their own emotional lability, constant rage, impulsiveness, and projective identification.

With chronic medical diseases, targeted group programs can increase coping, especially regarding the management of pain and physical limitations, as well as enhance compliance with the medical regimen.

Of special consideration is the schizophrenic patient, who is both troublesome and baffling to the primary care physician. Physical symptoms can reflect psychotic delusions, familiar examples being an odor which only the patients can smell that convinces them that their insides are rotting, a testicular pain that shifts sides frequently, or an abdominal pain that changes quadrants even during the physical examination. Other delusional physical symptoms can be more subtle, and the collaboration of the psychotherapist is essential. In addition, independent living programs can be conducted in various critical places in the environment, teaching schizophrenics how to buy underwear, order a meal, or buy a bus ticket without being overcome with psychotic anxiety. Although the psychotic thought disorder is incurable, the patients in such programs suffer fewer and fewer "crises" that provoke acute exacerbations of the kinds of ideation and behavior which require heavier doses of psychotropic medication or even hospitalization.

Prevention

Perhaps the most surprising finding is that when appropriate patients are assigned to appropriate targeted group programs, the demand for more intrusive and costly services is significantly, if not dramatically, diminished. This includes the reduced need for individual psychotherapy on the psychological side, as well as reduction of costly overutilization on the medical side. This is true prevention: services are no longer needed (i.e., the *demand* side in health economics), as contrasted with reducing services found in most cost-containment programs (the *supply* side of health economics). This is an important distinction because in this true prevention services are increased while costs still go down. Those medical patients who are prone to abuse hospitalization or emergency rooms, or those psychological patients who do the same by threatening suicide, learn to manage their lives without such drastic recourse. Chronic schizophrenics who require frequent and sometimes protracted hospitalizations learn to avoid exacerbation which triggers this need for hospitalization or restraint by medication.

PREVENTION VERSUS COST-CONTAINMENT

Reducing costs by reducing demand is certainly more desirable than rationing care, and is the very essence of both prevention and legitimate cost containment. In fact, the impetus for developing independent living programs for schizophrenics was the direct result of the discovery that the first capitated behavioral health Medicare contract of 140,000 covered lives included 8,000 persons in their thirties who were on social security by virtue of disabling mental illness. This was in 1988, and their average hospitalization rate of nearly 50 days per year could have bankrupted the coverage for the entire cohort, of which the vast majority were elderly social security recipients. A series of independent living programs rescued the entire contracted system by drastically reducing the need for psychiatric hospitalization (Cummings, 1997).

   Hospital days utilized can also be reduced in populations suffering from chronic medical conditions, along with significant reduction in emergency room visits and invasive procedures (Mumford, Schlesinger, & Glass, 1982; Schlesinger *et al.*, 1983).

TWO EXAMPLES OF TARGETED GROUP MODELS

Extensive descriptions of targeted group models are published elsewhere, and only two programs which have been successfully employed for several years are included here as examples. The first is the Hypertension Management Group Program (Kent & Gordon, 1997), which addresses a widespread medical condition with strong psychological and lifestyle components. It also is a medical condition with a potentially high mortality rate, yet it is among the lowest in compliance because the patient feels no symptoms. The second is the Bereavement Program (Cummings, 1997; Cummings & Cummings, 1997), which treats early bereavement, a psychological condition with overwhelming medical complications. It is a well-known fact that the first year after widowhood the surviving spouse experiences considerable physical symptoms, necessitating a great number of medical visits, tests, and procedures. This is especially true with marriages of over 40 or 50 year's duration.

THE HYPERTENSION MANAGEMENT GROUP PROGRAM

Essential hypertension is a medical condition that is potentially fatal. It has far-reaching psychological concomitants in that high blood pressure is exacerbated by stress. Since the patient feels no symptoms and is unaware of the condition, compliance tends to be very poor. The following protocol was developed at Kaiser Permanente in San Jose, California, by the chief of behavioral medicine, a psychologist, and the chief of medicine, a primary care internist.

The team consists of a primary care physician, a psychologist, and a medical assistant, all of whom are involved in other collaborative programs and teams.

The patients are invited to participate in the group program from the physician's panel. Inclusion criteria are: (1) diagnosis of stable, essential hypertension, with minimal other complicating medical diseases (although hyperlipidemia, mild diabetes mellitus, and mild coronary artery disease are acceptable), and (2) a willingness to participate in the program. The members are invited to participate by letter, phone contact, or a personal invitation from the physician.

The group size is set at a maximum of 15, with experience demonstrating that 12 is consistently the average number for the groups.

An introductory series of weekly sessions of $1^1/_2$ hours duration each, meets for 3 weeks to begin the program. These meetings cover group introductions, the completion of forms, the distribution of information/program packets, and educational presentations in the following areas: (1) hypertension diagnosis pathophysiology and behavioral and pharmacological treatments; (2) dietary considerations, including weight control and sodium and fat intake, as well as the importance of regular exercise; and (3) stress management and relaxation techniques. The group members are strongly encouraged to purchase a home blood pressure cuff and demonstrate competency in its use. All participants are required to keep a home blood pressure log, which they bring to the meetings. The work of Pickering (1994) suggests that home pressure readings are better predictors of how well blood pressure is controlled than blood pressure readings taken in medical settings. This is the so-called "white coat" syndrome, in which blood pressure is temporarily elevated because the doctor or nurse is taking the reading.

Clinical decisions regarding treatment modification are based on home blood pressure readings at the third session and at the four-month follow-up session. The appropriate treatment is based on input from the patient, the physician, and the psychologist. Telephone follow-up and treatment regimen modification is done by algorithm by the medical assistant after the initial sessions and between follow-up group appointments.

At follow-up meetings, which occur every four months, didactic information regarding hypertension, health topics, lifestyle interventions, and routine health maintenance measures are covered. It is also an opportunity for group support and "peer counseling." At all group meetings, participants are encouraged to discuss any health-related issues, which characteristically include psychological problems and stress, inasmuch as the patients do not differentiate between the mind and the body in an integrated system. There is no stigma because it is an emotional rather than physical issue. Finally, at these follow-up sessions the staff makes certain to address any acute health problems.

The researchers/clinicians found the following results: Recidivism for the group members who participated in the program has been negligible, and the patient satisfaction scales show unanimous delight, with an average score of 4.9 on a scale of 5. Blood pressure control has been excellent, with many patients able to decrease their medication and others able to discontinue it altogether. A financial analysis reveals that in the first year the program is slightly more costly than traditional approaches, with a reduction in costs thereafter. It is interesting, that for the staff, both psychologists and physicians, the satisfaction level is very high, which contradicts the fear of most practitioners. The authors conclude that the collaborative care of hypertension helps to address psychological aspects of the patient's life as they interface with their chronic medical condition. The biological, psychological, and social issues are seamlessly addressed. Their over all finding is that the model (1) improves clinical outcomes; (2) is cost effective; (3) improves patient and professional staff satisfaction; and (4) actively engages these patients in their own care (Kent & Gordon, 1997, pp. 114–117).

THE BEREAVEMENT PROGRAM

The Early Bereavement Program for widowed older adults was empirically developed and tested in Florida's "retirement strip," the 100-mile-long, 20-mile-wide section on the east coast from Miami to Palm Beach. This was in 1988 when American Biodyne received the first extensive behavioral health carve-out contract covering 140,000 Medicare lives from the Health Care Financing Administration (HCFA).

The target population is widowed older adults (over 62) who have recently lost a spouse, usually after many years of marriage.

An aggressive outreach program within the health plan identifies the patient shortly after the death of a spouse. Empathtic telephone contact invites the individual to the first session only, which is one-on-one.

There are a total of 14 group sessions, all of two hours' duration and spaced as follows: 4 semiweekly sessions, followed by 6 weekly sessions, and concluding with 4 monthly sessions.

Participants are assigned to groups of not less than 5 or more than 8 members, depending on the patient flow in the system. An even number is desirable as the patients are paired in a "buddy" support system.

Screening

In addition to the usual need for bonding, the initial individual first session is used to screen out patients who reveal severe depression rather than uncomplicated mourning. Reactive depression reflecting years of internalized rage stemming from marital unhappiness interferes with the healing process and is treated separately.

Medication

The patients are helped to use antidepressants sparingly, or not at all. These medications retard the process of healing and prolong and even postpone bereavement.

Education

The patient learns a great deal about the process of mourning and its painful but healing sequence. The grieving person is encouraged to cry, is given permission to spend a lot of time alone in spite of well-meaning friends, and is rewarded for reflecting on a lifetime with the deceased, recalling all the good and bad moments. It is normal to miss the deceased very much!

Self-efficacy

The patient learns to cope with being alone, and if the widowed patient was unduly dependent on the deceased in certain matters (finances, initiative, etc.) he or she is taught to unlearn the helplessness.

Support System

The pairing into a buddy system is particularly important for these patients, who at times would rather be with someone who is mourning than to be with well-meaning friends who often do not know what to say. The patient is also taught how to make friends more comfortable by releasing them from their self-imposed duty to make the mourner feel better. This results in making it possible for patient and friends to comfortably spend more time with each other.

The veteran is a patient who has completed a group but expresses a desire to continue the program because he or she needs the continued support. Such patients are encouraged to do so. Additionally, the presence of one or two "veterans" in each group helps and supports the newer patients. Their ability to say, "I remember when I felt exactly as you do, and this is what I did," is of inestimable value.

Homework

Since these patients spend a lot of time alone, appropriate reading assignments are welcomed. Not as welcomed is the homework to exercise, and they often must be cajoled into getting out and doing brisk walking. Once they try it, however, they feel so much better that they become fairly consistent in exercising. Mall walking early in the morning is a common older adult activity, so these patients do not feel out of place engaging in that form of exercise. At the appropriate time homework involving a *moderate* amount of social activity is assigned. This must be carefully tailored to the needs and abilities of each individual.

The Bereavement Program (Cummings & Cummings, 1997, pp. 343–345) has been found to dramatically reduce the somatizing that typically occurs during the first and even second years after the death of a spouse. Although it saves hundreds of dollars in needless medical services for each patient, even more important it saves the widowed person two years of needless physical suffering.

A VISION OF THE FUTURE

During the first part of the twenty-first century, behavioral health will take its rightful place as an integral part of the health system. Mind/body dualism, which has kept medicine and psychology apart for centuries, will disappear. Issues of parity between physical health and mental health will vanish; the system will be seamless, with biomedical and psychosocial care indistinguishable. The formidable resistance which perpetuates the fractionation of the medical and psychological, even in healthcare settings that are struggling to implement the collaborative model, will continue for a time and then crumble. Once the evolutionary process is in motion, it is only a matter of time. The senior author has seen this process in a number of activities in which he was instrumental. The reform of doctoral education and training in psychology was stalled until the spectacular success of the four campuses of the California School of Professional Psychology made them a model to emulate, both in existing universities and as freestanding schools. Up until he formed CSPP in 1969, the senior author had been working unsuccessfully with the Education and Training Board of the APA for more than a decade. The managed behavioral carve-out was invented by the senior author in 1976, which was long before its time. When he reintroduced the concept in 1983, the need was there and it took off like a rocket.

Similarly, collaborative care systems are still somewhat ahead of the wave, but once there are several successful programs demonstrating the superiority of care, the large employers of the nation will demand integrated care. If one has flown an amphibious airplane, she or he knows that it takes several more seconds of airspeed to break free of water than is required when taking off from land. The suction of the water prevents the craft from becoming airborne at speeds more than adequate on dry land. Once the suction breaks, however, the airplane lifts suddenly and rapidly. This is what will be seen in integrated primary care in the early part of the twenty-first century.

Experience in settings where collaborative care is implemented has shown that the prediction seems accurate that 50% of psychotherapy will be targeted group models, 25% will be time-limited group psychotherapy, and only another 25% will be one-on-one psychotherapy, most of it focused and problem oriented, and following the intermittent model throughout the life cycle. This will mean that most psychologists practicing today will need retraining in health psychology, a prospect that most will resist. The overproduction of psychologists will still leave more than enough practitioners who would welcome working in collaborative settings.

As has been seen, the new targeted models embody all of the elements of true psychotherapy. Yet they break the mold of tradition. Leaving the protected atmosphere of the solo practice office frightens many practitioners.

Let us not forget, however, that there will remain a smaller psychosocial system that parallels the newer collaborative model. There will always be clients who would prefer that model and will be willing to pay out of pocket or satisfy large deductibles. This traditional model will no longer be supported by the mainstream healthcare dollar. However, it remains to be seen if some entrepreneurial practitioners of the future do work out a financing mechanism that has yet to be conceived.

CHAPTER 7

New Notes on Old Masters

Psychology and social work entered the field of psychotherapy essentially in the post-World War II era of the late 1940s and early 1950s, a period that in retrospect can be designated as "the golden age of psychotherapy" (Cummings, 1975). The art of dynamic healing through verbal understanding became an essential service in the military whose casualties in the war just ended were one-third mental and emotional. The two decades immediately following World War II saw the popularization of psychoanalysis and the seemingly overnight public acceptance of private psychotherapists.

Psychoanalysis was inordinately successful, creating an enormous demand throughout the United States. There was no third-party reimbursement, but in its exuberance for this new treatment the public was eager to pay out of pocket. Psychologists imitated the medical model and rode the crest of this "golden age of psychotherapy." There seemed to be no end to the number of patients seeking psychotherapy, giving rise to the myth there could never be enough professionals trained.

This grand illusion not only helped spawn the paraprofessional movement also inspired ever-increasing legions of young people to seek careers in a practice that 35 years later would be overcrowded. In those naïve days we regarded as our only problem the eruption of three neuroses for everyone we "cured" on the couch. It was reasoned that given enough dollars psychotherapy could alleviate, if not actually eradicate, all the ills of a sick society. Accordingly, in the 1960s the community mental health centers were launched with this golden promise. Now we are painfully aware that psychotherapy not only oversold itself to patients and to society but also to future generations of colleagues, who believed the golden age would never end.

As the mental health professions themselves began to realize they could not make good their promise to the American public, the overselling collapsed and gave way to profound despair characterized by two self-destructive phenomena. The first of these was a pervasive, overly critical reevaluation of psychotherapy, which soon took on all the overtones of self-flagellation. The medical model needed to be criticized, but taken full-blown, the position of Thomas Szasz is an absurdity. Eysenck found no good in psychotherapy, and Schofield called it "paid friendship." Behavior therapies attacked dynamic therapies unmercifully, and everyone joined forces to make orthodox psychoanalysis the scapegoat for all of psychotherapy's tarnished promises.

The second symptom of despair, equally destructive by its intensity and excesses, was the espousal in the 1970s of every new kind of treatment that a seemingly endless array of proponents presented. During this turbulent era it was hoped that the next wild therapy would provide the solution to the failed promise.

Theory, empirical research, intensive training, and even seasoned experience were cast to the wind as professionalism was replaced by the guru's caftan.

The 1980s saw the return to professionalism, with many of the former "gurus" scurrying to regain respectability. Unfortunately, as is common following periods of excess, the professions overreacted. Our licensing boards and ethics committees have become overbearing and punitive, the plaintiffs' lawyers jump on our every therapeutic error with multimillion dollar lawsuits, and the public is proliferating psychologist jokes to the point they threaten the old standby, lawyer jokes.

The 1990s saw further decline in professional income and autonomy from managed care. The current clamor for data is perhaps the one sign of hope in a deteriorating practice climate, but the downside is that in cowering to managed care, exhibiting timidity in the face of malpractice suits, and joining the rush to "scientism" rather than science, the art in psychotherapy may be lost. It may be useful to reflect on the old masters who were practicing mid-century. For those of us who are older, they were our mentors. For those of us younger, they are among those who gave us our legacy.

The following notes, except for the final one, are narrated by the senior author from his own personal experiences. The last one of Milton Erickson's is narrated by his student, Jeffrey K. Zeig, Ph.D. (Zeig, 1980; 1990a; 1990b), who is the founding chair of The Milton H. Erickson Foundation. As you read these notes, reflect on the artistry of these colleagues, who as thoroughgoing professionals were not only grounded in theory but were also intensively trained and possessed vast experience. Their dedication to patient care is inspirational. Yet many of the notes would today raise eyebrows on ethics committees and might even mobilize overly zealous licensing boards. As Arnold Lazarus, Ph.D. laments, "We have become devoted to rules rather than doing what is helpful to the patient" (personal communication, August 1998).

SIEGFRIED BERNFELD, PH.D. AND
SIGMUND FREUD, M.D.

Dr. Bernfeld was instrumental in founding the San Francisco Psychoanalytic Institute. He had been analyzed by Dr. Freud, knew him intimately, and supplied Dr. Ernest Jones, Freud's biographer, with much of the historical information that otherwise would be missing. In spite of this background in Vienna, once Freud died and psychoanalysis "medicalized," Dr. Bernfeld's role in the San Francisco Psychoanalytic Institute was shamefully downgraded.

In the 1950s, after Dr. Bernfeld died, I was privileged to get to know his widow, who was also a lay analyst. One evening over coffee Madame Bernfeld told the following story.

Siegfried and Suzanne were both in psychoanalysis with Dr. Freud. In fact they met, courted, and fell in love while both were in treatment. This was taboo; two patients seeing the same analyst are regarded as psychoanalytic "siblings." They struggled to tell Freud but were fearful he would terminate treatment and throw them out of the Vienna Institute. Eventually they set a wedding date, and both knew they must tell their analyst before he heard it through the grapevine. They had a number of long discussions about who would be the one to tell him. Finally, Siegfried confessed that he totally lacked the courage to do so and Suzanne would have to be the one. The day they had set as the deadline to tell Dr. Freud came and Suzanne lay on the couch overcome with fear. Eventually she mustered the courage to tell her famous psychoanalyst. There was a long period of silence, during which Suzanne recalls shaking all over with fear. Then Dr. Freud arose, walked over to his bookshelf, and picked up an artifact she had frequently admired. Handing it to her while she still lay on the couch he said, "My wedding present to you and Siegfried."

FRIEDA FROMM-REICHMANN, M.D.

Dr. Fromm-Reichmann was a remarkable psychoanalyst who enjoyed treating schizophrenics. She was deeply influenced by her mentor, Harry Stack Sullivan, M.D., who had a real understanding of psychosis. In the 1940s I was privileged to work with Dr. Fromm-Reichmann for an all-too-short three weeks. It was one of the most profound experiences of my life.

The first time I accompanied her on her hospital rounds was an unforgettable morning. Psychotherapists active in psychiatric hospital care today have no idea what these institutions were like before the discovery of psychotropic medications. They were incredibly noisy, chaotic, and very brutal places. There was no way to effectively control patients in crisis except by physical restraint. The camisole was most frequently used, but for patients who could not be so tethered there was the wet sheet pack, which totally immobilized the patient. Then there was the unbelievable water restraint known as the "scotch douche." The patient would be placed in a tiled room and sprayed with pressure hoses that alternated very hot water with frigid water. This alternating spray was kept up until the patient collapsed in exhaustion. Perhaps the worst part was that violently acting-out psychotics had to be subdued by several burly male nurses before the restraint could be applied. Dr. Fromm-Reichmann was often distained because she would not permit these common, barbaric procedures.

She believed that schizophrenics may be speaking with us, but they are not really communicating until they allow us into their psychic space. It was they who chose whether to keep us out or, very infrequently, let us in. Dr. Fromm-Reichmann taught there were ways in which the psychotherapist could purposely enter the patient's space and, by virtue of the entry point, be let in. The first morning I went on rounds with her I witnessed the first of these.

Coming upon the not infrequent prepsychotropic-medication-era sight of a patient smearing feces, she sat down on the floor with the regressed schizophrenic. She donned a pair of surgical gloves and began smearing feces with the patient. After a time she removed the gloves, reached in the opposite pocket of her white coat, and pulled out a candy bar. Handing it to the patient, she said, "I would like you to consider which you like best, candy bars or feces. You don't need to tell me (the patient was mute). When I come by tomorrow morning I will know. If you are smearing your feces, I'll know you like feces better. But if you are not smearing feces, I'll know you prefer candy bars and I shall have another candy bar for you." This was repeated twice more before the morning rounds were completed. In one pocket she kept surgical gloves, and in the other candy bars. In the three weeks I was privileged to accompany her on her rounds I never saw the patient who did not give up feces for candy bars. She insisted that we cannot ask the patient to consider the matter until they hear us, which comes after they have let us into their psychic space. The act of smearing feces with the patient literally catapulted her into the space in which the patient could communicate. She or he could now hear and respond.

It is not well known that Dr. Fromm-Reichmann made a significant, fascinating contribution to the World War II effort, particularly in saving the lives of many of our paratroopers. The life of a paratrooper averaged three combat jumps, two for an officer. Troopers believed this, and as strange as it seems, it was psychologically helpful, enabling the paratrooper to jump into combat with the rationalization, "Nothing can happen to me because it is not my turn." The problem came on the fourth jump: "Now it is my turn." It was not infrequent for the paratrooper to freeze at the moment he was to jump, a phenomenon known as "jump door fever." It is very important that a platoon go out the door in a certain cadence. If it is too quick, the men will tangle in mid-air; if it is too slow they will be spread out too far from the target. The jump sergeant has the responsibility of maintaining the appropriate cadence, and if a trooper freezes at the jump door, pushing him out with his boot kicking the trooper's back. In such instances the trooper would hit the ground in a panic state and, forgetting all of his training in the face of the overwhelming anxiety, would soon be killed by the enemy. General (Doctor) William Menninger, who was chief psychiatrist for the army during World War II, reasoned that if a trooper could be talked out the door voluntarily he would not be killed while in a panic state. The problem was formidable: how do you talk a trooper willingly out the door in a matter of seconds?

Dr. Fromm-Reichmann had the answer. She taught a group of combat officers from the 82nd Airborne Division how to talk a trooper with jump door fever out the door in less than ten seconds, and usually within five. The paratrooper would be under the command of the platoon leader who had trained him and knew him well. The concept is simple but profound. Rage is a far more immediate, galvanizing emotion than love or any other feeling. In the service of health, rage can even be life saving. The officers were trained in how to so insult a trooper at the critical moment that he went out the jump door voluntarily, but in a rage. Rage and panic are incompatible emotions. The rage would save the paratrooper's life. To provoke the rage the officer would have to know the man well enough to choose the ultimate insult, which would be screamed at the "paralyzed" trooper while both were standing at the jump door with the roar of the engines, the deafening wind, and the turbulence of the aircraft.

I remember two such examples. One was with a 19-year-old soldier of Italian descent. It must be remembered that the Italian army disgraced itself during World War II and their missions had to be taken over by the German army. The soldier was very sensitive to being of Italian heritage and had been teased, often sadistically, by his fellow troopers. While frozen at the jump door he suddenly heard his officer scream, "Andy, are American wops as yellow-bellied as Italian wops?" The paratrooper uttered an insubordinate "Fuck you, captain," as he jumped out the door. In another instance a trooper facing his fourth jump had consistently demonstrated a concern for his manhood, even to the point of frequent aggressive homophobic remarks against his fellow soldiers. When he was overcome with jump door fever the officer yelled, "Don't jump, Donny" (a name hated by Don, who would hit anyone who called him that). "I've already prepared the papers for your transfer to the WACs" (Women's Army Corps, a segregated unit founded early in World War II). Don made a motion as if to punch the officer with his fist and then went out the door.

These are drastic verbalizations, uttered under extreme circumstances as the only possible way under combat conditions of saving a trooper's life. But consider these in the current world of political correctness. No matter that they saved many lives. No matter that no one was ever lost again with jump door fever in units where the officers were so trained. No matter that the trooper later understood the drastic measure and thanked the officer for saving his life. No matter that no one would recommend such incorrect talk in other than a live-or-die situation. I can just see Dr. Fromm-Reichmann furrow her brow and scowl at a charge of political incorrectness. After all, this was a remarkable woman so devoted to her patients that she would smear feces with them if that was what it took.

ERIK H. ERIKSON

Mr. Erikson, as he preferred to be addressed during an era when no one called his or her analyst or mentor by the first name, was a watercolorist who was spotted by Anna Freud for having the most remarkable rapport with children she had ever seen. She invited him to come to London and train to be a child psychoanalyst. He responded, "My paintings aren't selling so I might as well." He was never apologetic for not having a college degree of some kind in psychology, and he turned down a number of honorary doctorates. Whenever in my profound respect for this man I addressed him as "doctor," he shot back, "*Mister Erikson,* if you please!"

It was Erik Erikson who was the first truly developmental psychoanalyst, extending development beyond the first three years, which to Freud were the basis for the creation of the future personality. Mr. Erikson extended the development to stages throughout the life cycle, up to and including death.

As I fondly remember him, his understanding of children was as remarkable as that which Anna Freud had originally detected. He did not merely rely on this keen sense; he had an interesting evaluative procedure that he would employ before he began to treat a child and the family milieu. He would invite himself to dinner at the last minute so that artificial preparations could not be mounted. If the family declined or otherwise made excuses, he would refuse to take the referral. This dinner in the family home would be the first time he would see the child, and it would be in the natural setting with all the family interaction operating. He often would make interpretations in the middle of dinner, pointing out what was happening and suggesting more desirable alternatives. Sometimes this one "session," lasting several hours and continuing with the parents after the children were put to bed, was all that was required to bring about a resolution.

During my 44 years of practice I have often thought about Mr. Erikson and fantasized about present-day ethics committees and licensing boards accusing him of dual relationships and overstepping his therapeutic role, and remanding him to the play therapy room as a way of redeeming his suspended license.

ERIC BERNE, M.D.

Dr. Berne was a psychoanalyst and a respected member of the San Francisco Psychoanalytic Institute until he shook it to its foundations. Dr. Berne developed transactional analysis, a concept which purports that each of us has a child, adult, and parent in the way we respond. The trouble comes if my child is talking to your child, or my child is talking to your parent, and so forth throughout all the permutations. Mature, responsible relationships are present when my adult is talking to your adult, recognized by the phrase he popularized, "I'm okay, you're okay." He was the only psychoanalyst who ever inspired a Broadway musical. But through all of this he scandalized the orthodoxy of the San Francisco Psychoanalytic Institute, which both liked the publicity he brought to them and was extremely uneasy with his innovations. During the beginnings of our mental health services at Kaiser Permanente we were searching for anything that might be more efficient and effective than what was extant at the time. We engaged Dr. Berne as a consultant who would spend an afternoon a week with us.

Dr. Berne was a master of letting out his child as a way of teaching a difficult concept or driving home a point. He drove a Maseratti, an Italian sports car with rakish lines, which he called his mazeltov, a Yiddish word meaning congratulations. I never saw this car with its top up, even on the rainiest San Francisco day. When he entered the conference room he would remove an utterly squashed chapeau from his head, throw it on the chair, and sit on it for the next several hours. At the conclusion of the consultation, he would perch this disgraceful hat atop his balding head and nonchalantly walk out the door. He, his hat, and his mazeltov were inseparable. The man was brilliant and charming, but some colleagues never understood his delightful tongue-in-cheekbanter.

Several times while one of us would be presenting a case he would stop us and ask, "It is a psychotherapist's responsibility to cure every patient on the first session. What did you do this session to bring that about? And having failed, what did you do the next session to cure the patient in that otherwise unnecessary session?" One of our staff members, Dr. Jerry Travis, was a Jungian psychiatrist who took terrible umbrage with the idea that it was our duty to cure a patient in one session. He argued vociferously against what he called stupidity and nonsense, but Dr. Berne stuck by his guns. After a number of weeks Dr. Travis challenged Dr. Berne to present a case. He readily complied, described the patient, and said, "I would like to present the 11th session." Dr. Travis cajoled mercilessly, "I thought we're supposed to cure a patient in one session." Dr. Berne replied, it is our duty to cure each patient with one session. We do not always succeed, but in each subsequent session we try to cure the patient with just that one more session."

The lesson had been driven home and none of us present that day ever forgot it, all except Dr. Travis, who was so angry and upset that he transferred to another facility. This was radical stuff in 1960; amazingly, it is radical stuff to most psychologists even today.

FRANZ ALEXANDER, M.D.

Dr. Alexander was instrumental in founding both the Chicago and Los Angeles Psychoanalytic Institutes. In spite of this stature, when he and Dr. Thomas French wrote their book on brief psychoanalysis, a firestorm of criticism was unleashed. Few today are aware of the intriguing way he saw many of his patients.

He apportioned his time between his Chicago and Los Angeles supervisory activities, traveling regularly between those two cities on a fast, limited train known as the City of Los Angeles. In those days one could not simply jump on an airplane and make the trip in hours. Dr. Alexander could not spare from his practice three days to Los Angeles and three more back to Chicago every time he made the trip, which was at least once a month, so he hit upon an ingenious plan. He would take a compartment, his patients would book passage on the same train, and for three days they would file through his compartment for their 50-minute analytic session. While he spent the week in Los Angeles working they would vacation or do other things; then the procedure would be repeated on the three days back to Chicago. Some of his patients did not need any more treatment than would be provided in one sojourn, but most repeated this itinerary several times.

Since there is only one dining car on a train, was Dr. Alexander seen eating all his meals by his patients? Was there often mingling because of the nature of train travel? Of course. Fortunately, there were no investigators from a psychology licensing body aboard the train, probably because there were no such licensing boards yet. This was the late 1930s and the 1940s. In any of these encounters was Dr. Alexander anything but a thoroughgoing professional? Absolutely not. Did his patients benefit from such an unusual course of treatment? I would definitely bet yes.

PAUL WATZLAWICK, PH.D.

Dr. Watzlawick is the only one of our old masters who is still living. Anyone who has read his books, heard him lecture, or has seen one of his demonstrations can attest that he is truly a master therapist. His annual European lecture tour, in which he would lecture in several local languages, was always a sell-out. A key member of the Mental Research Institute, also known as the Palo Alto Group, Dr. Watzlawick is a remarkable brief, family, and strategic therapist.

Actually, there have been two Palo Alto Groups. The first of these was founded by Gregory Bateson, M.A., the late divorced husband of the well-known cultural anthropologist, Dr. Margaret Mead. Oddly enough, the first of the two Palo Alto Groups was never in Palo Alto, but next door in Menlo Park, California. Mr. Bateson formed the first Palo Alto Group (again, actually in Menlo

Park) in 1952 and disbanded it in 1962 when he considered his project completed. During that decade the group published over 70 articles and books, principally on schizophrenia, hypnosis, and therapy. The "double-bind" concept emerged from the Bateson group, which included Jay Haley and the late John Weakland. Don D. Jackson, M.D. and William F. Fry, M.D. were part-time consultants. As the Bateson project ended, a second Palo Alto Group, soon to be known as the Mental Research Institute (MRI), was founded by Dr. Jackson. Mr. Bateson and Mr. Haley refused to join that group, but Mr. Weakland did, thus infusing many of the Batesonian concepts into MRI. As previously stated, Dr. Watzlawick was also at MRI, along with Richard Fisch, M.D.; Jules Riskin, M.D.; Arthur Bodin, Ph.D.; Diane Everstine, Ph.D.; and a number of other prominent psychotherapists.

Family therapy, and more specifically systems theory, emerged concurrently in Palo Alto and the Ackerman Institute in New York. There is controversy as to who was first, and to this day I, myself, could not say which was. I first became acquainted with the Palo Alto Groups while at Kaiser Permanente when we retained Gregory Bateson (circa 1960) as a consultant, particularly in our behavioral health and primary care project. Not too much came of that relationship as Mr. Bateson was winding down his own project. But in 1979 to 1981 I was privileged to be the executive director of MRI. This was one of the most interesting periods of my career, particularly because there was much socialization and cross-fertilization among a number of colleagues who were pioneers in brief therapy, family therapy, systems theory, and strategic therapy. Along with all of the foregoing, there were others in the informal circle: Murray Bowen, M.D.; Jay Haley; Carlos Sluzski, M.D.; and Virginia Satir; as well as an array of other notables too long to list.

At MRI Dr. Watzlawick's inspired interventions with patients were legendary. One of my favorite stories was in regard to a single man he was seeing who was in his thirties. His mother was constantly on the phone warning her son about the wrong kinds of women. In her mind every single woman was a predator after her son. She even called Dr. Watzlawick to enlist his aid in protecting her son from such women. The son complained that his mother's incessant phone calls in this regard were extremely annoying and he wondered if the therapist could talk to her about the matter. Dr. Watzlawick had a congenial telephone conversation with the mother, during which he complimented her on her ability to know when her son was about to date the wrong type of woman. She would receive an intuitive message in this regard, prompting her to call the son with a warning. He suggested that someone as adept at receiving intuitive messages ought also be able to send such messages. Had she ever considered cultivating this potential? A few weeks later the mother called him to thank him for the guidance. She was always able to send a warning message in time for her son to avoid a woman he was about to date. Thus, he has remained free of trouble. In the meantime, the son had said to Dr. Watzlawick, "I don't know what you said to my mother because she never bugs me with telephone calls anymore."

FLORENCE MATEER, PH.D.

The private practice of psychology is essentially a post-World War II phenomenon. Prior to that time there were a number of female psychologists in private practice throughout the nation, mostly on a masters-degree level. They limited their practices to children, and they flourished because a maternal figure doing child therapy was not a threat to the male-dominated organized psychiatry of the pre-World War II period. A number of prominent women practicing with children did have their doctoral degrees, notably Drs. Nancy Bayley, Grace Fernald, Florence Mateer, and Jean MacFarlane, and they contributed a great deal to the literature and toward paving the way for the legion of privately practicing psychologists who were to come much later. One, Jean MacFarlane, Ph.D. was instrumental in the first government funding of training for psychologists within the Veterans Administration.

Dr. Mateer practiced for many years in Columbus, Ohio. As early as 1928 she was asked to appear in court as an expert witness on a case involving a child. At that time psychology had little or no standing in private practice. This was almost 30 years before the first psychology licensing law, and society saw psychology as essentially an academic, not a practice, endeavor. Once Dr. Mateer was on the stand, the judge set about considering her role, if any, in the court proceeding. He asked her what one needs to be a psychologist. Dr. Mateer replied in the crisp, incisive manner that was typical when she was annoyed, "First of all, Your Honor, one needs intelligence!" The judge was somewhat taken aback at first, recovered, and said, "The court finds Dr. Mateer qualified as an expert."

I was a student of Dr. Mateer's in her older years when she left Ohio and joined the psychology faculty at the Claremont Graduate School in California. She was extremely helpful in cases that involved children, and I often went to her. On one occasion, however, I felt desperation. I was scheduled to see an 11-year-old boy who was so hyperactive that he had destroyed the offices during the first sessions with two previous child psychologists and one child psychiatrist. The few child therapists in the community who had not seen him refused to do so after this story got around. I asked what I could possibly do that the three unsuccessful therapists had not tried. The boy's reputation was that he was like a cyclone. Dr. Mateer suggested that I had to do something that no one else had done, and it would have to be effective. I pondered this to no avail. Then she said, "You are a young man over 6 feet tall. You could pick him up by his ankles and stand him on his head until he agrees to settle down. He would never expect that, but I would guess he would welcome it. He is in a rage because he has no father and the ineffectual males (teachers, therapists) in his life are too weak to stop him. He wants to be stopped.

I thought this to be a terrible idea, but once confronted by Ronald I was desperate. He had smashed my telephone within five seconds of entering my office, and he was about to take on my typewriter. At this point I grabbed his ankles, swooped him up so that he missed the floor, and then lowered him until he was resting vertically, but upside down on his head. He was absolutely startled, tried unsuccessfully to wriggle free, but soon discovered that all resistance resulted in his banging his head on the carpeted floor. We carried on a conversation in this incredible stance, he upside down and I standing holding onto his ankles so that his head rested on the floor. Within a few minutes he agreed to behave, and he kept his promise. In the second session he tested my resolve and promptly found himself once again resting on his head, suspended by his ankles. From that time on Ronald and I were bonded. He simply worshipped our sessions together, and he was eager beyond all expectation to please me. He abandoned his reckless, destructive behavior, settled down in school and at home, and actually became a model student and son.

Dr. Mateer was uncanny in her discernment of this boy's needs. This was in the late 1940s and she was elderly and frail, but brilliant in her understanding of children. I cannot help but wonder if in the current climate this case would not have ended with the both of us, student and supervisor, accused of child abuse, and Ronald, prompted by a plaintiff's lawyer, testifying against us in a malpractice suit. The worst part of this scenario is that Ronald would have been given official sanction to continue his self-destruction.

MILTON H. ERICKSON, M.D. (AS NARRATED BY JEFFREY K. ZEIG, PH.D.)

I would name this case "the seeding and indirect suggestion in Erickson's couples therapy." In 1978 a group of clinicians came to Dr. Erickson (1901–1980) specifically for therapy. At the time it was more customary for those who sought out Dr. Erickson to attend a teaching seminar. In this instance, however, each member of the group brought a focal problem to Dr. Erickson, who sequentially provided hypnotic and strategic treatment.

The first hour of the first day concerned a man named Jim, and his wife Jane, both approximately 30 years of age. Jim requested help from Dr. Erickson, explaining that he became physically tense when he read and wrote. He was asked to what extent he had worked with Dr. Erickson before, and he replied that he had seen Dr. Erickson twice previously. The first was for help in stopping smoking and the most recent for couples counseling before he and Jane were married.

After a three-minute "diagnostic" interview, Dr. Erickson offered a hypnotic induction to Jim, who proved to be a good subject, responding readily to indirect instructions. The induction was Dr. Erickson's favorite—the early learning set, in which the therapist uses absorption in memory as an induction device. Jim was to vividly remember the details of learning to write the letters of the alphabet.

On superficial analysis, it was peculiar that Dr. Erickson chose the early learning set induction. Jim had seen the therapist twice before; certainly he had heard this induction previously. On deeper analysis, however, Dr. Erickson had a specific design and did not render the induction in his traditional way. Per custom he commenced by talking about the difficulty children have in learning to write letters. Then he diverged, saying that the same is true of numbers. "Is the 6 an upside-down 9, or is the 9 an upside-down 6? Which way do the legs of the 3 go? Is the 3 a letter 'm' standing on one end?" The subtle reference to numbers had strong sexual connotations. In most cultures, the number 69 refers to a sexual position, and talking about three legs can lead a man to think about his own sexuality.

Why Dr. Erickson made this sexual reference was not immediately clear. Did he pick up on a sexual problem, or was sexuality itself a metaphor for potency or masculinity or intimacy? At any rate, Dr. Erickson seemed to alert Jim on a covert level (remember there were other people present) that the therapist would be subtly working on aspects of Jim's marital life, in addition to helping him with the presenting problem.

That Dr. Erickson worked with a patient or student on multiple levels was well understood. Part of the unstated contract of being with him was that he would work intimately with students, helping them to bring out undeveloped physiological and psychological potentials.

In subsequent hypnotic work, Dr. Erickson used indirect hypnotic techniques to help Jim establish the hypnotic phenomenon of dissociation. Jim easily accessed the state, being a "bodiless mind," to solve his presenting problem. Being a bodiless mind is an ideal state from which to read and write comfortably.

After working with Jim for approximately 30 minutes, Dr. Erickson turned to Jane and said, "Jane, go way back, way, way back—maybe to the time you had pigtails and saw something funny. Slowly, gradually, way back. Then you will open your eyes and tell me what funny thing you are seeing. Open them very slowly."

This was a hypnotic suggestion for age regression; however, no induction of hypnosis was offered to Jane. Jane had closed her eyes when Dr. Erickson was working with Jim. The therapist had viewed Jane's behavior as a response and as an invitation to work with her hypnotically. It was, however, difficult to imagine that Jane could achieve age regression when no induction was presented to her and no intermediate steps, such as deepening the hypnosis or building responsiveness, were developed. As it turned out, Jane neither responded to the suggestion of opening her eyes slowly nor to the suggestion of experiencing age regression. She merely explained that she imagined herself as a child and noticed the pigtails and the part in her hair. Jane achieved some hypermnesia, a partial revivification of a memory, although no memory was relived.

Dr. Erickson then asked Jane to remember how she looked as a child, to become absorbed in that memory and then relive it with him. Jane was to close her eyes and have the regression. Again she was asked to open her eyes slowly. For the second time Jane did not open her eyes slowly and reported only a partial revivification of memory. Dr. Erickson tried a third time with Jane. He asked her to have an age regression and the additional phenomenon of a negative hallucination: She was to hear his voice but not see him. Again, Jane was asked to open her eyes slowly. But Jane did not open her eyes slowly. Moreover, she did not fully achieve the effects that Dr. Erickson tried to elicit. She reported seeing him. As Jane was internal referencing and not "seeing" Dr. Erickson, he used a paradoxical method where she would "win" on the social level by resisting, but he would "win" on the psychological level because she would "see" him.

The therapist was not to be denied. He tried a fourth time, using mostly direct suggestions. Again Jane did not achieve the age regression, but she did open her eyes gradually. At this point Dr. Erickson terminated the hypnotic directions to Jane. He looked down at the floor and related the following story to the couple in a methodical, hypnotic voice:

"One bitterly cold day in Wisconsin, on a Saturday, I was in high school. My father drove a condensary milk route. He gathered up the milk at various farms and took it to the condensary *nine* (italics mine) miles away. He took the entire forenoon to pick up the milk and deliver it to the condensary.

"He had made arrangements in Juno to stable the horses and give them a chance to eat and rest while he made arrangements to eat lunch in the warm kitchen of a resident in Juno. On that particular day, the weather was zero. I made the trip. I stabled the horses, fed and boarded them. I went into the house, knocked at the door, identified myself, and went into the kitchen.

"While I was taking off my overcoat and galoshes, a girl about *six* (italics mine) came in, walked around me, eyed me carefully from head to foot, walked around me *three* (italics mine) times. Then she turned to her mother and asked, "Who is that strange man?" Up to that moment, I knew I was a farm boy, just a 16-year-old farm boy. When that girl asked her mother, "Who is that strange man?" I felt my boyhood slide off my shoulders and the glorious weight of manhood descend on my shoulders. Never again was I a boy. I felt like a man. I thought like a man. I behaved like a man. I *felt* (Dr. Erickson's emphasis) like a man.

That little statement by that little girl, "Who is that strange man?" produced a lasting effect because every little boy wants to become a man desperately. Every little boy wants to feel his manhood comfortably. He wants to know that he has the strength of a man to do this or that, and to feel good while doing it."

Then Dr. Erickson asked Jim to close his eyes and really understand that story. And he pointed out to Jane that every little girl wants to be a woman sometime, "so close your eyes and recall vividly all of your feelings, all of your surroundings when you were convinced that you were a woman, by some little thing no more important than a little girl saying something to a boy and changing him into a man immediately."

Dr. Erickson continued his story. "The woman was named Virginia; she had a sister named Della. I never knew the little girl's name. I was standing in the kitchen facing east, and Virginia, the little girl's mother, was a few steps to my right. The little girl was in front of me about three feet away, asking her mother, "Who is this strange man?" Her hair was blonde. It was in *pigtails* (italics mine)."

This remarkable and sensitive anecdote described a girl empowering a boy. It was a bridge to create some good feelings between Jim and Jane. They were married in a religious or civil ceremony. Dr. Erickson was offering an "emotional" marriage. Note that Dr. Erickson did not merely tell the story to the couple. He prepared the anecdote carefully. He worked with Jim, who was quite responsive to hypnosis, and helped to elicit even more therapeutic responsiveness. He seeded the numbers 3, 6, and 9, and brought them back when he talked about the male protagonist in the story. Jim's numbers would help him to experientially identify more fully and dramatically with the protagonist of the story.

Dr. Erickson worked with Jane, who was characterized by more internal locus of control and was less responsive to hypnosis. He gave her a task to accomplish, namely regression, which she refused. He concomitantly asked her to open her eyes slowly. On the fourth try, when Jane responded to the latter suggestion and opened her eyes slowly, it was as if Dr. Erickson assumed that some of her "resistance" had been discharged. She had said "no" to him enough times. Now she could be more open to his ideas. Earlier, Dr. Erickson had unobtrusively seeded for Jane the idea of pigtails, an idea to which he knew he would later return. There was no reason to mention pigtails except seeding. The idea of pigtails would be brought back during the story and used to help Jane identify with the female protagonist. The numbers were Jim's cue, the pigtails were Jane's.

Seeding is a very powerful technique that is used by dramatists and fiction writers. It is called "foreshadowing" in literary circles. In social and experimental psychology the effect has been empirically studied under the rubric of "priming" (Zeig, 1990b).

We can surmise that when Dr. Erickson began the induction with Jim, he had already decided that he would tell the anecdote about his becoming a man. Then he seeded the concepts, built the responsiveness, and discharged the resistance. Only when the bed was fertile did he "plant" the target story.

Subsequently, Dr. Erickson told the couple another story about a senseless struggle that he encountered when he was at the university. He saw college "boys" competitively pushing a large ball across a muddy field. The "boys" on the winning side decided to cause mischief in the town, and he refused to participate in the vandalism. Instead, he remembered the time he became a man.

The college story was an indirect suggestion to the couple to avoid senseless struggle and use the reference experience that Dr. Erickson had created through the story of becoming a man. If Jim and/or Jane initiated senseless struggle, each could, perhaps unconsciously, remember the Erickson story and the concomitant feelings. They could be a "man" and a "woman." I call this technique a *process instruction*. It is a method of telling the patient how to use the resource (in this case, the respective feeling of being a man or a woman) that was developed in therapy.

This outline is a superficial description and analysis of a quite complex therapy. There are many additional facets to this session. For example, after the stories, Dr. Erickson worked with Jane, providing other stories and tasks to help her be more open and flexible. Dr. Erickson provided "insight" to Jim and told him what his problem was: He had not grown out of a once-useful pattern whereby children tense and use their entire body when reading and writing. Jim seemingly accepted Dr. Erickson's interpretation. (Note that Dr. Erickson used insight, but it was served as the dessert, not the main course.)

As a result of this therapy, Jim, in his own words, "wrote up a storm." He achieved his stated goal. The couple, however, eventually divorced. In the process of working with Dr. Erickson, they were confronted with their differences. Dr. Erickson tried to help them bridge their differences, but even his powerful methods were insufficient.

CHAPTER 8

A Sampling of
Current Masters

We contacted a number of psychotherapists who would not only
be regarded as current masters but who also would cover a wide
spectrum of approaches, and invited them to present a case that
was representative of her or his therapeutic point of view. We
asked each to present the case without theoretical comment. We
wanted a description of the patient followed by a straightforward
narrative of what it was the therapist did. However, asking a psychotherapist to refrain from commenting on his or her own case
may be asking too much. Although most did not succeed in
restraining themselves entirely, all did an admirable job of avoiding lengthy theoretical discussions.

Each of these master therapists has many years of experience
and is theoretically grounded, in addition to being a psychological

"artist." Most are also skilled researchers, and all are scholars. The cases are presented in alphabetical order by author. It is our contention that the therapist and the therapy are inexorably interwoven; thus, following each case presentation there is a "Nick and Janet Comment." It is here we shall try to bring to the reader the therapist as we know him or her as both a person and a professional, revealing some qualities and accomplishments that may not be well known. We take these liberties out of profound respect and affection for these colleagues who have given us so much, and to whom we are all indebted.

THE CASE OF GENE:
SIMON H. BUDMAN, PH.D.
ORIENTATION: BRIEF PSYCHOTHERAPY

Gene and I first met twenty years ago when he was a young graphics design artist living in Boston. At that time, he had major difficulties in regard to his parents, who lived in a distant city, and in his romantic relationships with women. He would also get into conflicts with his supervisors at work and, although he was talented, he went from job to job looking for the "perfect" employment situation.

Gene spent about 10 months with me in a time-limited group therapy. He did very well in this group, felt involved and supported, and left at the end of the group with the view that he had profited greatly from the treatment.

Over the next 15 years, I would see Gene periodically when certain major issues arose in his life. He saw me for about six sessions when he broke up with a woman at the end of a serious relationship. He returned when his father and mother died in a car accident and he felt grief and remorse about having never resolved the troubles in those relationships. I saw him again when he was considering getting married, and he came in with his wife when they were considering having children.

Through all these episodes of treatment, a thread in the background—like a dimly heard drum in a piece of classical music—were work issues. Gene would get a new job, keep it for approximately 12–18 months, and then something would occur. The things that would happen would differ. In one company he indicated that he had a very difficult boss who was always giving him a hard time; in another, the work that was being done was boring and unengaging. In yet another, a new company bought the firm for which he was employed and they went through a downsizing.

The issue of how he did at work was not viewed as central by Gene—even if I pushed the issue and wondered aloud how he felt about moving from place to place so frequently, Gene would basically reply that it was all the fault of his employer for placing roadblocks in his way that prevented him from doing well at the job. Furthermore, he could find a new job which would be better than the last. He would go back to a focus on the issue or issues which had brought him in for the current course of treatment.

Gene was a bright and insightful man in many ways. He understood that at least some of his difficulties at work related to his conflict with his father, who had been a very controlling and rigid man. Gene would chafe at being told what to do by authority figures and would figure out how to "get around them." He had little interest, however, in making any changes in this behavioral pattern.

At one point, after I had not seen Gene for many years, he called in an anxious state. "Can I see you soon?"

"Sure, what's going on?"

"Things at work are about to fall apart."

"In what way?"

"If I don't change, they will fire me."

Gene had been employed for several years with a large firm. He was well paid and had excellent benefits. He had, from the beginning, been in conflict with his boss. Gene felt that the boss was "a jerk" and didn't understand the business. Further, he was not as talented a designer as Gene.

Several days before Gene called me, his boss had returned to the office to find him in a meeting with one of the company's big clients. Gene had set this meeting up without letting his boss know that the client was coming. What Gene did was clearly a "slap in the face" to his boss and should not have occurred. His boss was discussing the situation with his own boss and was to let Gene know two days after his first meeting with me (in this episode of treatment) what was to happen. When Gene went into that meeting, he was immediately fired and ushered out of the building.

This firing was seen by Gene as more serious than his prior exits from other jobs. He was nearly 50-years-old. He had gone through many of the firms in the local area which were likely to hire him, and he felt that he might not get work again and could be "in the street" with his wife and two sons. In my view, for all of the times that I heard from Gene that he had lost his job this one most clearly represented a "teachable moment." He seemed more ready and motivated than I had ever seen him. *He* wanted to focus on work issues. I did not have to impose the discussion on him.

After losing his job, Gene initially became very depressed and, briefly, suicidal. Once the risk of suicide and his overwhelming and immobilizing depression had been dealt with, and to some degree had subsided (perhaps three weeks after the firing), we began to focus on his issues with work. First we focused on what had gone on in this job. "What role did you play in what happened?" "Sure, your boss may have been a difficult and incompetent person, but how did *you* contribute to the problems and issues?"

I had Gene write me a set of logs. These logs described in great detail what had happened on a daily basis (the best that he could remember) in his interactions with his boss. "What sort of things did you do that were provocative and got your boss mad at you?" We went over these logs together and looked at the interactions which Gene had had with his boss. For the next session I asked him to write me a "frank letter" from his boss, indicating what Gene was like as an employee. Simultaneous with these letter-writing tasks, I asked Gene to call and begin to meet with a vocational counselor whom I knew.

I met with Gene for about eight sessions over a five-month period. During this time, we worked intensively on the issue of how to make a work environment "livable" without fighting with his employer. We particularly emphasized how Gene could "take charge" of his own behavior. We discussed and role played ways in which he could discuss concerns with employers, rather than getting into contentious arguments and acting out problems. I also asked Gene to begin "coaching himself" in better job performance by writing letters to himself focusing on ways to improve his work-related behaviors.

Throughout the period of our meetings, Gene continued to go to vocational counseling and also applied for jobs. After being a finalist for several good positions but not getting them, he was offered a job. The firm that made the offer was a mid-sized, but not very prestigious, company. Gene was at first ambivalent, but decided that with his new tools he would be able to work effectively in this position. Shortly after he took the job, we tapered off our meetings. I met with Gene again 18 months after he began the new job. He was thriving. He reported, "I have never done better at a job. I don't get into arguments with my boss. I am very well liked and, because I am working out so well, I have already gotten two promotions."

Nick and Janet Comment

For the last several generations of graduate students, the volumes on brief therapy by Dr. Budman and his colleagues have been *the* textbooks. His original work with Dr. Gurman is regarded as a classic, even though it is still current and remains a part of contemporary teaching assignments. Nick met him twenty years ago when the HMO-enabling legislation signed under the Nixon administration facilitated the formation of the Harvard Community Health Plan (HCHP) in Boston. Dr. Budman, along with Michael Bennett, M.D., was instrumental in founding the mental health service under that new HMO. Nick had been chief of mental health at Kaiser Permanente for the preceding two decades, and when the Kaiser Family decreed the HMO technology should be given away to the fledgling HMOs, Nick eagerly accepted a series of invitations from Dr. Budman to go to Boston. Psychotherapy at the Harvard Community Health Plan was from its inception a system of effective, efficient treatment, and the experience and research findings inevitably found their way into Dr. Budman's books and journal articles.

Nick has always been proud and flattered that Dr. Budman has regarded him as a mentor. However, Nick looks upon him today as a gifted, brilliant, and innovative colleague. They have published together and have conducted workshops together. The two bonded early. At the first of several workshops Nick did for the emerging HCHP mental health group, he was handed a note while he was in the middle of a complicated presentation. It read, "Your daughter Janet is a hostage in a bank holdup in Davis, California. It is urgent that you call home." After many hours, everything turned out well. But neither Janet nor Nick will ever forget that workshop.

With the cross-fertilization that has occurred between us, it is no wonder that the case of Gene is really one of brief, intermittent psychotherapy throughout the life cycle. It should be noted that, like Nick, Dr. Budman believes psychotherapy should be efficient, not quick. Effective therapy is as long as necessary. One episode of group therapy with Gene was ten months in duration.

After leaving HCHP, Dr. Budman founded Innovative Training Systems (ITS) which for years provided retraining in time-sensitive therapies under contract with the managed care companies. ITS has branched into other innovative projects, but in the last several years Dr. Budman and his colleagues have provided more training than any other group in the nation. He remains one of the most gifted teachers in our field.

THE CASE OF BARBARA:
ELIZABETH AND JAMES F.T. BUGENTAL, PH.D.
ORIENTATION: HUMANISTIC/EXISTENTIAL
THERAPY

Barbara sits across from me, her ample body settling into the couch, her hands tightly clutching the purse in her lap. I know she is pleased to be here, although, as always, I feel the tension beneath her pleasant smile. A year ago when she first came to see me Barbara was drinking heavily and suffering severely from agoraphobia.

On her first visit her husband delivered her to the door and waited outside to drive her home. In the course of this year she has stopped drinking entirely and overcome her agoraphobia enough to join in several community activities, take a college course, and attend a regular exercise class. Lately, she has also joined Overeaters Anonymous. Her blood pressure, once abnormally high, has receded to within the normal range.

A good "therapeutic product"? No, but a good, though partial, gain. Barbara is still stuck, a compulsive eater, and an unwilling housewife and mother. She has suffered intermittent depressive periods for years, and they still recur. With two children in college, a boy of ten, and an at-home mini-farm, there is always work to do. She describes the laundry piled on the washer, the closets and cupboards that need sorting, and the unwashed dishes in the sink.

Her tone is alternately complaining and self-accusing. I know that during the day when she is home alone she is unable to take care of these chores. Yet, because she feels they are her responsibility she cannot let them go and do something else for herself outside her home. Her mother was a compulsive housekeeper and cook and did nothing else, dying in middle age a bitter and depressed woman.

Barbara's husband works hard and long hours. He expects to do so and feels successful in his work. Although he is an immigrant with little formal education, he provides well for his family by doing manual labor. His high energy, frugality, and good business sense have enabled him to make investments, with the result that they are financially secure.

In Barbara's view everyone in her household functions well except herself. She is full of self-reproach and blame, seeing herself as the nagger, the complainer—and sometimes the martyr, sometimes the tyrant. Thus, in her eyes she is at once the central figure and the freeloader.

In my office she talks nonstop the first few minutes, filling me in, reporting, unloading. Gradually, I find ways to connect with her beneath her words. I keep eye contact with her, stay with her in the moment, remind her that I know how sad she is, that I notice the tears welling up in her eyes. I let her know that I accept and affirm her sadness here and now in this room. There are two of us who know her pain, the desperation behind her apparently mundane account.

One way or another I insist on her presence, refusing to buy into the content of her words even as I hear what she has to say. Over and over she is telling me, "fix me; get me out of this." But we both know there is absolutely nothing I can tell her that she has not thought of many, many times. I wouldn't be so foolish or so insulting (depending on her mood on any particular day) as to try to tell her what to do. But I can be there with the person she is so ashamed to be, and gradually, over time, she has come to believe that I am indeed there.

Actually, Barbara was a professional woman when she was married. She never really wanted to stay at home all the time. Intermittently she has returned to work for short periods and enjoyed it, but always felt guilty for not being at home. She knows that there are enough adults in her household to share the responsibilities, and she is free to have a job of her own. Her husband and daughters encourage her to do so. But, in order to do that she must relinquish her mother in herself—her mother, who demands that she keep her house immaculate, prepare elaborate meals, and take care of everyone's needs. In her inner court it is unimportant that she isn't able to do that right now. Soon she will be, must be. Her fear of making that choice and the relinquishments that would be involved keep her stuck.

It would appear that over this past year Barbara has taken a great deal of action. On one level this is true. But, paradoxically, all of this action has only lifted the deadness of her depression enough to enable her to really experience its weight. No longer directly or indirectly suicidal, Barbara must now decide whether or not she chooses to live her own life as a separate person.

Sitting in her house alone for hours at a time, refusing to do the chores she feels she should do, nibbling compulsively as she stares out her kitchen window, Barbara must deal with the real issue. Can she let herself try to do what she wants, go for her own satisfaction and stimulation into the next phase of her life, become a separate person with power of her own? Gradually, with support, she is beginning really to experience her fear of this step, of confronting the resistive function of her depression.

In my office I continually remind her that her depression is a signal of a struggle trying to take place in her. Her yearning for a more complete life is pushing against her hesitance to make that change. Her deadness emerges from the impasse. We bring this deadness into the room, where we both experience it, quietly affirming it as her ally, not to be put aside, her system letting her know she is becoming ready for change. She is "on strike" until she can relinquish her guilt, her old identity inherited from her mother, to make way for the unfolding of the next phase. All the work she has done thus far is to reveal this lowest, most promising platform from which she may perhaps step out into a new experience of herself in the world. Making this move will be confronting an existential dragon—becoming the separate woman she has been terrified to become, fearing she will be nothing when she lets go of who she has been.

A first important step occurs after Barbara has come to therapy twice a week for three months. It is a beginning of letting me see behind her mask of angry self-disparaging. Barbara sits in one corner of the waiting room, somehow managing to appear small despite her heavy body. Her eyes dart quickly to me when I come to the door and as quickly flee to the magazine on her lap. The magazine, I notice, is unopened and probably upside down. I know it is a disguise in case anyone else should see her.

"Good morning, Barbara," I say with a smile. "Come on in."

"Oh," she pauses, starts to gather herself to get up, drops the magazine to the floor, scrambles to pick it up and nearly drops her purse. As she enters my office and takes the client's chair, the anger comes off her like waves of heat. "Clumsy bitch!" She bites off the words. She has yet to look directly at me.

"Clumsy bitch." I say it tonelessly except for a touch of questioning.

"All right." Her manner is a grudging concession to my implied question. "But I was clumsy."

"So...?"

"So I ... uh..." She trails off.

"I saw the clumsiness, if you insist on that. But where does the 'bitch' come from?"

"Well, I get so angry when I act like such a klutz."

"Uh-huh. So...?"

"So ... so I ... Oh, I don't know, I just feel like I can't really do anything right."

"So...?"

"I wish you'd stop those 'so's'."

"Um-hum."

"I know, I know. My mother wouldn't approve of my being so clumsy ... nor of my being angry and profane about it."

"And you?"

"I don't ... oh, what does it matter? I am clumsy and profane ... and angry and..." She pauses. I wait. She resettles herself in her chair, looks quickly at me and then away. "And so unladylike. That's it, isn't it?"

"Is it?"

A long silence. Barbara is busy inwardly but unable or unready to say anything yet. At last she meets my eyes and her body relaxes a bit. "It's been a hellish week. I tried to get myself to do something—clean the house better, go see about a part-time job, join a gym—anything. But when I got dressed to go out, I just slumped in my chair and didn't do anything. When I started to clean the house, I got distracted into reading an old magazine. I really wasn't interested in what it said and..." She takes a breath and her voice hardens. "And I don't even know what it said."

"So now you're beating yourself up."

"Well, why not? I haven't done anything worthwhile. I mean, I know it isn't going to do any good to get mad at myself, but..."

"But?"

"But at least..."

"At least?"

"At least I'm doing something."

"How much you must want to get out of the slump if even beating yourself is something."

She pauses, studying my face, listening inside herself. Then her eyes swim, and her whole manner changes. "Oh yes, yes, I do. I want to quit living this way, quit always making a mess of things. I want ... I want to have a little peace."

"A little peace." I say it softly, looking full into her eyes.

"Oh, yes, yes." She cries openly but quietly, fumbles for the tissue box, which I put closer to her hand. "Thanks." Even now she is polite!

It is some weeks later that she takes the next step. A summer day, and for the first time she is wearing something other than the drab wash dresses which have been her garb since starting therapy. I hesitate commenting on it because in the past such personal comments have sent her fleeing to stiff, impersonal distance.

Barbara watches me cautiously, recognizing, I think, that I'm aware of her changed appearance.

"So say it." She is amused!

"Yes, I will say it, Barbara. You look fresher."

She holds herself rather stiffly as she listens inside. "I think I am…" Her manner is cautious. We are silent together, contemplating the dangerous step she has just taken. Ironically, miserably, to recognize any change for the better is, for Barbara, stepping into a trap. In the past she has hastily covered up any such admission. ("Well, if I can do that, why can't I get my house in order, get a job, do any of the thousand and one things I should be doing? Lose weight, for example!" The last is the killing blow.)

I keep a low profile today and let Barbara set the pace. At first she is hesitant to get beyond superficialities, but a little past the middle of the hour she risks another step.

"I'm thinking that…" She pauses, catches her breath, steadies herself. "I'm thinking that I can go see the people at the library…" Another pause for breath and then a longer pause.

I wait patiently, reminding myself that this woman is fighting for her life, fighting to retrieve it from the dark place in her that has swallowed up so much of her hope and has converted it into smouldering anger and loneliness.

Suddenly she is impatient with herself. "Oh, I'm making such a stupid big deal out of nothing. You must think I'm an idiot. I … I uh … I want to kick myself for making such a ridiculous…"

"Stop it!" I say it loudly, sharply. "Stop knocking down your hope for yourself."

Barbara bursts into tears, turns away from me, grabs a tissue to dab at her welling eyes. "I can't help it," she sobs. "I am so ... so afraid."

"Yes, Barbara, I know, and I know how hard it is for you to do what you're trying to do now. Give yourself some room. Hang onto..."

She nods, still weeping, but with a firmer voice says, "I'm so glad you know. I forget ... I get scared and can't remember what I was trying to say."

I'm tempted to prompt her, but I know this is her battle, and I must give her space. Even support is dangerous for her to accept. I content myself with a subdued "Mmmm," which I hope will convey understanding and support.

"Why is it so hard?" It's more a wail than a question. But I think I can help a bit.

"Because you're trying to change what has seemed to keep you safe for so long. Of course, it's hard."

She doesn't speak, but with her head down nods understanding. This is as far as Barbara gets today, but it is a critically important turning point. Albeit not without hesitations and even brief episodes of flight into the old withdrawal, she never again gets so totally consumed by her fear as she had been for so long.

Therapist's Commentary

Barbara's psychotherapy extended over 11 months. The pivotally important work of establishing a truly therapeutic alliance is synopsized in this report. This account summarizes the third through fifth months. Barbara was coming three times a week until the eighth month, when she dropped to twice a week.

The alliance I have with Barbara has grown because I have refused to "fix" her, because I have shown her that I was aware of her self-punishing without feeling I must intervene, and because I have consistently addressed the person behind the more overt and obvious symptoms. Barbara might not be ready to put it in words, but she demonstrates my alliance is not with the Barbara who beats her up but with the Barbara who wants to get free.

Thus I am not a "cheerleader" for Barbara, nor am I concerned—as some affect-focused therapists might be—to bring out her emotions or to validate her despair.

As is often desirable with depressed and withdrawn clients, the work with Barbara centers around her ways of dealing with herself and her life. Obviously, she has taken over and carried on patterns which may have characterized one or both of her parents' attitudes. In a more traditional psychotherapeutic approach, we might spend more time uncovering this source. Barbara, however, shows an ability to work more directly on the disabling alienation from her own center.

By leaving the responsibility for the content of our conversations largely up to Barbara, we are able to get a fair sample of her struggle. Then we can begin to intervene in ways that simply highlight the intrapsychic conflict.

With some clients it might be necessary to encourage more review of the mother's attitudes toward the client and then to bring out how they have been perpetuated in the client's internal struggle.

My chief focus is on those processes within Barbara that defeat her wholeness and lead to her being split into the suffering victim and the punishing monitor. The implied (and sometimes explicit) message is, "You are a whole person and only by reclaiming your wholeness can you make a lasting change in your experience of life."

The portion of Barbara's psychotherapy which is examined here is not, of course, the whole story. Nevertheless, it is evident that she is beginning a change process which can eventuate in a less conflicted inner life.

Nick and Janet Comment

Nick first met the warm, engaging Dr. James Bugental in 1948 and has been a fan ever since. He has contributed enormously to our understanding of existential therapy, and to Janet's generation of graduate students he was known, along with the late Dr. Rollo May, as the voice of humanistic psychology. Elizabeth and Jim Bugental practice together in a Marin County suburb north of San Francisco and across the Golden Gate Bridge, where people seek them out from all over the nation.

Since Nick founded American Biodyne in the Silicon Valley, he has had the opportunity to know and work with many CEOs of firms ranging from Fortune 500 companies to technology startups. As a psychologist he is very often asked by these business leaders if he knows the Bugentals. These men and women are captains of industry, who have achieved great wealth and stature. When it came time to pause and reassess their lives, they went into treatment in Novato with the Bugentals who, as a team, conduct everything from individual therapy to weekened group programs. In the business world they are legendary.

The therapist in the foregoing case, Elizabeth Bugental, avoids falling into the trap of "fixing" Barbara, as the patient often wishes her to do. She knows that the depressive symptoms are a sign of Barbara's struggle, not the problem in itself. This is the art in psychotherapy: knowing when to take the traditional route of exploring that which was adopted from the parents, and when not to do so for the sake of a patient who must find her separateness in her own unique way, even if this means struggling a while longer.

MEDICARE—THE CASE OF SONYA:
PAULA HARTMAN-STEIN, PH.D.
ORIENTATION: FOCUSED PSYCHOTHERAPY

Sonya was an 82-year-old woman of Eastern European descent. Her primary care physician strongly encouraged her to obtain psychotherapy because she had tried numerous antidepressant medications that had proven to be ineffective or had produced negative side effects. Sonya's symptoms were somatic preoccupation, low energy, low appetite with a 15-pound weight loss, withdrawal from activities, frequent crying, and irritability. She became highly anxious before social events or when traveling. She called her PCP's office frequently over new minor complaints. The patient's daughter also was frustrated because health complaints became the focus of every contact with her mother. Although Sonya doubted the usefulness of a psychologist for her problems, she agreed to come for at least one visit, if only to quiet her daughter and primary care physician.

Sonya and her daughter were seen together for most of the initial session. The daughter's implicit contract with the psychologist was to get recommendations for anxiolytic medications for her mother. Sonya's implicit contract was to satisfy her family and doctor. Sonya expressed open annoyance about the appointment, contending that she was here because "I haven't been behaving." She agreed that she had been miserable lately. The daughter noted that her mother's frequent complaints about her health and symptoms of withdrawing from most activities started when her mother accidentally took two times the amount of her cardiac medications, mistaking them for antibiotics. No catastrophic outcome occurred, but the mistake resulted in Sonya's obsessing not only about the mistake but about all of her medical problems as well.

Given the possibility of memory loss complicating any therapeutic intervention, I administered a brief mental status exam in addition to a depression-screening questionnaire. The results revealed no obvious cognitive deficits, and the daughter corroborated that she saw no signs of significant memory loss or other declines in cognitive functioning. The geriatric depression-screening test indicated a moderate degree of depressive symptoms.

Sonya dated the first onset of similar depressive symptoms to when she was in her 30s, following the unexpected death of her first husband. The symptoms had been recurrent in nature, usually occurring following an identifiable stressful event. Sonya had been married to her second husband for over 40 years. Although he was in his mid-80s, he continued to work part time and lead an active life. Sonya had withdrawn from her husband, preferring to stay home on the couch while he engaged in numerous social activities. She expressed annoyance at his upbeat mood and unwillingness to listen to her complaints.

During the last 15 minutes of the session I explained what therapy could do for Sonya. I emphasized that she would become a partner with me in finding ways of coping with her physical problems. I explained to Sonya that during therapy I would ask her to "try on" new ways of thinking and behaving with the ultimate goal of improving the quality of her life. Much to the chagrin of her daughter, I discouraged the use of tranquilizers. I then became an ally in the patient's eyes because she did not want any more medications added to her already long list for high blood pressure, a hiatal hernia, chronic constipation, and a current urinary tract infection. With some reluctance Sonya consented to work with me. I wrote out the parameters of our agreement and her first homework assignment on an index card. She agreed to:

1. Attend approximately four individual half-hour sessions, one or two follow-up sessions with her daughter, and group therapy sessions.
2. Walk five minutes every day. I used a mild paradoxical intervention, emphasizing that she should not "overdo" any exercise or activities.
3. Engage in at least two pleasant events that she identified: playing a bridge game with old friends and renting an old favorite movie to watch with her husband.
4. Self-monitor her mood on a daily basis.

I thought the first session had gone very well until her departure from the office, when Sonya turned to me and stated smugly, "I'm only going to do this because it costs me nothing. I have excellent secondary insurance, and I sure wouldn't pay anything for this." With that remark I was less than optimistic of a successful outcome.

During the next individual session Sonya was surprisingly positive, reporting that she disregarded my warning about limiting her physical activity to five minutes a day. She proudly announced that she had gone swimming twice, walked a half hour three times during the week, played bridge for three hours, and went on a drive with her husband. She noted that her weakness and lethargy were much less. I reinforced her herculean efforts but cautioned her not to go too fast.

The content of this and the other individual sessions was the generation of coping thoughts, reinforcing efforts to engage in uplifting events, and life review. Coping thoughts that appealed to Sonya were, "All of my problems are hassles but none is life-threatening. I am still here, aren't I?" In tracking her mood, she admitted that her mood was better on days she had planned pleasant activities. During one session devoted to life review she discussed how her immigrant family coped with financial setbacks and other life crises. She clearly did not want to spend much time talking about the past, preferring to focus on her own here-and-now concerns of health and well-being.

Themes that recurred were her tendency to catastrophize about minor physical symptoms such as gastrointestinal discomfort or toothaches and her propensity to overdramatize her physical distress to her daughter. One homework assignment was to rate the satisfaction and enjoyment she experienced from conversing with her daughter when she purposely refrained from mentioning her health concerns compared to conversations when she intentionally complained about every ache and pain. By the fourth individual session I felt she was ready to attend group sessions.

The themes of the ten-session group were managing life stress and coping with transitions of age. We had eight members, all women, ranging in age from 68 to 82. Sonya was our most senior member. We met twice a month for 90 minutes. Prior to each session, participants filled out questionnaires to rate their mood (both the Beck Depression Inventory and the Geriatric Depression Scale). Each participant met the criteria for a mood disorder because of their physical problems or depression related to a variety of recent losses in their lives. The structure of the group included time for individual "contact" work, when each person reported on her individual homework assignment and progress or problems in meeting her goals. I also presented a mini-lecture on topics such as how thoughts affect mood, anxiety-reduction techniques, and how to be appropriately assertive with health-care professionals. We discussed assigned chapters from books such as *Optimal Aging* (Ellis & Velten, 1998) and *Enjoy Old Age* (Skinner & Vaughan, 1983). I designed much of the content and structure of the groups from ideas described in *Group Cognitive Therapy: A Treatment Approach for Depressed Older Adults* (Yost, et al., 1986).

During the first two sessions Sonya was disengaged, often not appearing to follow the content and pace of the group. She made minimal eye contact with others, rarely initiated responses, and stopped doing her homework. The third session was a pivotal one. One of the group members suggested that Sonya seemed very frail and increasingly anxious about tasks such as getting her banking done. The group member then pushed that her daughter needed to take over more. Sonya rose to the challenge. Her level of activity and exercise jumped exponentially over the next few weeks. She admitted that she drove her daughter and granddaughter crazy by complaining constantly, and said she was determined to stop that habit. Her daughter had her own life, and she did not want to burden her even more!

During subsequent sessions Sonya became appropriately confrontational with others when they slid into inertia, not meeting their own goals. I no longer needed to preach about the mood-improving power of pleasant events and uplifts. Sonya repeatedly pointed out to others that in tracking her own good days she now realized that they were directly correlated to the events she had planned. She also set a new challenging goal for herself: to fly in an airplane by herself to her granddaughter's home for a week without her husband. Two weeks later she proudly announced her success in doing so! This was the woman who had a full-blown panic attack and fainting spell on an airplane a year earlier.

Other obvious positive changes in Sonya included improvements in her demeanor, activity level, symptoms of depression based upon questionnaire scores, and her appearance. Two of the other younger group members had joked about how "old ladies" wear white sweaters wherever they go. Sonya pointed out to the group one morning, "You'll never catch me wearing a white sweater anymore." Indeed, her choice of clothes and haircut progressed to a more attractive look as the group continued. From my perspective, one of the most significant changes in Sonya was her marked decrease in somatic preoccupation. She had learned to put into practice the coping statements and thought-stopping techniques. Her primary care physician personally called me to remark how striking this improvement was in her patient. Apparently her implicit contract had been met!

Group therapy was a very powerful modality in bringing about change in Sonya. She far exceeded my expectations for her progress. Clearly, the idea of being viewed as an "old lady" who was increasingly dependent upon her family and in need of more medication was anathema to this patient. Through a combination of paradoxical intent, group support, cognitive techniques, and bibliotherapy, major improvements were achieved in this older woman. She openly agreed that her vitality was back and she was enjoying her life more. We met for a total of 16 sessions that included two family therapy sessions with the daughter present, ten group sessions, and four individual sessions. I expect that when the next health or family crisis occurs, Sonya will be back in treatment. We hope to be able to build upon the base of learning and trust that has already occurred.

Nick and Janet Comment

Dr. Hartman-Stein just smashed the myth that says all master therapists are older adults. Considerably younger than our colleagues in this chapter, she, nonetheless, has demonstrated the art of psychotherapy with a kind of patient with whom most therapists would not bother. Sonya was 82 and depressed, a prime candidate for pills, neglect, or both. How many therapists would even consider intensive, active psychotherapy with someone as elderly as Sonya? Ignoring Sonya's age, Dr. Hartman-Stein plunged into a tailored, focused psychotherapy and achieved stellar results.

In 1998 Dr. Hartman-Stein participated in our eight-day, 86-hour marathon Scottsdale Postgraduate Training in Behavioral Healthcare Delivery, along with two dozen other psychotherapists. At one point after her presentation of a case, Nick came down heavily on her. Janet wondered why, because he was not that hard on the others. Besides, she was potentially a star and showed that ability. Nick replied, "That is precisely why. She must come in touch with her genius, and that is both difficult and frightening." Dr. Hartman-Stein rose to the occasion. Stunned at first, she picked herself up and went on to learn focused psychotherapy. But that is learning not only a technique; it is she who turned the technique into art, applying it as no one else has. She heads the Center for Healthy Aging, has edited a definitive book on the treatment of older adults (Hartman-Stein, 1997), and writes a column for *The National Psychologist,* encouraging and inspiring our colleagues to address the psychotherapeutic needs of our Medicare population.

We welcome the opportunity to include her as our youngest master therapist, for she has shown us one is never too old for skillful, innovative, and dedicated psychotherapy.

DANNY—A CASE OF PANIC DISORDER: STEVEN C. HAYES, PH.D.
ORIENTATION: ACCEPTANCE/COMMITMENT THERAPY (BEHAVIORAL)

In my approach to therapy I am particularly sensitive to the tendencies many clients have to avoid private experience, to treat thoughts as literally true even when they are not functional, and to have difficulty following through with behavior change. Explaining *why* I do that is beyond the scope of this vignette (see Hayes, 1987; Hayes, Strosahl, & Wilson, 1999; Hayes, Wilson, Gifford, Follette, & Strosahl, 1996), but the case of Danny shows the issues well.

Danny came to me as he neared age 30 with a history of panic disorder that had been ongoing ever since adolescence when he saw a severe automobile accident. His panic attacks were frequent and intensely physical. He was afraid of dying and focused very heavily on his bodily sensations during panic attacks. A very intelligent man, he had dropped out of college because of the anxiety. He avoided restaurants, bridges, tunnels, stores, trips, phone calls, public speaking, and many other situations in which anxiety would be difficult. He could not hold a job, did not date, and stayed near his home most of the time, with some notable exceptions described below. He felt as if he were completely alien compared to other people, and when looking at other people he would often compare himself negatively to them. He was chronically depressed by most measures, and the depression seemed to have followed in time his struggles with anxiety.

Danny had been in treatment for much of his life, and had been referred to me by a therapist who had worked with him for years. His treatment history included most major forms of pharmacotherapy, cognitive therapy, biofeedback, relaxation, and insight-oriented psychotherapy. None was notably helpful, but he was very attached to some of his past therapists and appreciated their efforts.

Danny's early history had been difficult. His father had left the home when Danny was very young. Danny had only a limited relationship with him, in part because he was often perceived by Danny to be extremely critical. Danny's stepfather, whom he cared for deeply, left the family suddenly following an accusation of sexual abuse directed toward his sister. His mother was an alcoholic, and tended to control Danny's behavior with guilt. She was overly involved with Danny's daily life. For example, when he went to college some distance away, she called almost every day, frequently encouraging him to move back home. Similarly, she used him as a confidant even for intimate issues. She was irresponsible with money and drew Danny into various get-rich-quick schemes.

Danny was self-effacing, emotionally flat, and withdrawn. His attitude was that of someone who thought life simply wasn't fair. He was resigned to his fate, but was angry about it. He rarely expressed his anger outwardly, in part because he was afraid of exploding, since he had experienced a number of intensely aggressive incidents, mostly in childhood, to back up that fear. He was afraid to stand up for his rights, in part because he feared that doing so might precipitate a panic attack.

Danny had achieved local notoriety as an outstanding extreme sports athlete. He became quite anxious in these events (for example, riding mountain bikes on steep, snowy slopes) but did not mind anxiety in that situation "because it is normal."

Looking ahead to life, Danny saw little that was attractive. He denied an interest in a family, intimate relationships, or work. He was interested in travel but viewed that as a vain hope.

In our view, Danny had an emotional avoidance disorder (Hayes *et al.*, 1996). At the time he came to me he was afraid of dying, afraid of his body, and afraid of his fear. Suicidal thoughts were his constant companion, and he described himself "at the end of my rope. If this [therapy] doesn't work I can't see any hope for me."

The initial source of the problem was his difficult history (feed-
ing him a stream of worries and anxieties) combined with the
encouragement of dependent behaviors and active punishment of
his attempts to create an independent and successful adult life.
Over time, however, the emotional struggle became functionally
autonomous. He anxiously tried to avoid anxiety, and produced
more anxiety as the natural result. This led to round after round
of fearful focusing on bodily signs of anxiety, followed by active
forms of avoidance and escape, followed by more fearful focusing.

The goal of therapy with Danny was to increase his willingness
to feel anxiety and its bodily accompaniments without running
away, and to make active choices in his life. After a short psychoeducational intervention (to explain the nature and source of
anxiety), considerable effort was spent on undermining the
agenda of emotional control. I pointed to his direct experience in
this area, which revealed that trying to avoid anxiety produced
anxiety. I also attempted to undercut the rough equivalence Danny
had created between the future he constructed verbally and the
one actually experienced. Instead, I tried to teach a kind of mindful dispassionate observation of his thoughts as mere thoughts,
not as what they purported to be.

This approach seemed very interesting to Danny, who had
heretofore believed that the only way to succeed was to win the
war with anxiety. He began to be more willing to experience what
it felt like to have his heart beat quickly, or to feel faint. As this
occurred, he also began to be more willing to feel other emotions,
such as sadness, hurt, and anger.

As these changes occurred, I began to encourage Danny to go
deliberately into fearful situations, while simultaneously encouraging emotional openness and a careful process of observing
thoughts as they unfolded without either believing or disbeliev-
ing them. For example, in imagination I created situations from
his childhood that were painful or anxiety provoking and
attempted to relive these without any attempt to avoid the emo-

tions that were present. In an *in vivo* exercise, we hiked into the desert and spent some time feeling waves of fear and waves of catastrophic thoughts. We worked on exposure to the interoceptive cures associated with anxiety. For example, we walked up hills to create a rapid heart rate and practiced letting go of any struggle with that sensation.

As the emotional and cognitive struggle subsided, Danny became more able to stay with his fears without avoidance or escape. The natural next step was more outwardly directed: toward values' clarification and behavioral commitment. His first overt behavioral steps were in the area of travel, and over a period of time he took a series of short trips by car and plane. As opportunities arose, we tried to take advantage of them. For example, he was offered a free ticket on an extensive ocean cruise. After a lot of soul searching, he accepted the offer and went on the trip. We practiced every step of the journey in imagination, making room for even the most frightening thoughts, feelings, or bodily sensations that might emerge. The trip itself, as we expected, created a great deal of anxiety at times, but he generally did not try to defeat the anxiety and instead rode the emotional roller coaster his history presented him with. The trip was a huge success.

As Danny's behavior began to change, he realized he had to confront such issues as resolving his relationship with his father, which he did to a large degree. We practiced in therapy what he might say, feel, or do, so that this step would not seem too large. He became seriously involved with a woman who cared for him and was fairly together. He traveled more frequently, and stopped taking tranquilizers. We periodically agreed on willingness exercises, such as leaving the pills home for a day (rather than carrying them with him).

After about 40 sessions, Danny could no longer be diagnosed as an agoraphobic. Panic attacks were rare and nontraumatic. Therapy gradually faded out. He checked in periodically, but he increasingly progressed on his own. He got married, took a job in human services for a time, started his own successful business, and made a conscious choice to have children—steps that he originally thought were simply impossible.

Danny came to a class of clinical psychology students one day to talk about his journey in therapy (itself a difficult exposure exercise). Here is a section of the transcript from that class:

> Danny: I had never conceived or even dreamed possible that it was OK to have your thoughts and your feelings. I began to consider that I didn't need to run or hide from my own thoughts and feelings and bodily sensations, that I didn't need to be afraid of them, things like that, and it was OK and there's as much life and living in a moment of pain as there is in happiness or whatever. To me that was a revelation. I just never even considered it. And so it was things like that which would just leave me reeling. It just really started breaking the ice.
>
> Student: Before that had you consciously thought about "Well, my thoughts and feelings are not OK, I should try to control them?"
>
> Danny: Oh, absolutely. Yeah, I mean I would be "better" or "fixed" as soon as I quit having these thoughts and these feelings and so that was my mission in life was to get rid of these and so, um, it was really a 180 to consider having all that instead. As I learned I can't get rid of it anyway, and then to go on with it, uh, I just found that to be absolutely just a revelation.

Nick and Janet Comment

It often takes a master therapist to break through a case like Danny, who has been in treatment for panic disorder, and subsequent or attendant depressions, for most of his life. Of all our master therapists, Dr. Hayes is the most dedicated to the unification of practice with science. The founder of the Practice Guidelines Coalition, he demonstrates a gift for consensus building, moving the professions forward in spite of themselves. We can just imagine that same kind of approach with his patients, who find themselves working with a firm, knowledgeable, and optimistic behaviorist, yet one with infinite patience and regard. He and his colleagues have developed acceptance and commitment therapy (ACT), an empirically based radical behaviorism which is applicable to a variety of psychological conditions (Hayes, Strosahl, & Wilson, 1999; Hayes, Wilson, Gifford, Follette, & Strosahl, 1996).

We have seen the same kind of patience and dedication as Dr. Hayes moves the Department of Psychology at the University of Nevada, Reno through consensus and toward becoming the nation's cutting-edge program in behavioral health. He defies the prevalent notion among many private practitioners that a dedicated scientist can not also be a master clinician.

JOHN—THE PRESENT IS A GIFT: MICHAEL F. HOYT, PH.D.
ORIENTATION: BRIEF INTEGRATED PSYCHOTHERAPY

The case presented here was a one-session clinical demonstration interview (see Barber, 1998) conducted at the "Brief Therapy: Lasting Impressions" conference held in New York City during August 1998 under the sponsorship of the Milton H. Erickson Foundation. The client, "John" (a pseudonym), was a mental-health professional attending the conference. The session started quickly and intensely:

> Hoyt: I appreciate your volunteering to join with me in this, John. What's up?

John: I have a baby daughter—she's 11 months old. And my mom died, died last year. [chokes up] And she never saw the baby, but before she died she told me that she always felt she worked too hard and didn't spend enough time with the kids. Well, having seven kids she had to work hard—a good Catholic family. And I really want to spend more time with my daughter and I'm a hard worker, too, so I'm kind of struggling with being with my daughter and not working too hard. I'm just worried I'll work too hard and not spend enough time with her.

Hoyt: How can I be helpful to you? What would you like to change?

John: I guess I just kind of need to slow down and just, just enjoy her. I'm feeling some pressure: she's facing major surgery and...

Hoyt: Your daughter is?

John: Yes. It's nine-hour surgery...

After some additional discussion about the impending surgery (scheduled for a Wednesday a couple of weeks hence), having established some initial alliance and comprehension of the presenting situation, I endeavored to clarify the client's goal in seeking the consultation:

Hoyt: After the surgery, when things are better and she's recuperating, it sounds like you want to learn to slow down.

John: Yeah, well, I want to do it now. That's one reason I've been doing things with her, but also you know, with my wife, too, because that gets neglected for Grace [the daughter], and I just want to not always feel like I have to work.

Hoyt: What do you call this pressure, this sort of not being able to relax? Does it have a name?

John: Mmm. What do you call it? [musing to himself] Anxious, I guess. Does it have a name? Yeah. Anxious.

Hoyt: From what you're telling me, it sounds like sometimes you're able to control it, and sometimes it controls you.

John: Yeah.

Hoyt: What's the difference? When are you able to manage it and when does it seem to get the best of you?

John: Ah, if I don't think about work and just enjoy what's happening and that work will take care of itself; it's not going to go away. I don't always have to be on top of things, always kind of rushing, and so what if things are done a day later, this whole notion that it has to be done today.

Hoyt: So that's how you manage anxiety. How does it sometimes trick you and take over?

John: Hmm, trick me and take over. [long pause] Sometimes, like I don't know what to do, I guess is the only thought that comes to my mind. I get restless. I don't like waiting. I wouldn't do well in New York—you have to wait a while.

Hoyt: Right.

John: I don't like to wait.

Hoyt: Uh-huh. So when you have to wait, that's when anxiety can work on you?

John: Yeah, because I could be doing something, you know; I could be off getting things done. Which is sometimes a good thing.

Hoyt: So during this time while you're having to wait for a couple of weeks, what do you need to do so anxiety doesn't take you over while you're waiting?

John: Ah, stay out of the future.

Hoyt: Stay out of the future and keep staying in the moment, huh?

John: Yeah, not think about the surgery and stuff. I mean it's all been taken care of; there's nothing else we can do but be there Wednesday morning. Um, and just don't think about that.

While I would usually, in solution-focused fashion, have inquired after details of times when John had "stayed in the moment," the connection with his deceased parents seemed almost palpable, so I inquired:

Hoyt: How did you learn to worry so much about the future?

John: Probably from my mom.

Hoyt: Your mom?

John: Yeah, yeah.

Hoyt: Tell me more, how did she teach you that?

John: Um, well, she worried you know about how to take care of a large family and just worried about taking care of us, and sometimes my dad drank too much. I think she probably worried about that and I think sometimes he wasn't real faithful, you know…

Hoyt: So she had some real things to worry about.

John: Oh, I worried, too.

Hoyt: Do you find yourself now sometimes worrying about things you don't need to worry about?

John: Yeah, yeah. I do well in my practice and I don't need to worry about that. I'm successful and it doesn't seem to kind of penetrate, you know, that I'm doing very well, very nice lifestyle. We can do lots of things my parents couldn't really afford to do. There doesn't ever seem to be enough.

Hoyt: So what do you say to yourself in your head; how do you keep yourself scared about "never enough"?

John: How do I keep myself scared?

Hoyt: That's my way of putting it; you may have a different way of thinking about it.

John: Right, right. I guess I don't like being scared, but I get scared. [sighs] I guess "I'm not good enough" is what comes to mind. But I am, I mean, I'm successful.

Hoyt: As you think back, can you think of a time when you got that message, "you're not good enough; you haven't done enough"?

John: My dad was pretty critical and stuff. I'd help him fix things but he'd always criticize my mistakes. [pause] You know, I'd be a hard worker. I work hard. [cries] I guess a lot to please my dad.

Hoyt: Sounds like no matter what you did, it wasn't going to be enough for him, huh?

John: Well, he wasn't always critical, I mean he bought me things. He bought me a beautiful bike. I kind of smashed it after a week. I ran into a fire hydrant. So he's done some nice things for me, too. But I kind of like my mom more than my dad. I think my dad knew that. Maybe that's what some of that was all about. I liked them both; I loved them both.

Hoyt: Sure. You said when we sat down you didn't want to be so pressured and so critical.

John: Uh-huh.

Hoyt: What will it take, do you think, for you to finally say, `I love my parents but I'm not going to march to my father's demands'?

John: I want to do that. Some of the stuff was between my mom and dad. You know, I somehow got in the crossfire of some of their stuff; it had nothing to do with me.

Hoyt: True.

John: Yeah. I could just be me and they can whatever … I don't have to fix that.

Hoyt: When you say that now, does it sink in? Do you feel that all the way through?

John: [sighs] I kind of feel less nervous. I'm a parent now and, you know, while Carla [his wife] and I have our dis-agreements, it has nothing to do with Grace. She's not responsible for that. I mean I want my baby to like me a whole bunch and she's really close to her mom and that's really great and I enjoy seeing those two play together and she loves me, too, and I guess that's what's triggering all this is that, you know, I'm a parent now so I can understand. Plus I can see from the other side.

Hoyt: Yeah.

John: And ah, understand more about that. I like being a parent.

Hoyt: Good.

John: You know. I started a little bit late, but that's all right.

Hoyt: Me, too. I have a small son.

John: Oh, do you?

Hoyt: Oh yeah. Is this helpful, what we're talking about?

John: Well, yeah, I never thought about my dad really in some ways, probably being jealous because I was closer to my mom. I was. Not that it was a bad thing. He was working, he worked a lot, my dad, and he was gone a lot, he worked really hard. And so I was with my mom more.

Hoyt: Is your dad living now?

John: No, both my parents are deceased; dad died a long time ago. I'm going to live longer than him, I hope. He died when he was 70.

Hoyt: Uh-huh. Is there something you wish you had said to him?

John: I wish I told him I loved him. I tried. Before he died, I tried to as much as I can express the love—it's not easy for me. I guess I was afraid of how he would respond.

Hoyt: What did you think he would do?

John: I was hoping he'd say he loved me, too. I think he would say that. I wasn't the best of kids. [laughs] I certainly gave them gray hairs over the years. But it helps me being a parent and knowing that in terms of my own daughter. She can't date until she's 30; that's the rule! [laughs jokingly] I laugh about that. I think he would have.

Hoyt: Even if he wouldn't of, can you still feel good about yourself?

John: Well, if he couldn't, he would just have difficulties saying that. That'd be his difficulty. I think he did, but I just think he may have had trouble saying that. I don't know. I wish he had saw [sic] my daughter, too. [looks down, sadly]

Hoyt: Sure. What are you thinking of?

John: Oh, that my dad died in August, around this time, and my mom died in July, so the anniversary and the sadness with that and that they won't see my little daughter and—she's really beautiful.

Hoyt: Yeah, that's hard.

John: Yeah.

Hoyt: We had the same situation in our family. My wife's mother passed away just before our child was born. It was just a couple weeks, and she was ill with cancer and I remember we were talking with her, and feeling sad of course, and she said, "It just can't be helped," and that's true, and it was sad.

John: Well, my mom was laughing about me going to be a father; she thought that was quite funny. [chokes up]

Hoyt: What are you holding back?

John: Just some sadness. I did tell my mom I loved her and I hugged her before she died, so I feel good about that. Of course I miss her.

Hoyt: Especially this month and surgery coming and…

John: Yeah. One of my sisters died and she was six months old and I remember that. It was tough for my mother. I was talking with my mother and she had hydroencephalitis [sic], water on the brain. So I thought about that … my mom knew there was something wrong with the baby and they didn't want to believe it, and then finally they realized there was something wrong, so she died when she was six months. I remember that was really tough on my mom—I know she felt bad about that. You know, she was telling people, "There's something wrong," and they didn't have shunts back then and it was all experimental and stuff, so she didn't survive the surgery. So my mom would have been real supportive.

Hoyt: Does that come up now in terms of your own daughter's surgery?

John: Well, as I think about it, it does now. I didn't really think about that until just now. You know, it was tough on my mom.

Hoyt: Of course. How do you remind yourself that your sister's not your daughter, that what happened with your sister doesn't mean anything in terms of the outcome of your daughter?

John: Oh, it doesn't. I mean it's a totally different thing. The prognosis for my sister was really low; it was experimental.

Hoyt: Sure.

John: With my daughter, the technique, the procedure, they do the surgery like every other week. It's very common. Well, it's not an uncommon problem to have. I'd never heard of it before, but one out of 200 babies has this problem, and the doctor has never lost anybody.

Hoyt: Good.

John: Better not lose this one either; he'll be in deep trouble. He's real perfectionistic—I guess you want that for a plastic surgeon, though.

Hoyt: Yep. When we first sat down you mentioned being critical and pressured.

John: Yeah. Well, it's okay to be sad.

Hoyt: Yeah.

John: You know, and have those feelings. They're just feelings, nothing wrong with them. I guess sometimes I work to avoid those feelings. Yeah, sometimes they're not very pleasant.

Hoyt: I'm impressed by how much you've got going on right now. As a father, thinking about my child who's facing surgery in two weeks ... my voice even trembles saying it now.

John: Umm.

Hoyt: I'd be nervous, worried, scared, trying to keep my mind in the present, but it'd be very hard not to also be thinking ahead and how many more days and what's going to happen and...

John: [nods] I guess I really want to enjoy Grace and have her have a nice experience in New York, and she's having a great time. So am I. It was my idea to come here just before the surgery, and so the biggest worry now is if the airline goes on strike, we may be here longer, which wouldn't be so bad. So I'm not really going into the future at this point. I mean, I know that it's going to be uncomfortable and I can't change that. It's going to be...

Hoyt: ...cross it when you get to it, huh?

John: Yeah, really. Not much more I can do about that. I'm not feeling guilty about it. We thought this through and it's for her benefit to have this surgery. And she won't remember it at all; she won't remember New York either, for that matter. You know, so I just want to get that behind us—I kind of want to skip September and enjoy Halloween or something with her.

Hoyt: So, when it's Halloween or down the road...

John: ...yeah...

Hoyt: ...and you're enjoying her. What are some of the things you're looking forward to doing with her?

John: Well, go out for Halloween, get her dressed up. She won a prize last year. We went to a benefit for some people. There was a fire, their house burned down so we went to a benefit. We dressed her up as a pumpkin and she won a prize. She got two free ice cream cones, which she gave to her cousins. So we'll take her out for Halloween and...

Hoyt: Do you know what she's going to be yet this year?

John: No, I haven't even thought about that yet. Her charming self, that's for sure. Then we want to go to Scotland next year, that's our plans, and want to do a lot more vacations with her in the summer. Find a conference someplace in either California or Colorado, take her there, and just spend some real vacation time with her. And just show her things that either I've seen already and just let her enjoy vacations with her ... that way I can spend more time with her on vacation. I'll take more vacations. I don't need to work all the time now. I don't want to wait until my retirement like my dad did. I can do it sooner.

Hoyt: How are we going to help you remember this?

John: Remember?

Hoyt: Smell the roses, be in the moment, take a vacation.

John: [long pause] I guess I'm planning to do those things. I'm really realizing I've got to spend more time with my daughter and to enjoy it. The best way is to do it is through vacations and stuff ... and not work so much on weekends.

Hoyt: So, in a few months from now when it's Saturday or Sunday and you're tempted to get on the computer or do whatever you do [John laughs in apparent self-recognition], how are you going to say, "Wait a minute, I'm supposed to take it easy here"?

John: Well, part of it, I'll remember what my mom said that she had some regrets about not spending enough time with us, and I do tell myself that. And, I guess, just sit back and have my feelings I may have about things. I guess I'm still grieving my mother's death and stuff. I do talk to my daughter about my mom and, ah, the world's not going to fall apart if I'm not in there on the computer.

Hoyt: Do you think your mom would be glad to see you taking more time?

John: Oh yeah, she would be, I think she's be pretty pleased about how I'm being a father and a parent. I think she'd be real happy.

Hoyt: And in a few months when you're tempted by anxiety to get on the computer...

John: Oh, not me! [laughs]

Hoyt: She'd approve of you taking it easy, huh?

John: Oh yeah, she'd be okay with that.

Hoyt: It might even be a way of kind of honoring her memory.

John: Yeah. [nods thoughtfully] I wish she [daughter] knew my mom and my dad, too. But in a way she does through me. I mean, I'm like my mom and dad, in different ways, so in that way she'll kind of know them and I just have to tell her the stories about them, you know.

Hoyt: Yeah, I've come to think that if we don't want to completely lose somebody, we have to take the qualities in them that we love and manifest them, carry it on. Otherwise they get lost, the parts that should be carried forward.

John: Yeah. Yeah.

Hoyt: I think your daughter is very lucky to have such a good dad.

John: Thanks.

Hoyt: Yeah.

John: Yeah, we're pleased.

The desired changes are further future-paced and also explicitly linked to his social system.

Hoyt: When you begin to make some of these changes now and into the next months, who else is going to help you with that? Your wife?

John: Yeah, yeah. We both are making a more strong commitment to slow down. That's certainly possible because my income flow is increasing, and by not even doing more work, which is even nicer. So that's really happening. I do some contractual work and getting a substantial increase in income by doing the same amount of work, so I can work on just Fridays and not Saturdays and do fine.

Hoyt: Is there anything you should ask your wife or partners or anybody to help you stay on track with this?

John: Well, we just need to plan our weekends and our time together, because if I don't plan it, it tends not to happen. So we just need to plan things together.

Hoyt: I found with my life, it helps me with my appointment book if I block out the times—like nature abhors a vacuum and if I don't schedule time not to do things there's always something interesting to do. I don't know if you're similar, but in some ways it sounds like you need to…

John: …I do that at work. Yeah, my wife and I just need to plan our leisure time more.

Hoyt: For me I find that the world has got all these demands that kind of impinge, so I wonder how you're going to deal with the outside world's demands on your time while you're telling yourself "I want to slow down, be with my daughter more."

John: Financially we're doing fine. I don't have to accomplish everything so quickly. I have these goals, I have my daughter's education kind of paid for in the next couple of years.

Hoyt: Wow.

John: I don't want to work my whole life, so I'd like to at least semi-retire in my early 60s.

Hoyt: It sounds like in some ways you want to take a very different path than what your folks did.

John: I'm able to.

Hoyt: You're able to.

John: Yeah, but I don't know if they were able to—with seven children, you're kind of stuck working, you know. I value some parts of my father, though, in terms of being a real hard worker and real persistent, and my mom, too. So I have this work ethic. It's okay, but also I can enjoy the fruits of my labor, too. So, it would be fun to have more time off with my daughter, take her to things and do things. You know, my dad used to watch me play football and I used to enjoy him being there, and so I'm sure my daughter would want me to be there when she's doing various activities. I'd like to be there. Not a super parent, but just to enjoy her.

Hoyt: In a couple of minutes we'll stop, but I wanted to ask you before we stop—what's been helpful in our talking? What's something you'll carry with you?

John: [pauses] I guess not being in a hurry to get anyplace. Kind of just sharing with you what I was feeling and just being me and just talking about it and having my feelings, whatever those were. They've kind of subsided and it's nice being able to talk about my mom or my dad without crying. It doesn't mean I don't love them. It's okay to be sad. Now I'm able to breathe. I'm enjoying that, not really feeling anxious.

Hoyt: Good.

John: For a compulsive, you know, that's kind of a trick. I'm not as compulsive as my sister, though. And just realizing that I am making plans to spend more time with my daughter, I'm actually doing that, and it's starting to happen and it's real joyful. That it's really going to happen, I'm going to have a real good life, for her and my wife and myself, and just really enjoy that. It's like we're enjoying New York.

Hoyt: The other day, I was obsessing and a friend of mine said something...

John: You obsess?

Hoyt: Of course! [laughter] And when she said it, it was just
       `Wow!' She said—let's see if I can get the words
       [pauses]—"Yesterday is history and tomorrow's a mystery,
       today is a gift, and that's why they call it the present."

John: [laughs] That's great!

Hoyt: Yeah, even though it's sort of corny, probably five or six
       times in the last week when I've started to obsess, I'll say,
       "the present, a gift—be here now."

John: Yeah, I can do that at times. It's been very valuable to do
       that. I just need to acknowledge my feelings and I don't
       need to be in a hurry. I don't have to worry so much
       about other people. Just take care of me. It's an occupa-
       tional hazard being a caretaker, you know, taking care of
       others. Take care of me. I think that's what I need to do.
       If I take care of me, I'll be taking care of my daughter. She
       needs me to do that.

Hoyt: Yeah. You need to do unto yourself as well as you do
       unto others.

John then mentioned that he and his wife had taken the time to
enjoy a night out together. This provided a reinforcement opportunity.

John: That's true. We went out last night and saw the play
       "Rent." It was really fantastic. It was all about love. I
       don't know if you've seen the play or not. I didn't under-
       stand all the words of the play—I was just getting into
       the feelings and just raw emotions and I didn't have to
       figure things out. It's just a real emotive experience, you
       know.

Hoyt: How did you do that? That's fantastic!

John: All of a sudden in this play I began to see the beautiful
       lust, and see the attraction and struggles with the
       attraction.

Hoyt: Yeah.

John: And they're all struggling towards attachment and the difficulties with that and I didn't. I couldn't understand the words too well, but I didn't need to.

Hoyt: You got the message.

John: Well yeah, the message was really into the emotions and the feelings they were having and their struggles. It was a very beautiful night—expensive but very beautiful. But that's all right.

Hoyt: You're worth it.

We then concluded:

Hoyt: I'll be thinking about Wednesday next, wishing you well.

John: Oh, thank you, I appreciate that. I could use the warm thoughts. I'll think about you at that time.

Hoyt: Yeah, prayers are with you.

John: Thanks.

Hoyt: Would this be a good place for us to stop?

John: Yeah. Certainly.

Hoyt: Thank you.

John: Thank you.

Therapist's Comment

I like this session because it appeared to be quite helpful to the client. The work was relatively straightforward, nothing fancy. My personal involvement and "use of self" is fairly typical. I could certainly relate to both the client's concerns as a father and his tendencies toward worry and overwork. People attending the interview commented on the sense of presence and intimacy, which may not be well conveyed in the written form of a truncated transcription.

I have had no further contact with John. If we met for (an)other session(s), I expect I would ask about his daughter, of course, and also follow up (and attempt to amplify) practical, behavioral details of how he was taking time to "smell the roses." I find that many times we mental health professionals know about our "issues" and what we need to do—a superificial level of "insight" (see Kaslow, 1984)—but may not actually follow through to make the changes we desire. I was impressed by all that John had going on. I hope things work out well for him and his family.

Nick and Janet Comment

Dr. Hoyt has long been affiliated with the Kaiser Permanente Health Plan, the largest staff model HMO in the world. He is a leading figure in the development and theory of time-sensitive therapy, and he is the author or co-author of several important books in the field (Hoyt, 1994, 1995, 1996, 1998; Budman, Hoyt & Friedman, 1992). He refers to his approach as "integrated brief psychotherapy," as he seeks to increase effectiveness and efficiency by drawing upon different schools and methods. In this way he believes that the clients' (he prefers that word to patient) sense of choice is enhanced, and there is a fuller utilization of their competencies and resources. So at various times Dr. Hoyt's work resembles narrative and constructivist therapy, but essentially, in his own words, "whatever works."

At one time he almost drove Nick up the wall when he took Nick's findings with Dr. Follette in the 1960s which showed that fully one-third of patients were helped with one session when the first session was purposely therapeutic, and then developed with Dr. Moshe Talmon a one-session therapy. After his initial reaction, Nick settled into the realization that anything that will prompt us toward efficiency along with effectiveness (Dr. Hoyt's ever-present message) is positive. This comes through in his one session with John, as well as his down-to-earth straightforwardness with this client. This is quite typical of the skills of this warm, direct, and affable master therapist.

THE CASE OF GILDA—SHOTGUN
THERAPY: ARNOLD A. LAZARUS, PH.D.
Orientation: Behavior Therapy

Let's call her Gilda. A close colleague had begged me to see her. The preliminary details were not encouraging. She had already seen two previous therapists to no avail. A 52-year-old attorney, Gilda had been married for 12 years. Her husband John, also a lawyer, was threatening to leave. Her 9-year-old son had called her "a nut case." Gilda's only sibling (a younger sister) had not spoken to her for the past seven months. Her parents had distanced themselves from her, and since moving out of state a year ago, they had deliberately avoided having much to do with her. The senior partner at her law firm had intimated that she would be fired unless she "shaped up." What "shaped up" meant had not been specified at that time.

When I told my colleague that her description of Gilda's presenting problems was rather daunting, she implored me to see her, saying, "I just know that you will be able to help her." She had seen Gilda four times in so many weeks. "You will see from the Multimodal Life History Inventory (Lazarus & Lazarus, 1991) that her problems fall mainly in the cognitive and interpersonal areas ... I know you have the tools to fix her." I reluctantly agreed to see her.

Gilda looked much younger than her chronological age. She was well spoken and outwardly at ease. She was fairly attractive despite being considerably overweight. Professionally attired in a jacket, blouse, and skirt, her overall demeanor nevertheless conveyed a slight aura of dishevelment. As the session continued, it became apparent that Gilda was very bright and extremely articulate. She described her interpersonal style as "polemical" and said that people had called her "the lawyer" as far back as her fifth grade. Her argumentative style had often landed her in hot water, but it had also held her in good stead, especially in the courtroom. It was only in the past year or two that matters had somehow escalated and deteriorated and had resulted in alienation from several quarters. Her upbringing seemed unremarkable, except for the fact that she described her mother as "chronically depressed," and reported that her parents were not overly demonstrative or affectionate.

A clear-cut treatment objective had become apparent within the first 10 or 15 minutes. Dichotomous reasoning seemed to characterize her cognitive style. Good–bad, right–wrong categories dominated her outlook. I commented on this penchant, outlined the advantages that accrue when switching from a black-and-white perspective to one in which a broad continuum provides gradations in place of absolutistic appraisals. Although Gilda seemed to possess what I sensed as some borderline personality qualities, on the face of it our initial session went well.

At our second meeting, however, before she even sat down, Gilda announced that during our initial meeting I had infantalized her and demeaned her, and that I had also attempted to undermine her self-confidence. How should one respond to such allegations? The clinician has a few milliseconds to emit a response. One might elect to say nothing and wait for the client to elaborate. The therapist may opt to use reflection: "You feel that I have infantalized, demeaned, and undermined you." Perhaps an apology might be in order—"I'm sorry I gave you this negative impression." An exploratory stance may be proffered—"I'd like you to tell me exactly what I said to make you feel this way." A simple, "Please tell me more," may suffice. The range of possible responses is quite broad. I decided to use *confrontation* because I have found that it is essential to challenge the manipulative responses of people with borderline tendencies—and the sooner, the better. The dialogue proceeded more or less as follows:

> Me: We are in trouble. I have one aim in mind, one exclusive goal, and that is to be maximally helpful to all my clients. I try my utmost to be of service, to use my knowledge to its full extent for one purpose and one

purpose only, and that is to assuage suffering and enable my clients to achieve personal fulfillment. Now if someone feels that not only am I not being helpful, but that I am actually being hurtful and intent on insulting or sabotaging him or her, something is terribly wrong. It is then incumbent on me to think of someone to whom I can refer this person, a colleague who will manage to convey his or her beneficent intentions. So give me a few moments to come up with the name of someone who might succeed where I have failed.

Gilda: Oh great! My parents have rejected me, my sister has rejected me, my husband and boss are threatening to reject me, and now my therapist also wants to reject me! You're not supposed to do that. I've read enough psychology to know that you are supposed to provide your clients with unconditional acceptance.

Me: Really? Unconditional acceptance is something a loving parent offers an infant or very young child. Are you suggesting that if a client goes berserk, starts busting up my office, and threatens me, I am going to *accept* such behavior? I'd leave the room, grab the phone, and dial 911 within seconds.

Gilda: How have I threatened you?

Me: You haven't threatened me. I'm not about to dial 911, but you have *falsely accused* me of something that goes to the core of my professionalism. I repeat. I have one goal, a single intent in mind, and that is to be maximally helpful to all my clients. I am not here to undermine or to insult anybody.

Gilda: Okay. Okay. I get the point.

Me: What point is that?

Gilda: Perhaps I was mistaken; maybe I misread things.

Me: You're darn right you did. But if you did it once, you'll do it again. I can't work with someone who does not

> fully believe that I would never try to undermine
> them.
> Gilda: Let's not be hasty. I believe I deserve a second chance.
> Me: Very well. But if you pull such stuff on me again I'll have
> to refer you to someone else. Now I want you to help me
> understand exactly what it was that I said or did that led
> you to conclude that you were being infantalized,
> demeaned, and undermined by me.

My tough-minded stance was predicated on several factors. The colleague who had referred Gilda to me was typically gentle and supportive. Her two previous therapists (whom I knew fairly well) were also both extremely nonconfrontational. Given that she had derived no discernible benefits from their ministrations, it seemed logical to switch gears and come on strong. Besides, as I mentioned above, the manipulative responses that borderline clients typically display need to be nipped in the bud. In a different context, I have emphasized that "relationships of choice" are no less important than "techniques of choice" for effective psychotherapy, and that proficient clinicians need to be "authentic chameleons" (Lazarus, 1993). In other words, far from offering empathy and warmth to all comers, decisions regarding different relationship stances are called for and include when and how to be directive, supportive, reflective, cold, warm, tepid, formal, or informal.

From time to time Gilda resorted to her attack stance in therapy and accused me of offenses, to which I always pleaded "Not guilty!" Whenever this occurred, I said something such as, "You're doing it again. You are questioning my commitment to be nothing but helpful. Is this your way of asking me to refer you to someone else?" She would then capitulate immediately. This proverbial gun to the head, or what I am calling a "shotgun" approach, was consistently effective in maintaining her cooperation. Thereafter, we typically examined the bases behind these denunciations. It seemed that she needed to test me from time to time, and she also tended to "mind rape"—assume that she knew what I was thinking and feeling without checking it out. This proclivity, of course, was not confined to our relationship. It required a significant degree of cognitive retraining.

Gilda's treatment trajectory encompassed two primary objectives: (1) Her penchant to categorize everything on a two-dimensional plane required a serious course of cognitive restructuring and (2) her aggressive interpersonal style necessitated a regimen of role-playing scenarios wherein she was taught to deal in a non contentious fashion even with emotionally charged issues. I remember telling her: "There is one dichotomy I want you to uphold, and that is the difference between in-court and out-of-court behaviors." There was a third component that soon became evident. Gilda seemed to be depressed. She balked at my recommendation to consult a psychiatrist to determine if a course of antidepressant medication might be indicated. I decided not to use the shotgun in this instance because I was not entirely sure that medicaiton was called for. We continued working on her faulty reasoning, which included the disputation of her paranoid perceptions of various family members. I said that I would like to arrange a meeting with her and her husband. After conducting a shorter than usual "legal grilling," Gilda agreed to invite him to attend our next session.

John, who specialized in tax law, was a couple of years younger than Gilda. He was very tall, distinguished-looking, soft-spoken, and eager to be of assistance to Gilda and their marriage. He described her as a loving wife, good companion, excellent mother, and a first-rate lawyer whose major problem was that she often "went off the deep end, flared up at people, and landed in hot water." It angered him when she would fly off the handle and attack him for crimes he had not committed. "It reached the point where I was threatening divorce," he said. I asked if he had noticed any change in this regard since she had been in therapy with me. "Oh yes," said John. "It's like night and day. My big question is whether it will stay this way." I asked Gilda if she would like to air any complaints about John, and she said that other than the fact that he worked too hard and was somewhat overzealous about watching sports on TV she had no major complaints.

I met with Gilda at approximately ten-day intervals for hourly sessions, although when I had nobody else waiting to see me, we'd often run over the hour and sometimes spent 90 minutes or more. I was quick to point out that when this occurred, I did not act like a typical lawyer and levy an extra fee. After three months, we had met approximately eight times. She then announced that despite her significant gains, she finally acknowledged that she was depressed and had asked her internist for medication. He prescribed Prozac. Due to various external circumstances we did not meet again for five weeks. At that juncture she arrived for what turned out to be our final session. As she walked into my office she said, "Do you notice anything different?" "You've got to be kidding," said I. "No one in his right mind would bite at that piece of bait. Tell me what it is that I am supposed to notice." Gilda smiled and said, "I've taken off ten pounds." Basically, she reported that things were going very well for her. Her mood was significantly better. There had been no flareups at work and her boss had given her an unexpected bonus. She visited her parents and "it went well." She also got together with her sister and had a productive discussion. She gave me (undue) credit for having made her over into a much nicer person. "Inside, you were always a nice person. All I did was help you wash away the gunk and gook." We parted with the understanding that if she felt the need for further therapy she would let me know.

After about 6 or 7 months I sent her an e-mail inquiring about her well-being. She wrote back saying that she was doing just fine and once more expressed her thanks for my help. About three years later I saw her and her husband in a restaurant. They came over to my table and we had a brief chat, during which they both stated that things were going very well for them.

Nick and Janet Comment

To say that Dr. Lazarus' orientation is behavior therapy is to be redundant. He is not only its progenitor, but he coined the term, and he is the essence of behavior therapy. A prolific writer and a powerful speaker, he has written 18 books, and has had two books written about him.

On a personal level, Dr. Lazarus is the epitome of both charm and modesty. A genuine human being, he lets you forget you are talking to a great man. In fact, when one alludes to his stature in the field of psychotherapy, he responds, "Then I must be one of psychology's best kept secrets." We shall never forget when in 1995 Janet called him to inform him he had been selected to receive the first annual Cummings PSYCHE Award along with its $50,000 tax-free prize (our nation's most prestigious mental health award). He accused Janet of being one of his graduate students pulling a prank. At Janet's request Nick had to call and tell him the award was real. It is interesting that only after he received this award did the American Psychological Association begin to recognize that Dr. Lazarus is, indeed, a national treasure.

In the case of "shotgun therapy," Janet paid Nick the supreme compliment when she said, "Dad, this is the way you might have handled it." She was referring to Nick's writing during the past 25 years that motivation for psychotherapy can be dramatically increased by skillfully and paradoxically denying treatment to the unmotivated patients. Thanks, Janet, but this is really vintage Lazarus. How can one forget the time with a troublesome patient when he alluded to the freshly spaded flowerbed outside his office window as the place he buried his failures? Dr. Lazarus is renown for the aplomb and irresistible charm with which he therapeutically confronts a patient.

LORRAINE—BREAKING THROUGH DEFENSES TO GRIEF: LEIGH McCULLOUGH, PH.D.
ORIENTATION: SHORT-TERM PSYCHODYNAMIC PSYCHOTHERAPY

> Patient: Our appointment last week felt like I didn't do my part. Like I was a failure. I felt like, "What's wrong with me that I can't get in touch with my feelings, or whatever it is that is blocking what I feel." I have a sense of failure.
>
> Therapist: Isn't that a lack of compassion for yourself? After all you've been through, to think that you can change a lifetime pattern without difficulty? What we need to do is to erode the blocks away in bits that you can bear. In fact, we began to do some of that last week.
>
> Patient: Yes, we did.

Lorraine is a very courageous 64-year-old woman who came to therapy to work on her depression from a lifelong block to feelings, particularly to a series of losses and abuse, as well as her relationships with her daughters. The session is number 18, double length as she travels a great distance. She had been suffering from depression since the death of her brother in the last month, but could not cry. The previous week I had focused constantly on her feeling of loss, and although we did not get a breakthrough of grief, we did come to understand the factors that prevented her from grieving. She saw that she acted as the family's caretaker who could not let herself cry or ask for care herself. Her mother had died when she was girl and she had never been allowed to have feelings of grief or anger. She married a sadistically abusive husband and was for years unable to leave him even though he would both beat and rape her. He would do so with particular pleasure when she was physically ill. Finally, a caring therapist forcefully guided her through a divorce but did not get to her feelings about the gross mistreatment. She was so ashamed of having passively sustained such abuse that she had never spoken of it since. In later life she became a hospice counselor, helping others grieve, but she never could grieve on her own behalf. Therefore, our first 10 sessions involved unearthing the grief and rage around her husband's abuse. We then linked these traumatic events, as well as her conflicted relationships with her daughters, to the emotional neglect in her childhood.

My goal in this session was to help her become able to bear her feelings enough to grieve and thus relieve the profound depression she had suffered in the past few weeks. Her brother's death had seemed to tap into the loss of her mother, but I was concerned because she was quite blocked to these feelings.

> Therapist: Last session we looked at it closely, and it was very clear how you shut down.
>
> Patient: My daughter pointed out how I wasn't letting myself react when we lost our dog. She said she was really concerned that I wasn't letting myself feel what was happening.
>
> Therapist: Are you numbing your feelings?
>
> Patient: I don't know. Maybe I am. I didn't listen to the audiotapes on my way down like I had planned. (I provide audiotapes and/or videotapes of each session so patients may review them if desired. This is a powerful way to move therapy along). But I do feel that despair. I do!
>
> Therapist: Well, let's stay with that, because you left here saying that maybe you could have a good cry.
>
> Patient: Well, I didn't. I didn't. I went to the movies that night.

Therapist: So you got away from it. (I confront her defense of avoidance of grief.)

Patient: I have been numb, I think.

Therapist: That's like your getting busy rather than letting yourself cry with your brother before he died. And through your life you've comforted yourself these ways (pointing out the benefit of the defense).

Patient: These ways have served me well.

Therapist: Yes, these have been stoic ways to get through unbearable feelings (validating the defense).

She then tells how she can't tell people that she feels despair.

Therapist: So just stay with that. Where is the despair in your body? Where do you feel it the most?

Patient: In my stomach and in my chest. Tightness, tenseness ... the opposite of letting go.

Therapist: What words would the despair say to you if it could speak? What would it look like?

Patient: I guess it would look like all the cumulative outrage, sadness, aloneness. It would look like all the loneliness which I have never acknowledged. But I've never perceived myself this way. I generally want to be alone.

Therapist: But if you are alone there are no arms to hold and comfort you.

Patient: Right, that was graphic last week. I would love to have someone else holding me and sharing my pain.

In the previous session we had discovered that she could not cry because she had never allowed herself to become vulnerable enough to let someone put their arms around her.

Therapist: And the tragic thing is that your brother would have held you before he died. As he did his wife and children laying next to him on the bed.

Patient: Yes, he would have put his arms around me if I had shared my pain with him.

I hold the focus on the feelings of despair for several minutes with little effect. She described how angry she would become as a teenager if anyone showed pity for her. She also noted that her father never talked with her about her mother's death. Then a memory came up about the death of her son in childbirth.

> Patient: This is not a hard rock of despair at all. It feels mal-leable. But I don't think I let myself get in it. The only time I ever did was when I screamed uncon-trollably when I lost my newborn son. And that was so horrible that I never wanted to feel that again.

I feel worried at this point because I do not know how strongly she will resist facing the emotion she is so phobically avoiding.

> Therapist: What was the worst part of that?

If the experience of the loss was so horrible that she couldn't bear it, she must be helped to bear it before proceeding. She told of feeling totally powerless when her son was taken away, and also when her husband beat her and raped her. She said how hard it was for her to feel despair, so I focused on the greatest loss: her mother.

> Therapist: What were your last images of your mother?

I am intentionally trying to elicit memories that might bring up the feeling of despair. It is 11:35 and she has driven several hours for a double session. I am aware that I need to break through her defenses or I will send her home to face several more weeks of depression.

> Patient: In the hospital she was so haggard. She didn't look like my mother. She tried to smile. I was rhapsodic on my birthday with this bracelet Ronald had given me. It never occurred to me to ask her how she was. I was 14 and self-centered, wanting her to be excited about my bracelet. I was angry at her lack of response, and I was angry when she said,

"Don't let Ronald hurt you." Those were the last
words she said to me. I never saw her again. It did-
n't occur to me that she was dying then and that I
would never see her again.' The fact that she was
dying was not talked about, not ever.

She had often wondered if her mother knew how violent
Ronald could be, and if she had ever warned her father.

Therapist: What did she look like? You said she looked so hag-
gard.

Again I am trying to intensify the imaginal experience to elicit
the grief she is spending so much energy holding back.

Patient: She had dark hair. I remember that her face was
more jaundiced than my brother's face. I don't have
distinct memories ... but how thin, and her eyes.
She was a beautiful woman, but it was not a beautiful woman in that bed there. She did not reach out
and hug me. (Then with emphasis:) She did not
reach out and hug me! She didn't! She did not reach
out and hug me. I did not put my head on her chest
or lap. I did it a lot at home, but not at the hospital.
I remember going into her dressing room and hugging her, and she would hug me.

Therapist: There's so much warmth and tenderness in that
memory of home, but in the hospital there must
have been part of you screaming inside.

Patient: (blandly) But it was never heard, not even by me.

I was attempting to intensify the inner struggle, but it did not
elicit the feeling. It was time to try something else.

Therapist: Did you ever see her face again?

Patient: No. I just remember the funeral in New Haven. The
minister got her name wrong.

She was still dry-eyed, so I persisted with the imagery to elicit the feelings.

Therapist: Was she buried?

She began to describe where the ashes were buried, but she immediately expressed a sense of failure that she could not remember more. Instead of grieving she attacked herself. Then I changed perspectives by saying, "But if you had a patient who had lost her mother, how would you feel toward her?" I hoped this would help her take a step toward compassion for herself. But this seemed to have no effect. She talked about going very wild that summer, with boys and cars. She then said the happiest times were when she was riding her horse. She would not go off alone and cry, yet the relationship with the horse was nurturing.

Therapist: What are you feeling as you talk about this?
Patient: Sad, for this little girl. A longing for her being alone. I never thought of myself as being alone. I was always with friends, groups.
Therapist: Some part of you knows you were aching with loneliness and soothed by the horse.

The word "aching" brought up a pained response. She mentioned her brother's death and recent problems with a grandson which had been upsetting to her. She then responded with some intensity.

Patient: It takes us most of our life to recognize our despair. At least it's taken me most of my life. Then once I recognize it and greet it and embrace it and work with it ... I don't know ... it doesn't mean it will go away. It won't alter the facts.

The feeling of "What's the use?" is a very common block to grieving. It is the fear that nothing will change and the feeling will be unbearable. So I employ an anxiety-regulating perspective that often helps people to face their feelings.

> Therapist: No, we can't alter the facts, but you can alter your reaction to what happened, perhaps.
> Patient: It's the ignoring. It's the ignoring of the despair as a girl. I guess I could be angry at having had to ignore it, and wish someone had recognized that.

She is beginning to feel some anger at someone other than herself. This is the first sprout of self-compassion. But it is not my intent to blame her parents. Instead, it is to assign correct responsibility in a compassionate way for what happened so that she will stop blaming herself.

> Therapist: And I wonder if you longed for some arms to hold you, a lap to put your head in, and to be allowed to cry. Isn't there such an aching in you for that?

In the next few minutes she tells how she would have loved to be able to break down in the memorial service and "let her rip." But she was resigned that it was impossible to just let go and cry.

> Therapist: (gently) What do you mean you couldn't let go?

I spoke for a moment about the natural human grieving process which is so often suppressed by our culture. I also reminded her why it was so hard to give birth to crying for her brother, because so her own needs were blocked and unfulfilled.

> Patient: (after along silence) I get so angry with myself. I get so angry. I am angry.
> Therapist: You know, getting angry is such a convenient way to pull away from the grief. If you were compassionate with yourself you might break down and sob. It's so much easier to feel angry at yourself and feel like a

> failure than it is to feel the anguish you've been car-
> rying around all these years.

Patient: (leaning back in the chair, looking up) Yet I do allow
> myself to be worried about myself. I can do that
> because I am worried about myself. But I am mad at
> myself for not having more energy. I can't seem to
> accept the fact I have no energy.

Therapist: It takes a lot of energy to hold back the grieving and
> all the wailing, screaming, sobbing that's in you. It's
> throughout your body; small wonder you're
> exhausted.

The patient went into a long silence. I had hoped my comment
would help her feel more, but it did not seem to. So we talked for
a while about crying with her mother, and how she can cry for
other people, but not for herself. I pointed out that there seems to
be some category of tears that has to do with her losses, and this
seems forbidden to her.

Therapist: But let's pay attention to your feeling moment to
> moment, right now. How does your body feel? How
> sad are you?

Patient: I'm not feeling much of anything. Empty, empty.

Therapist: Had you been feeling sadness earlier in the session?

Patient: Yes.

At this point I felt concerned that I had not helped her keep up
the building of the feeling.

Therapist: You know, I should have monitored this much more
> closely because I'm sitting here feeling sad as we
> talk. I assume you felt the same.

Patient: No, I do feel sad, though it's elusive. The quality of
> the sadness, as I think about the various losses, there
> is a different quality to each one. There's less anger
> mixed with my brother's death. There is anger mixed

with sadness around my mother's death. And there is
a great deal of anger mixed with my son's death.

Therapist: (focusing on the most painful loss) Let's go to that.
Go to your mother's death.

Patient: I can imagine a screaming anger. (She does not say
with whom she is angry.)

Therapist: At whom?

Patient: It's very difficult imagining being angry at my mother.

Therapist: What's difficult about it?

Patient: That's like kicking someone when they're down.

Therapist: So you're mixing up your feelings with your actions.
Because when people we love are dying, they can be
infuriating the way they deal with the issues.

Patient: I certainly wouldn't have been allowed to have any
anger toward my mother at the time. It wouldn't
have occurred to me. It hardly occurs to me now! I
can't allow that now!

Because no image is arising, I asked her to follow my images. I
am concerned because time is passing and she has said she is feeling very little.

Therapist: Can you imagine now taking your mother by the
shoulders and saying to her firmly, "You're not talking to me about this! You're not letting me grieve.
You're trying to pretend that this is not happening!
How can you do this? How can you leave me alone
with these feelings?" What would your mother's
eyes tell you if she heard you say that? (The images
I present are intense and vividly interpersonal,
involving eye contact.)

Patient: She wouldn't have been able to deal with it, probably.

Therapist: If she hadn't been able to deal with it, what would
she have said?

There is no reason to let her mother's inability to respond stop the patient's own feelings or fantasies of what she might do.

>   Patient: Maybe she would have said, "I'm so sorry. I'm so sorry."
>   Therapist: (pushing for the feeling) What does that bring up in you?
>   Patient: I remember her in the kitchen telling us she's going to the hospital for another operation and not to worry, like she was going to Florida or something.

We discussed how her mother thought she was doing the right thing in trying to protect her, but how difficult this avoidance of feelings has made it for her. Thus, we validate both her mother's feelings and her own.

>   Patient: Now I'm feeling headachy, kind of constricted.
>   Therapist: It suggests to me that you're really angry and that it's being taken out on you. Let's stay with the images in the kitchen.

These images elicited both anger and grief and led to a strong breakthrough of feeling. The images poured out with great intensity.

>   Patient: I would have liked to say to her, "You know you're not going for a little operation. Tell me what's really happening. (with voice building) Tell me, for Christ's sake, tell me what's really happening (voice cracking). Tell me! (head in hands, voice high and pained). Tell me, fuck it, tell me (sobbing hard). Yes, I could shake her, Leigh. Yes I could! (She raises her cupped hands, making intense shaking motions, alternately screaming and softly intensive.) Tell me, for Christ's sake, let me know you're dying. Just let me know. Let me grieve with you, mother! Let me grieve with you (sobbing loudly). Let me in, let me

in! Let me be there! Let me hold you! Don't protect me! Don't! (crying and looking directly up at the therapist as if she is speaking to her mother). I'm fourteen years old! I can take it! I could take it when I was nine instead of pretending ... instead of pretending all along! Just let me participate! It's not all right. It's not! (She is crying so hard that I say "mmmm" over and over again to let her know I'm with her.) Just lie back there, mother, and let me crawl in bed with you. Let me hold you, and you hold me (crying)." I have the vision of her in the bathtub with her jagged scar from her mastectomy. She would take a bath, with bubbles all around her, and the door was wide open. We would all go in and out, and I always thought of her being open. She was not at all ashamed of this horrendous scar, and she would laugh about her prosthesis which would fall down. She'd say, "Oh, I have to fix my breasts." She was very open about that, but she was never open about pain, (whispering) never the pain. That's what I see in her the last time I saw her, the horrendous pain! And her pain that I was involved with Ronald, and knowing she wouldn't live to protect me. She did the best she could in saying what she said. But if she didn't tell my father to put a stop to that relationship, then I'm angry at her for that! I *am* angry at her for that. And she didn't teach me to speak up. She never did. She could have said, "Speak up, Lorraine. You're going to have to learn to speak up." She could have said that (crying). "Speak up, Lorraine." She could have allowed me in to help plan. "What are you going to do, Lorraine? How are you going to manage? Let's plan together how you're going to manage. How are you going to deal with your father? That is going to be tough for you. He's not an easy person to deal with." No one prepared me. No one dared say anything. Just tiptoeing right through it. Right around it. But there's no ever changing the pain on her face, and the pain she endured.

Therapist: (haltingly and in a low voice so as not to break the feeling) But there's changing now how you react to it (gently) and that voice that didn't say, "Speak up." You're saying it now to you. (later) They didn't know what to do with feelings, either sad or aggressive. That led to your being robbed of your autonomy (remembering that she was unable to leave a husband who sadistically abused her). You so needed to learn to speak up. And you needed to cry.

Patient: Never. Never! She should have told me, "You need to cry. You need to cry!" I can't imagine what her voice would have been like if she had been able to say that. I guess what I longed for the most was to hear that. (silent for a time, and then calmly and no longer crying) I feel now I might have inched a bit closer. I can envision getting closer to her in the hospital, and being able to put my arms around her.

Therapist: Let yourself do that right now.

Patient: (putting her head down). I can imagine being able to do that.

Therapist: What would you want from her?

Patient: I don't know if she would have had the strength to mover her arms to embrace me, but I could have embraced her. (whispering and barely audible) I could have. It's okay. I forgive you (sobbing). I do (sobbing). I do forgive her (openly crying). It just never occurred to me that I had anything to forgive her for (sobbing). She did the very best she could

> (crying). I can feel her holding me now. When I feel
> her presence (holding her hands up as if holding her
> mother's shoulders), I feel her spirit all around me.
> I feel held by her now. I feel more held by her in
> death than when she was alive.

The image of her mother not holding her had been transformed into the image of being held by her. She can now cry because she does not feel so alone. The unbearable quality of grief was related to the feeling that she never had anyone to hold her, so she avoided feeling it. Like so many patients who experience this type of breakthrough to intense feeling, her depression lifted in the following week. She was free to respond to life more fully and with vigor. Although this process will need to be repeated several more times in therapy to ensure that it becomes a response she can rely on, this session demonstrates one way of eliciting the type of affective experiencing that undergirds adaptive functioning. Two months later, when asked if the session had helped her depression, this is what she reported.

> Patient: Definitely! Yes, definitely! Although I didn't walk out
> of here and have everything go well, I was relieved
> and in shock when I went back to my car. But then
> increasingly the inner tension almost melted. Then it
> helped when I watched the video and I could cry
> some more, and be in a place again with my mother
> so I could be sure the feeling was real. (pausing) It
> was so stunning. I have revised the scene in my mind
> and have written another ending to it. It feels much
> more appropriate. It's not denying the way it was, but
> as you have often said, it allows me to have a voice.
> It's not the voice of a 64-year-old. It's the voice of that
> 14-year-old crying. And it's the voice of the mother of
> that baby. Somehow my screams have been heard
> now, by you, by me, and by the world. Because I am

able to acknowledge it so much more, I am no longer excluded from that hospital room. I'm not standing at the edge of the door sill. I'm in there hugging her. There's an acceptance around that last visit with my mother. It has a different flavor, with more compassion for myself. The depression? I'm not sure how to say it, but it lifted the way the fog lifts. I haven't felt depressed after that session.

In her own words, the patient went on to describe how meaningful it was to come to a resolution regarding the first loss, that of her mother. She alluded to earlier sessions in which her over-idealization of her mother was discussed. "I was highly resistant to seeing my mother as anything but perfect. Now I can acknowledge her shortcomings. She was only a human being. She did the best she could."

Nick and Janet Comment

Dr. McCullough is with the Beth Israel Medical Center in Boston, after previously being on the staff of the Beth Israel Medical Center in New York, where she directed the short-term psychotherapy research program. She is also currently a clinical assistant professor and director of the Short-Term Psychotherapy Research Program at the Harvard Medical School. She is well acquainted with the Davenloo school of psychodynamic therapy, and she has written her own book with modifications on that approach, *Changing Character* (McCullough-Valiant, 1997). Dr. McCullough is a visiting professor at the University of Trondheim in Norway, where her therapeutic skills are highly regarded and emulated. She has published extensively on therapy, training, and research in short-term psychodynamic psychotherapy, and is among its most gifted practitioners. Yet, as seen in the case of Lorraine, she did not hesitate to incorporate when appropriate gestalt and other approaches, all for the benefit of the patient.

The case of Lorraine is an outstanding example of short-term therapy in an era when psychodynamic approaches are neglected by researchers and replaced by clinicians with strategic and behavioral techniques. Her work exemplifies how psychodynamic therapy can integrate with the more popular gestalt, behavioral, and strategic therapies. Her continued research in short-term psychodynamic therapy remains a beacon for researchers who take the expediency of more quantifiable behavioral variables.

EMMA—HYPERCONSTRICTION AND COMPLEXITY : KIRK J. SCHNEIDER, Ph.D. ORIENTATION: EXISTENTIAL THERAPY

(This case is reprinted from Schneider (1988a) by permission of Guilford Publications.)

> The moment I meet with someone, for example, Emma, I immediately attune to how we are together. What is the "taste," feel, and texture of our contact? How do we sit with one another, position ourselves, and make eye contact? How does this person before me sit, move, and gesture? Is she in-my-face, or is she soft, pliable? Is she effusive, or is she subdued? Does she quiver, or is she composed? How does she dress? What vocal fluctuations does she display? What is her energy level and where do I feel pulled in this relationship? All of these questions are clues for me, microcosms of a dynamic, evolving picture, and portents of challenges to come.
>
> Emma entered my office on a bright and cloudless day. She was of medium build, approximately 40 years old, and Caucasian.
>
> Emma was charming. She was vibrant and articulate—and it was clear that she had "been around." She dressed with style, spoke in clear, firm tones, and got right to the point (as she understood it at the time). "There is something terribly wrong with my life," she declared. "I am at the end of my rope."

As I "sat" with this last statement and with Emma herself, I saw a person of solid conventional resources. She knew the societal "game" and how to play it. There was a hardness to her look and her makeup was formed by sharp and careful lines. It was clear that Emma—if she so desired it—had weight in the world.

There were, however, signs of strain beneath Emma's tough veneer. There was a fearfulness in her eyes and a melancholy about her face. Her otherwise resonant voice was interrupted by moments of urgency and breathlessness. It became increasingly evident to me that somewhere, deep in the recesses of her world, Emma was in turmoil.

When I invited Emma to elaborate on what was "wrong" in her life, this is what I discovered: She derived from a family of four—her mother, father, and slightly younger brother. When Emma was 3 years old, her father deserted the family, never to be seen again. It was at this point that her paternal uncle, roughly the same age as her father, gradually began to replace his brother as "head of the household." Although Emma's mother was devastated by the desertion of her husband, in her weakened state she accepted and even encouraged the uncle's developing new role. The mother and uncle exchanged some romantic feelings, according to Emma, but this was short-lived. Basically theirs was an arrangement of convenience, which everyone in the family grew to recognize.

Although Emma's memories of those early years were vague, by age four she knew something was askew. She felt like she experienced something with her uncle that no one else in the family had experienced and that to the degree they did experience it, they suppressed it. According to Emma, the uncle possessed a terrifying demeanor. He was very tall—well over 6 feet—of stocky build, and bullish. Her main memory of him at this early age was that of his booming voice and rancid breath.

Emma's memory clarified significantly as she recalled her late childhood (e.g., age nine) and early adolescence. In no uncertain terms, Emma conveyed that she had been brutalized by her uncle at these ages. She literally recalled him throwing his weight around with her—bellowing at her, pushing her, shoving her on her bed. She had a clear memory of him forcing a kiss on her and of being enraged when she rebuffed him. Although she did not recall being overtly sexually molested by her uncle, her dreams teemed with this motif and with many other sinister associations.

As I and others have found typical, Emma's reaction to these brutal scenarios was complex. The terms "helpless" or "hopeless" are too facile to describe this reaction. Indeed, virtually all words—from the ample lexicon of modern psychology—fail to address her layers of response. The closest she could come to describing her earliest feelings was a sense of paralysis. Beyond being an oppressor, her uncle acquired a kind of metaphysical status before Emma, and she, in turn, felt virtually microbial before him.

Yet Emma was no "shrinking violet." By adolescence, she became "wild," as she put it, displaying a completely new character. She became heavily involved in drugs, smoking, and seducing young men. She would leave home for days, periodically skip school, and associate with a variety of "bad boys." Speed (methamphetamine) and cocaine became her drugs of choice because they made her feel "wicked"— noticed, special, above the crowd. She didn't "take any shit," as she put it, and she occasionally exploded at people (usually males) if they got in her way. She even began raging at her uncle for brief periods, despite his continued dominance of her.

Emma's hyperexpansions, however, were short-lived. They were blind, semiconscious, and reactive. Beneath them all, her world was collapsing—narrowing, spiraling back on itself. The clearest evidence of this was the essential vacuity of Emma's life. She concealed herself behind makeup and laughter. She felt ashamed around peers and classmates. While she was popular for a period, her substantive relationships were a shambles. The men she involved herself with would beat her. She, in turn, would lash back at them, but with woefully limited results.

Emma was condemned by her past. As desperately as she endeavored to escape that past, she chronically reentered it. She repeatedly sought out boys and men like her uncle, repeatedly hoped that something—perhaps she or some magic—could "save" (or redeem) them from being violent men like her uncle, and repeatedly felt let down by such men and fantasies.

In sum, Emma was traumatized by hyperexpansion. The godlike power of her uncle made Emma feel worm-like. He came to symbolize her world—perpetually alarmed, perpetually confined, perpetually depreciated. Emma found ways, albeit transient and semiconscious, to counter this worm-like position, but her basic and unresolved stance remained worm-like, permeated by dread.

Emma's chief polarization, therefore, clustered around hyperconstriction. Her secondary polarization clustered around hyperexpansion and many gradations in between. In keeping with my theoretical stance, I attempted to help Emma confront her polarized states as they emerged, gradually proceeding to their core.

Emma's experiential liberation unfolded over four arduous years. We experienced the gamut of emotions during our intensive contact, from searing personal vulnerability, to panic, to rage, to bottomless grieving, to disappointment with, fury at, and terror of me. I worked with her to personally and intensively stay present to these feelings and to use role play, rehearsal, journal writing, exploration of our relationship, embodied meditation, dream analysis, and even a six-month stint of emergency medication, to facilitate this engagement. I also struggled with Emma over her tenacious resistances. First I assisted her to explore these resistances, then to mobilize her frustration with them, and finally to overthrow and transcend them.

The core of Emma's dysfunction was the dread of standing out. The closer we came to this core, the more Emma fought to deny it. This was understandable: not only did Emma fear standing out before her uncle, she feared the fuller implication of that fear—standing out before life. While the former fear was explainable and discussable, the latter fear exceeded explanations and words; it had to be experienced. By tussling with and remaining steadfastly present to this fuller fear, Emma was able to enter a new part of herself. She was able to "hold" that which was formerly unmanageable. As a result, she became more resourceful, trusting, and bold. She was also able to declare herself—not merely before me and her abusers—but before life itself. Today, Emma is in a nourishing and committed relationship, is active in her community, and asserts firm boundaries with her uncle. She still suffers, but she does not equate herself with that suffering. She equates herself with possibility.

Nick and Janet Comment

Dr. Schneider is a clear and aggressive voice for humanistic psychology and existential therapy, and a strong opponent of the manualization of psychotherapy. Lamenting the death of clinical romanticism in American psychology, he sought to reopen the debate about its rightful place in psychotherapy by organizing a special pro-and-con debate, which he submitted to the *American Psychologist*. He asked Nick to present the standardization view, not realizing he is a closet romanticist. For four long years Dr. Schneider persisted, revising his submission time and again until it was finally accepted and published (Schneider, 1998b).

By reopening this debate Dr. Schneider has done psychotherapy a great service. It is a lively debate, with the retort that clients deserve empirically supported treatments, not romanticism (Perez, 1999). Dr. Schneider is sticking by his thesis that clients deserve relationships, not merely "treatments" (Schneider, 1999). Nick and Janet would say unequivocally that we need both.

Dr. Schneider does not stop with mere advocacy. He is responding to the criticism that existential therapy does not subject itself to experimental verification by devising a methodology to do just that. If he succeeds in stimulating empirical research into romanticism, he will have made a monumental contribution, for at the present time most psychotherapy research limits itself to readily quantifiable behavioral variables. He will have extended our horizons immeasurably by making it possible to include a broader range of therapeutic endeavors than is part of our current research activity.

THE CASE OF BOB—FAMILY THERAPY WITH A PROBLEM CHILD: JEFFREY K. ZEIG, PH.D. ORIENTATION: ERICKSONIAN STRATEGIC THERAPY

Harold called me because he was concerned about his 10-year-old son, Bob, who was phobic about gravel roads. Bob's phobia had generalized to the extent that he had become reticent about leaving his home. Harold was the primary caretaker as his blue-collar job allowed him to set his own schedule. The mother, June, was a low-level professional, working full time.

Baffled by Bob's phobia, Harold and June contacted a psychologist. The psychologist said that he would need four sessions at $100 an hour to do an assessment before he could suggest treatment options. Harold and June had limited finances and no insurance. Having heard about hypnosis, Harold called me.

I told Harold that I would be willing to provide a one-hour consultation, if he would bring his wife and his son. I was a bit shocked by my own boldness, but I had faith in Harold's motivation, and my own ability to utilize whatever they would bring. We confirmed an appointment for two weeks later. I told him that although I use hypnosis, I do not use it in all cases, and I would not guarantee that it would be needed in this case.

The family showed up a week early, justifying my faith in their motivation. Fortunately, the scheduled patient had called to say she was running late. I explained the situation and she gladly rescheduled.

Bob was the most hyperactive child I have ever seen in my private practice. Based on the phone call, I had no idea that ADHD was part of the constellation. Bob couldn't stop fidgeting. As he entered my office, he poignantly announced. "I'm the crazy person." My heart went out to him.

I did not want Bob to assume a negative self-definition. I gave him a very difficult wooden puzzle consisting of two pieces that fit together to make a pyramid. Bob struggled but could not solve the puzzle. I told him I could not solve the puzzle either when I first got it. I called the friend who gave it to me and asked, "Where's the third piece?" There was no third piece.

I took Bob out of the office and into the waiting room. I showed him how to solve the two-piece pyramid puzzle. Then I instructed him to give the puzzle to his mother and father. Smiling, he strolled back into the office. Then Bob and I watched as his mother and father struggled to put the puzzle together. They could not easily do something that he knew how to do. Now Bob was one up.

Building on the situation, I said to Bob and his parents, "I'm an expert in helping families solve puzzles." I wanted to define the solution as existing within the family.

Harold told me how Bob's problem began. The family was driving on a gravel road when suddenly a mechanical failure caused the car to spin out of control. A very good driver, Harold brought the car to a safe stop, but the grandmother, who was in the back seat with Bob, completely panicked. Then Bob panicked, and subsequently refused to get into a car. Eventually he refused to be in any place where there was a gravel road.

When Bob went on to say that he was afraid of being out of control, Harold had a new insight. He had not previously understood that aspect of his son's problem. I asked a few more questions and I discovered Bob was not taking any medication. It was summer and he was on a medication holiday.

I remembered a dictum from Gestalt therapy: "If you're in terror, play out the terrorizer." If I can get the fearful person to play the part of the fear monger, it may breed a solution. Continuing my definition of the familial problem, I said, "Mr. Fear has attacked the family." Then I asked Bob to show me Mr. Fear. Bob went to the far corner of the office and became Mr. Fear, attacking the family.

I knew from experience that analogies can generate a solution, so I inquired, "Tell me, what is Mr. Fear like?" Bob asked me if I watched Power Rangers, which I knew only vaguely. "Mr. Fear is Drilla Monster," he continued. I did not know Drilla Monster, but I proceeded, "Be Drilla Monster and attack your family." So Bob pantomimed being Drilla Monster attacking his family.

Next, I thought about the Eriksonian principle of eliciting resources. I knew that there must be a resource in the family to deal with Bob's fears. Since Bob had offered the metaphor of Power Rangers, I asked him, "What power do you have?" "I know karate," Bob replied. "Show me how you can use karate to fight off Drilla Monster," I said. Bob successfully fought back the imaginary Drilla Monster. Then I asked him, "Please tell me, what power does your mother have?" "My mother has a very powerful scream," Bob replied. Suddenly, a systemic aspect of Bob's situation became clearer. I refrained, however, from interpreting underlying dynamics because I do not believe it to be helpful. I moved on: "Please tell me what power your father has." "Well, my father is a Sumo wrestler," Bob offered. Harold had a wiry build and was of average weight, but to this 10-year-old he looked like a Sumo wrestler.

Next, I explained the therapy. Whenever Mr. Fear, Drilla Monster, attacked the family, they were to stop and convene a meeting of all the Power Rangers, who would decide together how to use their powers to defeat Drilla Monster. Then I added, "I have two other therapies that I would like you to practice." Because June seemed exhausted and overwhelmed, I directed the tasks to the father and son. Harold was bright-eyed and seemed to have a lot of energy to devote to Bob. I explained that each morning for a week, Harold and Bob should practice being out of control. Bob would go into the backyard and play being out of control and Harold would coach him about being out of control. My covert design was to turn a problem component into a game. They agreed to the therapy.

Then I offered, "I have another therapy for Bob. I want you to write your name in my driveway." I live in Phoenix, Arizona, in the desert. My driveway is made of gravel. I told him that I did not even allow my daughter to write in the gravel, but that I would like him to leave his mark there showing that he had been at my office. My technique was a symbolic desensitization. Bob would have to slide on my driveway as he shuffled his shoes around to put his name in the gravel. I would have him violate his phobia about gravel. Adequate psychotherapy with a phobia can be achieved when one gets the patient to violate the phobic pattern, even on a symbolic level.

Then I said to the family, "Now that I have given you these assignments I'm going to give myself an assignment." I said I was going to Japan two months later, and I would send Bob a postcard of a Sumo wrestler. So I took their address, and when I got to Japan I did send Bob a postcard of a Sumo wrestler.

The entire therapy had taken thirty minutes. In the remaining time, I asked Bob to play with my daughter, who was a few years his senior. In the meeting with the parents, I empathized with their struggles with a special needs, highly sensitive child, and we discussed some strategies for providing structure for Bob.

It would be impossible to recapitulate that highly individualized therapy. I had a series of tricks—heuristics that could generate solutions. In this case, the most important heuristic was faith. There were three components to this faith: One, I had faith in my ability to utilize whatever they brought me. Most of my professional contributions in print during the past ten years have been explications of Milton H. Erickson's utilization method. I have made utilization a center point of my therapy. The second aspect of faith also came from what I learned from Erickson. I had faith in the family. I had faith that they had a resource in their system that would be adequate for solving the problem. The job of the psychotherapy would be to help them access that resource experientially. Finally, the third part of this faith was in myself. I knew that I had surmounted similar problems. I also had used methods to cure myself that were similar to those I prescribed for them. If I could do it, I knew they could, too.

Nick and Janet Comment

Dr. Zeig is undoubtedly the profession's outstanding exponent of Ericksonian strategic therapy. He sought out Dr. Erickson and became one of his earliest students. Even though Dr. Erickson said repeatedly during his lifetime he did not want to be known as a school of psychotherapy, nonetheless, after the death of his mentor, Dr. Zieg was instrumental in establishing The Milton H. Erickson Foundation, which he continues to head. It can be said that without Dr. Zeig there might not be a Milton H. Erickson Foundation. It is headquartered in Phoenix, Arizona, where Dr. Erickson practiced, taught, and wrote for many years with an energy that belied the pain associated with his postpolio syndrome. There are Ericksonian branches all over the world, and Dr. Zeig makes frequent and highly anticipated trips to them.

Dr. Erickson was committed to the patient's well-being with efficiency, professionalism, innovation, and dispatch, and Dr. Zeig has followed in his footsteps. This remarkable one-session treatment of a childhood phobia, following in the wake of a traditional psychologist who first required four assessment sessions, is not atypical of his work. Living in the shadow of his mentor, Dr. Zeig modestly gives all of the credit to Dr. Erickson. Yet through his prolific writing and teaching, he has expanded and enriched our knowledge of strategic therapy.

A FINAL COMMENT

All of the examples from this sampling of current master therapists have a number of things in common. Each therapist is profoundly devoted to helping the patient, and each is conscious of the patient's pain, with a desire to ameliorate it as soon as possible—sometimes in the face of severe resistance. Some have expressed concern that their interventions may not be adequate to the task. All are conscious of time. And each is "weeding the patient's garden, allowing the flowers to grow." Although there are stylistic and a parochial differences, the communality is startling.

These master therapists may counsel their patients, but they demonstrate that psychotherapy is more than just counseling. Each has strong relationship with the patient, but psychotherapy is not mere paid friendship. Supportive, empathic, and respectful of the patient's problems and resistance, they are, nonetheless, appropriately confrontational and active.

These master therapists began honing their skills long before the advent of managed care. They did it for the effective and efficient care of their patients, not out of cost consciousness. There is a lesson to be learned here for the beleaguered psychotherapy profession, as well as the industry which has turned managed *care* into managed *cost*. We have at our disposal the knowledge and techniques to fulfill the "patient's right to relief from pain, anxiety, and depression in the shortest time possible, and with the least intrusive intervention." And this is for the sake of the patient, not in response to the demands of a Wall Street that has no clinical focus, on the one side, and a profession that has been buffeted and has dug in its heels, on the other. Psychotherapy can be effective and efficient in itself, not merely in response to managed care.

CHAPTER 9

Extreme Therapy:
The Power of
Psychotherapy

Few psychotherapists have experienced the degree of power to which our profession is capable, and rightly so. What might be termed "extreme therapy" should never be undertaken lightly, or by anyone other than a master therapist. It is also not for the faint of heart. However, there are situations in which extreme therapy can save lives, as was illustrated by Fromm-Reichmann's "rage in the service of health," as adapted and used to save the lives of paratroopers in World War II.

In the case of paratroopers, the process that eventually led to destruction was at first facilitating and utilitarian. That the average number of combat jumps was three (two for an officer) was well known among the airborne divisions. By adopting the view that "It is not my turn to die until the fourth jump," it was possible to go into combat with confidence and without the debilitating fear that would interfere with survival. But when, inevitably, many paratroopers were assigned a fourth combat jump, they were so certain they were about to die that it became for too many a self-fulfilling prophesy. The bold intervention of substituting rage in the service of health, delivered within the time frame of a few seconds at the jump door, was ingenious and certainly fulfills the definition of extreme therapy. Many World War II paratroopers today owe their lives to the ingenuity of a master therapist, Dr. Frieda Fromm-Reichmann, who not only devised this intervention, but also imparted the skill to combat officers within a remarkably short six-week training period.

There are psychological conditions in which an unconscious destiny seems to be accelerating as if it were a runaway train on a railroad track at the end of which is the inevitable destruction. Some suicides seem to be of this kind. Ernest Hemingway put a gun to his head and killed himself at the same age his father died by a self-inflicted gun shot to his own head. The destiny, though unconscious, seems predetermined. When a psychotherapist encounters such a patient, will the self-destructive process be recognized at all? And if it is, will the therapist be sufficiently skilled to alter the inevitable through the overwhelming of the resistance, an effective form of extreme therapy that has proven effective?

If combat officers with no psychological training can learn in six weeks to effectively save the lives of their troopers, it is our contention that all psychotherapists are obligated to similarly hone their skills. It should be possible to save the lives of their patients even when this does not seem feasible or plausible within the context of ordinary psychotherapy. It is one thing to counsel homesick college students who have left home for the first time, to treat bored or overly ambitious middle-class patients, or to empathize with the self-anointed "victim." The real challenge lies in the patient who requires extreme therapy. The following is such a case.

DAN'S DATE WITH DEATH

Dan was 21-years-old when he came for death and dying counseling. He was suffering from lymphoma and had come to this distant city to be treated at the university hospital by one of the nation's leading experts with this form of cancer. When first seen, he had lost all of his hair from radiation and chemotherapy. In spite of this, he was still a tall, handsome young man. However, he was depressed and resigned, as his lymphoma had not responded favorably to the extensive medical treatment. He had been told by his oncologist to get his affairs in order.

The patient had moved into an apartment built on a hill, as is common in San Francisco. To one side of the ground floor was an unfinished room that was taken up mostly by the sloping hillside. The landlord planned to have it excavated and turned into a storeroom. Dan decided to help. Every morning on his way out he would fill a small paper bag full of dirt and then deposit it in the nearest public trash can. The patient was practicing a kind of magical behavior typical of those who know they are dying. At the rate of one paper bag a day, the large mound of dirt guaranteed that Dan would live a long life. The denial, of course, is that he cannot die until the task is completed. He was also looking forward to buying a car that would be more reliable for transporting him daily to the hospital. He still had his "clunker" because the bank balked at extending him the very unusual auto loan period of seven years as he had requested. This intended magic, coupled with the removal of the dirt, would presage a life much longer than that predicted by his oncologist, who had given him only weeks.

Death and dying counseling was abruptly interrupted when something Dan said alerted the therapist. The discussion had focused on the lack of responsiveness to medical treatment in spite of the patient's youth and otherwise vigorous health, belying the initial optimistic prognosis rendered by his physicians. Almost as an aside, Dan tossed out the statement, "I feel as if I've made a pact with the Devil that I would die." He was unable to account for this statement and, under questioning, dismissed it as his pessimism in the face of death. The psychotherapist would have none of it and began to probe. This had to be conducted aggressively in the face of Dan's attitude, "What difference does my past make? I'm dying anyway." His resistance was fierce, matched only by the ferocity of the therapist's digging. Little by little facts emerged.

Dan had lost both parents at age eight in a tragic freeway auto accident. They had been on a motoring vacation to Yellowstone while Dan and his three-and-a-half-year-old sister were staying with their grandparents. Upon hearing the tragic news, the extended family gathered at the grandparents' home. Dan was awakened in the middle of the night by the crying and wailing of the family members. One by one his four grandparents came to Dan's bedside and expressed the wish that God had taken them instead of his parents. Each stated, "I've had most of my life. Their death, on the other hand, leaves two orphans." This is all Dan remembered, and even this was painfully recalled and extracted over several sessions.

There had to be more; something of defining importance was missing. At such a time many therapists would consider hypnosis as a way of accessing the nonaccessible. The therapist considered it briefly, but for strong reasons he dismissed the procedure in favor of the hard work of psychotherapy. The value of the repressed material had to be within the context of making possible the patient's *real* determination to live, not just temporarily through magical attempts such as disposing of bags of dirt or paying off a seven-year auto loan.

There followed a series of turbulent sessions in which the therapist unrelentingly insisted that the patient recall whatever it was he was hiding. The questions were blunt, forceful, repeated, and insistent. Dan reacted with increased violent behavior, often writhing on the floor insisting there was nothing more. Eventually, in a particularly intense session during which Dan kicked a chair across the room, he suddenly remembered.

On each of the occasions when his grandparents expressed a wish that they had been taken instead of Dan's parents, the patient recalled with much emotion how he thought to himself that he was glad he was not taken. He also recalled thinking that his parents, whom Dan now recalled as quite cold and rejecting, really deserved to die. This was complicated by the anger Dan harbored at the time because he was not allowed to accompany his parents on what was regarded as a dream vacation to Yellowstone National Park. Then, several nights later, either in a nightmare or in a childhood hallucination, he was awakened by the Devil who came to claim the life of this ungrateful son. Dan recalled crying and pleading with the Devil, "I'm only a little kid. Let me live until I'm 21 and I'll go willingly." The Devil agreed to what seemed a lifetime of reprieve to an eight-year-old. But shortly after his 21st birthday, Dan was diagnosed as suffering from lymphatic cancer. The day of reckoning had arrived.

On learning of these powerful events, the therapist made no promises, but stated that the therapy could well question a contract to die made by a distraught child. The next several months were spent in examining his hostility toward his parents. Dan's mother was a self-centered woman. He could be doing his homework in his second floor bedroom, and when she drove up she would honk. He would have to come out and open the garage door so she would not have to get out of the car to open it herself. There was incident after incident like this in which nobody else's time mattered but hers. His father was "out to lunch" and never around either physically or psychologically.

Often, as Dan externalized his anger, the therapist was the recipient of stormy, hostile emotions. At other times, to facilitate expelling of the introjects, the therapist mimicked what he had learned had been typical parental behaviors. The stormier the therapy sessions, the stronger Dan became physically. Eventually, the patient, who had been declared terminal, was found by his physicians to be in remission. His oncologist was skeptical and insisted Dan see him weekly. Dan resisted, but the therapist pointed out that the skeptical oncologist was his best friend: "If there is even one cancer cell in your body he will find it." Finally, it became obvious to his oncologist that the patient was in full remission. Oncological treatment was terminated. Therapy was also interrupted, with the admonition that if Dan ever felt a swollen node to call immediately for an appointment.

Dan called three years later. He had since been married and had a daughter. His wife was in the process of divorcing him, and in his distraught state Dan noticed a swollen node. He came in for more therapy, during which time he was helped to separate from his wife, whom he had likened to his cold mother who had previously rejected him through death. He saw his ex-wife more objectively, and he reconciled himself to the visiting privileges he would have with his daughter. His cancer did not recur.

Over two decades passed before he was seen again. He had read a profile of his therapist in the newspaper and became aware for the first time of the psychologist's advanced age. He came in saying, "I hope you live for many more years. But I did not have the opportunity to say goodbye to my father, and I want to make certain I say goodbye to you." He then went on to tell the psychologist about his successful second marriage, his children by that union, and the fact that his first daughter had elected to live with them instead of with her mother. He described his successful and innovative career. He confided that he had followed from afar his therapist's lifelong innovations and confessed how proud he himself was to have innovated in a totally different occupation. It was striking that Dan did not seem to be talking with his therapist but to his father.

Dan's innovation is, indeed, remarkable. Unfortunately, it is impossible to reveal what it is without disclosing the patient's true identity. We ask that the reader accept our word that Dan has made an extraordinary contribution. None of this would have been possible without his having derailed his own destined rendezvous with death at age 21.

Extreme therapy is simultaneously rewarding and exhausting. It is unquestionably hard work, and one must eschew the temptation to take easier avenues such as hypnosis. It can be risky, but the risk is mitigated by an insightful conceptualization of the problem, coupled with the skill to unravel its destiny. We are doubtful that hypnosis would have elicited the true memory intact with all of its emotions. We have seen too many recovered memories that are incredulous—including abduction by space aliens—where there is enslavement to the memory, not freedom from its effects. The memory develops a life of its own, becoming the reason for living. The memory grows, the abductions increase, the multiple personalities multiply, and there is forever elaboration without resolution.

Extreme therapy is hard work for not only the therapist but also for the patient. Its reward is the release from the memory to pursue a productive life. In the case of Dan, twenty years later we saw a successful man, spouse, and father. He hardly remembered the cancer, much less the destiny to die at age 21, and he smiled as the therapist alluded to it. He summed it up by saying, "It was probably the most significant event of my life, but I never seem to think of it. It's like a bad dream set aside, forgotten but not forgotten, as there is family to be loved and life to be lived." Then, upon leaving, he hugged the therapist and uttered a parting word, "Thanks."

CHAPTER 10

Epilogue

In a thriving metropolitan area with a population of approximately 950,000, there is a brilliant surgeon practicing in a desirable community that has attracted more surgeons than are needed. Most of his colleagues are "underemployed," while he jokes he only works half-days, which is 12 hours a day, although most days he works more. As this is an actual story, let us call him Dr. Paul— not for the sake of protecting his privacy, but rather that of his less competent fellow surgeons who might well be embarrassed. In this city a consumer group biennially has physicians rate each other, then publishes a list by rank order. Anyone residing in this city can consult the list for the standing of the doctor being seen or about to be seen. This is a consumer-oriented service that is gaining momentum throughout the United States, even though in some areas organized medicine has put a stop to it. In the Phoenix area, which is now the nation's sixth largest metropolis, such a list is highly regarded and widely utilized by intelligent consumers. In his community, Dr. Paul occupies the top-ranked tier in general surgery all by himself. He is so good that his peers regard him as "peerless."

Surgery is the most manualized of all the healthcare professions. The manuals even carry "maps" showing not only where to make the incision, but how long and how deep. There is no question that this technology in surgery has lifted the practice to a much higher precision and quality than would have otherwise been possible. There is no question but that manualization/standardization will do that for any healthcare profession, albeit standardization is more difficult to achieve in some than in others. Our dilemma is this: since everyone is using the same manual, how does there emerge the uniqueness of a Dr. Paul, who is head and shoulders above his colleagues? How does one 43-year-old become *the* master surgeon in the community's glut of surgeons?

We learned about Dr. Paul from a retired primary care physician who underwent a botched surgery and would have died if Dr. Paul had not taken over the case and redone the procedure. Our physician friend knew the "paper" credentials of all the surgeons, and on that basis picked what he thought was the best in the community. In hindsight he now asks: What are the real qualifications that make a master clinician, as opposed to the so-called "credentialing?" This, indeed, has been the quest of this book in regard to our own field of psychotherapy, one that is far more elusive than surgery. The licensing boards would say that all licensed practitioners have leaped over certain hurdles and they are all equally qualified. The American public no more believes this than it believes the myth that all lawyers who are members of the bar are honest because they subscribe to the American Bar Association's code of ethics.

The morning we were to interview Dr. Paul was a Sunday, and Mrs. Paul had graciously invited us to Sunday brunch at their home. Dr. Paul's week was too overcrowded with surgeries to permit him to give us time during office hours. Dr. Paul was over five hours late. A baby was born with a very complicated perforated bowel, and no one in the community would tackle the surgery. Called early in the morning, he then spent nine hours in surgery with a one-day-old infant.

When he returned home he offered only a perfunctory apology for being late. Rather than being exhausted from the ordeal, he was full of enthusiasm for the work he had done that Sunday, acknowledging that when he first examined the infant, who would surely have died without surgery, he was not at all certain he could save his life. He was not even sure how the procedure should be done. He boldly, confidently, and enthusiastically plunged in, and he summed up his day's work simply, "I learned a lot in this case. If I ever see another case like it I'll know exactly what to do."

We learned some remarkable things about Dr. Paul. He did not attend a prestigious medical school; his grades were mediocre in his undergraduate years. Once in medical school, however, he was at the head of his class. During his internship he decided on what he had suspected all along: he definitely wanted to be a surgeon. His medical school may have been so-so, but he chose one of the best surgical residencies in America. After three years he journeyed across the country to enter a five-year residency in trauma surgery. The hospital was located in the inner city, and he told us that after five years and several hundred of the most incredible trauma surgeries, he was no longer afraid of anything. Then he rounded out his training with a three-year residency in pediatric surgery, itself a unique and complicated field. He had come to the present community in which he was practicing only three years previously at the age of 40; yet in that short time he came to be regarded as the surgeon among surgeons.

We were not surprised to learn that his fees were moderate, and far from the highest in the community. Our own surveys in the past revealed that the best do not necessarily charge the most, be they surgeons or psychotherapists. His house was comfortable and new, but not extravagant. It was sparsely and inexpensively furnished in keeping with the fact there were two very active growing boys in the home.

The subject of teaching came up. We wondered if his talents might be best put into use by his teaching others to do what he does. He responded that he had many offers to teach, but his competence as a surgeon depended on his continuing to do a lot of surgery. He frequently operated in a surgical amphitheater where colleagues and students could observe, and those who showed the greatest interest and promise were allowed to assist him. He cautioned us to beware of the surgeon whose office is in a fashionable part of town, who does teaching and consulting but very little surgery, and who is at every prominent social function, which is the source of his clientele. He does routine surgery, charges high fees, and refers difficult procedures to others. Repeatedly it has been shown that a surgical procedure has the best outcome and the lowest mortality in the hands of the surgeon and the surgical team that have performed more of these than anyone else.

In his own practice Dr. Paul approaches every surgery, be it routine or complicated, with the determination that it will be the best he has ever done. Do some of the cases frighten him, especially severe physical traumas or frail patients whose vital signs are failing? Yes, they do bother him. His mortality rate is extremely low, but he recalls each death sadly and with a query about how he might have saved that life. Does mortality, when it does occur, increase his surgical timidity? Quite the contrary, from each he has learned a great deal that will serve his patients in the future. We were also not surprised to learn that in this medical/surgical community that is saturated with managed care, his recommendations and charges are never questioned by the third-party payer. Within the first few months after hanging out his shingle, he acquired the reputation of being competent and straightforward, doing excellent but never unnecessary surgery.

Admittedly, this story is anecdotal and as such must be relegated to the level of a parable. But it is a true parable, and there seem to be remarkable similarities with what we have found among psychotherapists. Master therapists are well grounded in their theoretical structure, have had intensive training, and keep honing their skills by seeing a lot of patients over many years. They do not dabble in their profession. They are extremely patient-dedicated, and when needed they never hesitate to respond. A common characteristic possessed by all of them is that they *enjoy* doing psychotherapy, and that the more needy the patient, the greater the joy with the outcome. They see what others call difficult or hopeless cases as challenges, and it would never occur to them to refer them on. Rather, they begin treatment boldly, confidently, and enthusiastically. Two of the lamest excuses we hear repeatedly from psychologists is that the patient is schizophrenic or suicidal and therefore needs to be referred to a psychiatrist. Translated, this means these cases would be too difficult, time-consuming, or risky. In the words of one colleague, "I became a psychotherapist to have a comfortable practice where I see a few well-chosen patients, and then do a lot of teaching and consultation." Such a colleague is upset that managed care forces her or him to see the run-of-the-mill kind of patient rather than the carefully screened "psychologically minded client" who causes no trouble and never telephones during off hours.

Beneath his or her practice, the master therapist is a scientist who works only with documented, verified techniques, and does not get sidetracked by the latest therapeutic fad. The less-than-competent therapist is more committed to magic than the patient, always looking for that new twist that will make up for lack of skill. We are not just referring to outright quackery, such as crystal therapy, uncovering past lives, or treating post-traumatic stress follow-

ing abduction by space aliens, all of which are embarrassingly practiced by some colleagues. We refer also to the endless array of wild,
unverified approaches—what we call the *therapy du jour*, which
even before it is found lacking is rapidly replaced by another. Competent therapy is based on science, not pop psychology.

There are characteristics that seem to be prerequisites to being
a master therapist. Long before becoming a psychotherapist, this
person was a real human being who genuinely liked people. After
becoming a psychotherapist, she or he does not lose this quality
but continues to be genuine, enjoying each patient and taking
seriously the challenges they bring to us. They are hard-working,
dedicated, and there when needed. There is no such thing as a
patient that cannot be helped, and it is always remembered that
patients come to us to be helped, not just supported or enlight-
ened. They are free of bias and are open to understanding the
uniqueness of each patient without being hampered by trendy
postmodernism or political correctness. They are the kind of person we enjoy having lunch with. In the old days we used to call
this person a *mensch*.

REFERENCES

Adler, A. (1982/1930). *The pattern of life.* Edited by W. Beran Wolfe. New York: Cosmopolitan Book Corporation.

Albee, G.W. (1992). The future of psychotherapy. *Psychotherapy, 29,* 139–140.

Alexander, F., & French, T.M. (1946). *Psychoanalytic therapy: Principles and application.* New York: Ronald Press.

Austad, C.S. (1996). *Is long-term therapy unethical?* San Francisco, CA: Jossey-Bass.

Barber, J. (1998). Miracle cures? Therapeutic consequences of clinical demonstrations. In J.K. Zeig, & S.G. Gilligan (Eds.), *Brief therapy: Myths, methods, and metaphors* (pp. 437–442). New York: Brunner/Mazel.

Beardsley, R.S., Gardocki, C.J., Larson, D.B., & Hidalgo, J. (1988). Prescribing psychotropic medication by primary care physicians and psychiatrists. *Archives of General Psychiatry, 45,* 1117–1119.

Beck, A.T., & Haaga, D.A.F. (1992). The future of cognitive therapy. *Psychotherapy, 29,* 1, 34–38.

Bickman, L. (1996). A continuum of care: More is not always better. *American Psychologist, 51,* 689–701.

Bloom, B.L. (1992). *Planned short-term psychotherapy.* Boston: Allyn and Bacon.

Budman, S.H., & Butler, S. F. (1997). The Lilly Family depression project; primary care prevention in action. In N.A. Cummings, J.L. Cummings, & J.N. Johnson. (Eds.), *Behavioral health in primary care: A guide for clinical integration* (pp. 219–238). Madison, CT: Psychosocial Press.

Budman, S.H., Hoyt, M.F., & Friedman, S. (Eds.). (1992). *The first session in brief therapy.* New York: Guilford.

Budman, S.H., & Steenbarger, B.N. (1997). *The essential guide to group practice in mental health.* New York: Guilford Press.

Chapman, A.H. (1978). *The treatment techniques of Harry Stack Sullivan.* New York: Brunner/Mazel.

Cooper, K.H. (1995). *It's better to believe.* Nashville, TN: Thomas Nelson.

Coyne, J.C., & Liddle, H.A. (1992). The future of systems therapy: Shedding myths and facing opportunities. *Psychotherapy, 29,* 44–50.

Cummings, J.L., & Cummings, N.A. (1997). Holistic and alternative medicine: Separating the wheat from the chaff. In N.A. Cummings, J.L. Cummings, & J.N. Johnson (Eds.), *Behavioral health in primary care: A guide for clinical integration* (pp. 347–368). Madison, CT: Psychosocial Press.

Cummings, N.A. (1975). The health model as entree to the human services model in psychotherapy. *The Clinical Psychologist, 29*(1), 19–21.

Cummings, N.A. (1977). Prolonged (ideal) versus short-term (realistic) psychotherapy. *Professional Psychology, 8,* 491–501.

Cummings, N.A. (1988). Emergence of the mental health complex: Adaptive and maladaptive responses. *Professional Psychology: Research and Practice, 19*(3), 308–315.

Cummings, N.A. (1990). Brief intermittent psychotherapy throughout the life cycle. In J.K. Zeig, & S.G. Gilligan, (Eds.), *Brief therapy: Myths, methods, and metaphors* (pp. 169–184). New York: Brunner/Mazel.

Cummings, N.A. (1991). Brief intermittent therapy throughout the life cycle. In C.S. Austad, & W.H. Berman (Eds.), *Psychotherapy in managed health care* (pp. 35–45). Washington, DC: American Psychological Association.

Cummings, N.A. (1995). Unconscious fiscal convenience. *Psychotherapy in Private Practice, 14*(2), 23–28.

Cummings, N.A. (1997). Approaches to preventive care. In P. Hartman-Stein (Ed.), *Innovative behavioral healthcare for older adults* (pp. 1–18). San Francisco: Jossey-Bass.

Cummings, N.A. (1999). Was the death of clinical romanticism by murder, suicide, or natural causes? The standardization view. *Journal of Humanistic Psychology, 39*(3), 38–46.

Cummings, N.A., Budman, S.H., & Thomas, J.L. (1998). Efficient psychotherapy as a viable response to scarce resources and rationing of treatment. *Professional Psychology: Research and Practice, 29*(5), 460–469.

Cummings, N.A., & Cummings, J.L. (1997). The behavioral health practitioner of the future: The efficacy of psychoeducational programs in integrated primary care. In N.A. Cummings, J.L. Cummings, & J.N. Johnson (Eds.), *Behavioral health in primary care: A guide for clinical integration* (pp. 325–346). Madison, CT: Psychosocial Press.

Cummings, N.A., Cummings, J.L., & Johnson, J.N. (Eds.). (1997). *Behavioral health in primary care: A guide for clinical integration.* Madison, CT: Psychosocial Press.

Cummings, N.A., Dorken, H., Pallak, M.S., & Henke, C.J. (1993). The impact of psychological intervention on healthcare costs and utilization: The Hawaii Medicaid Project. In N.A. Cummings, & M.S. Pallak (Eds.), *Medicaid, managed behavioral health and implications for public policy, Vol. 2: Healthcare and utilization cost series* (pp. 3–23). South San Francisco: Foundation for Behavioral Health.

Cummings, N.A., & Follette, W.T. (1976). Brief psychotherapy and medical utilization. In H. Dorken (Ed.), *The professional psychologist today*. San Francisco: Jossey-Bass.

Cummings, N.A., Pallak, M.S., & Cummings, J.L. (1996). *Surviving the demise of solo practice: Mental health practitioners prospering in the era of managed care*. Madison, CT: Psychosocial Press.

Cummings, N., & Sayama, M. (1995). *Focused psychotherapy: A casebook of brief, intermittent psychotherapy throughout the life cycle*. New York: Brunner/Mazel.

Cummings, N.A., & VandenBos, G.R. (1979). The general practice of psychology. *Professional Psychology, 10,* 430–440.

DeLeon, P.H., & Williams, J.C. (1997). Evaluation research and public policy information: Are psychologists collectively willing to accept unpopular findings? *American Psychologist, 52,* 551–552.

de Shazer, S. (1982). *Patterns of brief family therapy*. New York: Guilford.

de Shazer S. (1985). *Keys to solution in brief therapy*. New York: W.W. Norton.

de Shazer, S., & Berg, I.K. (1992). Doing therapy: A post-structural re-vision. *Journal of Marital and Family Therapy, 18,* 71–81.

Ellis, A., & Velten, E. (1998). *Optimal aging: Get over getting older*. Chicago and La Salle, Illinois: Open Court Publishing Company.

Erikson, E.H. (1950). *Childhood in nature and society*. New York: W.W. Norton.

Erikson, E.H. (1963). *Childhood and society*. New York: W.W. Norton.

Freud, S. (1933). *Collected papers*. London: Hogarth.

Freud, S. (1915/1957). *Repression*. In J. Stackey (Ed.), *The standard edition of the complete psychological works of Sigmund Freud (Vol. 14)*. London: Hogarth.

Garfield, S.L. (1998). *The practice of brief psychotherapy*. New York: Wiley.

Goldfried, M.R., & Gastonquay, L.G. (1992). The future of psychotherapy integration. *Psychotherapy, 29,* 4–10.

Haley, J. (1973). *Uncommon therapy: The psychiatric techniques of Milton H. Erickson, M.D.* New York: W.W. Norton.

Haley, J. (1977). *Problem-solving therapy: New strategies for effective family therapy*. San Francisco: Jossey-Bass.

Hartman-Stein, P.E. (Ed.). (1997). *Innovative behavioral healthcare for older adults*. San Francisco: Jossey-Bass.

Hayes, S.C. (1987). A contextual approach to therapeutic change. In N. Jacobson (Ed.), *Psychotherapists in clinical practice: Cognitive and behavioral perspectives* (pp. 327–387). New York: Guilford.

Hayes, S.C. (1998). Practice guidelines are coming—practice guidelines are here. *Behavior Therapist, 21*(8), 153–156.

Hayes, S.C., Strosahl, K., & Wilson, K.G. (1999). *Acceptance and commitment therapy: Understanding and treating human suffering*. New York: Guildford.

Hayes, S.C., Wilson, K.W., Gifford, E.V., Follette, V.M., & Strosahl, K. (1996). Emotional avoidance and behavioral disorders: A functional dimensional approach to diagnosis and treatment. *Journal of Consulting and Clinical Psychology, 64,* 1152–1168.

Hoyt, M.F. (Ed.). (1994, 1996). *Constructive therapies, Volumes 1 & 2.* New York: Guilford.

Hoyt, M.F. (1995). *Brief therapy and managed care: Readings for contemporary practice.* San Francisco: Jossey-Bass.

Hoyt, M.F. (Ed.). (1998). *The handbook of constructive therapies.* San Francisco: Jossey-Bass.

Hoyt, M.F. (2000). *Some stories are better than others: Integrative essays and interviews.* Philadelphia: Taylor & Francis.

Kaslow, F.W. (Ed.). (1984). *Psychotherapy with psychotherapists.* New York: Haworth.

Kemeny, M.E. (1996, February 2). The immune system: Minding the body and embodying the mind. Presented at *Mind Matters Seminar,* Phoenix.

Kent, J., & Gordon, M. (1997). Integration: A case for putting Humpty Dumpty together again. In N.A. Cummings, J.L. Cummings, & J.N. Johnson (Eds.), *Behavioral health in primary care: A guide for clinical integration* (pp. 103–120). Madison, CT: Psychosocial Press.

L'Abate, L. (1999). Taking the bull by the horns: Beyond talk in psychological intervention. *The Family Journal, 7,* 206–220.

Lazarus, A.A. (1993). Tailoring the therapeutic relationship, or being an authentic chameleon. *Psychotherapy, 30,* 404–407.

Lazarus, A.A., Beutler, L.E., & Norcross, J.C. (1992). The future of technical eclecticism. *Psychotherapy, 29,* 11–20.

Lazarus, A.A., & Lazarus, C.N. (1991). *Multimodal life history inventory.* Champaign, IL: Research Press.

Levis, D.J. (1985). Decoding traumatic memory: Implosive theory of psychopathology. In W. O'Donohue, & L. Krasner (Eds.), *Theories in behavior therapy,* (pp. 173–207). Washington, D.C.: APA Books.

Mahrer, A.R. (1992). Shaping the future of psychotherapy by making changes in the present. *Psychotherapy, 29,* 104–108.

Manaster, G.J., & Corsini, R.J. (1982). *Individual psychology: Theory and practice.* San Francisco: F.E. Peacock Publishers.

Marques, C. (1998). Manual-based treatment and clinical practice. *Clinical Psychology: Science and Practice, 5*(3), 400–402.

McCullough-Valiant, L. (1997). *Changing character: Short-term anxiety regulating psychotherapy for restructuring defenses, anxieties, and attachments.* New York: Basic Books.

Miller, I.P. (1996). Some "short-term therapy values" are a formula for invisible rationing. *Professional Psychology: Research & Practice, 27,* 577–582.

Morgeson, F.P., Seligman, M.E.P., Sternberg, R.J., Taylor, S.E., & Manning, C.M. (1999). Lessons learned from a life in psychological science. *American Psychologist, 54,* 106–116.

Mumford, E., Schlesinger, H.J., & Glass, G.V. (1982). The effects of psychological intervention on recovery from surgery and heart attacks: An analysis of the literature. *American Journal of Public Health, 72,* 141–151.

Norcross, J.C. (1998, August). Symposium on psychotherapy integration. Presented at *Brief Therapy Conference* sponsored by the Milton H. Erickson Foundation, New York.

O'Donohue, W., & Krasner, L. (Eds.). (1995). *Handbook of psychological skills training: Clinical techniques and applications.* Boston: Allyn and Bacon.

Oss, M.E. (1998). What are "best practices," anyway? *Behavioral Health Management, 18*(3), 3–4.

Pallak, M.S., Cummings, N.A. Dorken, H., & Henke, C.J. (1994, Spring). Medical costs, Medicaid, and managed mental health treatment: The Hawaii study. In N.A. Cummings, & M.S. Pallak (Eds.), *Managed Care Quarterly, Vol. 2.* Frederick, MD: Aspen Publishers.

Perez, J.E. (1999). Clients deserve empirically supported treatments, not romanticism. *American Psychologist, 54*(3), 205–206.

Pickering, T. (1994). Blood pressure measurement and detection of hypertension. *Lancet, 344,* 31–35.

Reik, T. (1949). Listening with the third ear. New York: Farrar, Straus.

Rosenhan, D., & London, P. (Eds.). (1968). Foundations of abnormal psychology. New York: Holt, Rinehart and Winston.

Robinson, P. & Hayes, S.C. (1997). Acceptance and commitment: A model for integration. In N.A. Cummings, J.L. Cummings, & J. N. Johnson (Eds.), Behavioral health in primary care: A guide for clinical integration, (pp. 177–203). Madison, CT: Psychosocial Press.

Salzinger, K. (1998). Placebo therapy. *The Scientist Practitioner, 8*(2), 1, 7.

Schlesinger, H.J., Mumford, E., Glass, G.V., Patrick, C., & Sharfstein, S. (1983). Mental health treatment and medical care utilization in a fee-for-service system: Outpatient mental health treatment following the onset of a chronic disease. *American Journal of Public Health, 73,* 422–429.

Schneider, K.J. (1998a). Existential processes. In L. Greenberg, J. Watson, & G. Lietaer (Eds.), *The handbook of experiential therapy* (pp. 103–120). New York: Guilford.

Schneider, K.J. (1998b). Toward a science of the heart: Romanticism and the revival of psychology. *American Psychologist, 53,* 277–289.

Schneider, K.J. (1999). Clients deserve relationships, not merely "treatments." *American Psychologist, 54*(3), 206–207.

Sechrest, L., & Walsh, M. (1997). Dogma or data: Bragging rights. *American Psychologist, 52,* 536–540.

Seligman, M.E.P. (1995). The effectiveness of psychotherapy: The *Consumers Reports* study. *American Psychologist, 50,* 965–974.

Seligman, M.E.P. (1998, December). Why therapy works. *APA Monitor, 29*(12), 6.

Shaffer, I. (1999, January 7–9). Effectiveness and cost in managed care. Presented at *Nevada Conference on Behavioral Health and Managed Care,* Reno, Nevada.

Shapiro, A.K. & Morris, L.A. (1978). The placebo effect in medical and psychological therapies. In S.L. Garfield, & A.E. Bergin, (Eds.), *Handbook of Psychotherapy and behavior change* (2nd Edition). New York: Wiley.

Skinner, B.F. (1952). *Science and human behavior.* New York: Free Press.

Skinner, B.F., & Vaughan, M.E. (1983). *Enjoy old age: A program of self-management.* New York: W.W. Norton & Company.

Strupp, H.H. (1992). The future of psychodynamic psychotherapy. *Psychotherapy, 29,* 21–27.

Tourney, G. (1967). A history of therapeutic fashions in psychiatry, 1800–1966. *American Journal of Psychiatry, 124,* 784–796.

Wiggins, J.G., & Cummings, N.A. (1998). National study of the experience of psychologists with psychotropic medication and psychotherapy. *Professional Psychology: Research and Practice, 29*(6), 549–552.

Williams, R., & Williams, V. (1994). *Anger kills.* New York: Harper Collins.

Yost, E.B., Beutler, L.E., Corbishley, M.A., & Allender, J.R. (1986). *Group cognitive therapy: A treatment approach for depressed older adults.* University of Arizona: Pergamon Press.

Zeig, J.K. (1980). *A teaching seminar with Milton H. Erickson.* New York, NY: Brunner/Mazel.

Zeig, J.K. (1990a). Ericksonian psychotherapy. In J.K. Zeig, & W.M. Munion (Eds.), *What is Psychotherapy? Contemporary perspectives.* San Francisco: Jossey-Bass.

Zeig, J.K. (1990b). Seeding. In J.K. Zeig, & S.G. Gilligan (Eds.), *Brief therapy: Myths, methods and metaphors* (pp. 221–246). New York: Brunner/Mazel.

INDEX

A

Acceptance/commitment therapy, 188–193
Accepting, overly, compulsion to be, 50
Achievable goals, focus on, 83
Actualization, as goal of therapy, 83
Addiction
    iatrogenic, targeted program, 130
    psychodynamics, 92
ADHD, 235–239
Adler, Alfred, 84
Adolescence, focused psychotherapy, 102
Adversity, sense of coherence in, 131
African American community, 95
Agoraphobia, 128, 191
Alexander, Franz, 155–156
Alliance, therapeutic, formation of, 83, 179
Aloneness, cope with, 141
American Psychiatric Association, protocol production by, 3
American Psychological Association, protocol production by, 3
Anger, psychotherapy and, 47
Antidepressants, use of, 140
Anxiety, 54, 128
    psychodynamics, 92
    release of, 46
APA. *See* American Psychiatric Association; American Psychological Association
Approach-avoidance conflicts, 68

B

Asthma, 128
Attention deficit hyperactivity disorder, 235–239
Autonomy, professional, decline in, from managed care, 147

B

Back pain, low, 129
Base of competence, elevation of, 5
Bateson, Gregory, 156
Bayley, Nancy, 158
Beck Depression Inventory, 185
Behavior, changing first, *vs.* feelings, attitudes, 98
Behavioral aspect, of psychotherapy, 25–27
Behavioral interventions, 88, 130
Behaviors, new, assisting of patient toward, 84–85
Bereavement, postponing of, 140
Bereavement programs, 128, 137, 140–142
Berne, Eric, 153–155
Bernfeld, Siegfried, 148
Best practices, defined, 1–19
Bill of rights, patients, 94
Black-and-white perspective, cognitive style, 210
Blood pressure
    monitoring of, 131
    psychotherapy and, 47
Bodin, Arthur, 157

Borderline personality disorder, 92, 128
Boundaries, construction of, 93
Breast cancer program, 129
Buddy system, 130
Budman, Simon H., 168–181

C

Cancer, therapy programs, 129, 243–247
Cardiovascular disease, psychotherapy
   and, 47
Catalyst, therapist as, 54–56
Catharsis, via psychotherapy, 46–47
Challenge, master therapist and, 253
Change, psychotherapy and, 51–56
Chicago Psychoanalytic Institute, 155
Childhood, focused psychotherapy, 102
Chronic fatigue syndrome, 129
Chronic headache, daily, program for, 129
Chronic illness in general
   focused psychotherapy, 102
   stress management with, 130
   targeted group model, 135
Chronic pain, targeted program, 130
Clinical romanticism, 16–18
Clinically determined psychotherapy, vs.
   clinician-determined psychotherapy,
   44
Closeness, interpersonal, problems with,
   66–67
Cognitive nature of psychotherapy, 27–30
Cognitive restructuring, 88, 130
Coherence, sense of, 131
Colon cancer program, 129
Compassion, psychotherapy and, 41–43
Competence
   base of, elevation of, 5
   of patient, emphasis on, 84
   psychotherapy as amalgam of, 21–39
Compulsion, repetition, 52–54
Compulsive personality, psychodynamics,
   92
Confidence, 131
Conflicts, inner, of patient, 66–73
Confrontation, use of, 210
Constructive confrontation, 93
Context, of patient, therapist knowing, 97
Contract
   implicit, in first session, 89

   therapeutic, 59
   formulation of, in first session, 89
Coping behavior, exercise and, 132
Corrective emotional experience,
   psychotherapy as, 47–51
Correctness, political, elimination of, 6
Cost-containment, vs. prevention, 136
Countertransference, 64
Courtship, focused psychotherapy, 102
Creative power, 84
Cultural context, of patient, 95

D

Death, focused psychotherapy, 102
Death and dying counseling, 243–247
Denial
   as defense mechanism, 93
   psychodynamics, 92
   of treatment, as strategic intervention, 88
Dependency
   fostering of, in psychotherapy, 42
   transference relationship and, 58–59
Depression, 129, 131, 140, 216
   exercise and, 132
   psychodynamics, 92
   reactive, 140
Desensitization, 130
   meeting for, 130
   symbolic, 230–234
   systematic, as behavioral intervention, 88
Despair, 216–230
Destiny, unconscious, acceleration of, 242
Diabetes, program for, 129
Dichotomous reasoning, cognitive style,
   210
Diet, insulin, monitoring of, 131
Disability, focused psychotherapy, 102
Divorce, focused psychotherapy, 102
Doctor, psychotherapist as, 82
Doing unexpected, as strategic
   intervention, 88
Double bind, as strategic intervention, 88

E

Eating disorders, 129
Economic pressures, prolongation of
   therapy and, 44

Educational component, of targeted program, 130
Effective psychotherapies, elements shared by, 82–86
Effectiveness, therapeutic amalgams, 22–24
Elements shared by effective psychotherapies, 82–86
activities, definition of, 83–84
competencies, with expectation of change, 84
goals, focus on, 83
here, now, emphasis on, 85
patient strengths, emphasis on, 84
perceptions, behaviors, new, assisting of patient toward, 84–85
responsibilities, definition of, 83–84
time-sensitive nature of therapy, 85–86
Eliciting resources, Eriksonian principle of, 237
Emotional experience, corrective, psychotherapy as, 47–51
Empathy
with patient, 49
therapist lacking, 50
Energy level, 230
Enjoy Old Age, 185
Enjoyment, in doing psychotherapy, master therapist, 253
Epstein-Barr syndrome, 129
Erickson, Milton H., 160–166
Erikson, Erik, 152–153, 235–239
Ethical codes, 4
Everstine, Diane, 157
Evidence, in formulating future psychotherapies, need for, 2
Excellence, professional, 18–19
Exercise, 132
Existential therapy, 230–234
Explicit contract, 89
Exposure treatment, as behavioral intervention, 88
Extrapunitive patient, psychodynamics, 92
Extreme therapy, 241–247

F
Fernald, Grace, 158
Fibromyalgia, program for, 129
Fidgeting, in child, 235–239

First session, ideal, 88–91
Fisch, Richard, 157
Flexibility, of scheduling, 85
Free association, as psychodynamic intervention, 88
French, Thomas, 155
Freud, Sigmund, 148
Friendship, paid, psychotherapy as, 42
Fromm-Reichmann, Frieda, 149–152
Fry, William F., 157

G
Garlic, onion psychodynamics, 91–94
Geriatric Depression Scale, 185
Gestalt therapy, 86
Goals, specific, achievable, focus on, 83
Golden age of psychotherapy, 146
Grief, 216–230
bereavement program, 137, 140–142
case study, 31–32
Group Cognitive Therapy: A Treatment Approach for Depressed Older Adults, 185
Group therapy, as modality, 186
Growth, psychotherapy and, 51–56
Guided imagery, targeted program, 130
Guidelines
drive toward, 2
organizations publishing, 3
standards, differentiated, 4–5
Guilt, 68–70, 92, 93

H
Haley, Jay, 157
Hartman-Stein, Paula, 181–187
Harvard Community Health Plan, 172
Hayes, Steven C., 188–193
HCHP. See Harvard Community Health Plan
Headache, chronic, daily, program for, 129
Helplessness, learned, 131
Hemingway, Ernest, suicide, 242
Here, now, emphasis on, in therapy, 85
History-taking, in first session, 89
Homework, assignment of, 59–60, 88, 101–122, 131
in first session, 91

Honesty, without blaming, 90–91
Hope, in first session, 90
Hoyt, Michael F., 193–208
Humanistic nature, of psychotherapy,
    35–37
Humankind, love of, psychotherapy and, 42
Humoring resistance, as strategic
    intervention, 88
Huxley, Aldous, 82
Hyperactive child, 235–239
Hyperconstriction, 230–234
Hyperexpansion, 230–234
Hypertension, 129
    group program, 137–139
Hypnosis, 244
Hypomania, psychodynamics, 92
Hypotheses, creation of, in first session, 90
Hysteria/conversion, psychodynamics, 92
Hysteric, 92
    obsessional, 104

I

Iatrogenic addiction, targeted program,
    130
Iatrogenic reactions, 71–73
Ideology, practice based on, 6
Illegal behavior, patient in, 90–91
Implicit contract, in first session, 89
Impulse neuroses, psychodynamics, 92
Impulse schizophrenia, psychodynamics,
    92
Income, professional, decline in, from
    managed care, 147
Incorrect treatment, case study, 37–38
Independence of children, focused
    psychotherapy, 102
Independent living programs, for
    schizophrenics, 129
Infancy, focused psychotherapy and, 102
Inner conflicts, 66–73
    interpretation of, as psychodynamic
        intervention, 88
Innovative Training Systems, 172
Insight, in psychotherapy, 45–46
Insulin, monitoring of, 131
Insult, screamed at paralyzed trooper, 151
Intention, paradoxical, as strategic
    intervention, 88

Intermittent psychotherapy, throughout
    life cycle, 1–254
Interpersonal closeness, problems with,
    66–67
Intrapunitive patient, psychodynamics, 92
Isolation, 55–56
ITS. See Innovative Training Systems

J

Jackson, Don D., 157
Joining delusion, as psychodynamic
    intervention, 88
Judgmental nature, test of, 91
Jump door fever, 150

L

Language, of patient
    incorporation of, 111
    speaking in, with schizophrenics, 97
Last resort, psychotherapy as, 52
Lateness, case study, 25–27
Lazarus, Arnold A., 209–216
Learned helplessness, 131
Life cycle
    Erikson and, 153
    intermittent psychotherapy throughout,
        81–100
Life stages, intermittent psychotherapy
    throughout, 102
Lilly Family Depression Project, 48
Long-term therapy, transition to brief
    therapy, 43
Los Angeles Psychoanalytic Institute, 155
Loss of parents, focused psychotherapy,
    102
Love
    of humankind, psychotherapy and, 42
    tough, provision of, 42
Low back pain, 129
Lymphoma, therapy and, 243–247

M

MacFarlane, Jean, 158, 159
Maladjusted behavior, patient in, 90–91
Managed care companies
    impact of, 1

professional income, decline in, 147
protocol production by, 3
Manuals. *See also* Protocols
proliferation of, 3–4
Marriage therapy, 28–30, 102
Master therapist
concept of, 87
qualities of, 249–254
Mateer, Florence, 158–160
McCullough, Leigh, 216–230
Mead, Margaret, 156
Medication
with depression, 140
psychotherapy and, 14–15
reliance on, 129, 130
programs designed to reduce, 129
Meditation, in targeted program, 130
Mental Research Institute, 156, 157
Middle age, focused psychotherapy, 102
Milton H. Erickson Foundation, 147
Modular formatting, 132
Modus operandi-parataxic distortions, of
patient, 64–66
Morbid obesity, 129
Mourning, 140, 141. *See also* Grief
MRI. *See* Mental Research Institute
Multimodal Life History Inventory, 209
Multiple phobias, 128

N
Narcissistic personality disorder, 36–37,
128
psychodynamics, 92
NASW. *See* National Association of Social
Work
National Association of Social Work,
protocol production by, 4
Non-guilt reaction, 70–71
Novelty, in first session, 90

O
Obesity, 129
Obsessional patient, 55–56, 92, 104
Old age, focused psychotherapy, 102
One-session therapy, 208
Onion, garlic psychodynamics, 91–94
Operational diagnosis, in first session, 89

Optimal Aging, 185
Optimistic psychotherapy, 84
Outcomes, treatment, variability in, 5
Overvictimization, 96
Overwhelming resistance, as strategic
intervention, 88

P
Paid friendship, psychotherapy as, 42
Pain
back, low, 129
chronic, targeted program, 130
education, management programs, 129
management, targeted program, 130
medication, reliance on, targeted
program, 130
Palo Alto Group, 156
Panic disorder, 53, 128, 188–193
Paradoxical intention, as strategic
intervention, 88
Parataxic distortions, of patient, 64–66
Paratroopers
use of extreme therapy, 150, 241–247
Parenthood, focused psychotherapy, 102
Parents, loss of, focused psychotherapy,
102
Partnering, with patient, 59
Past, emotionally reliving events of,
catharsis and, 46
Patient, acceptance of, 49–50
Patients' bill of rights, 94
Perceptions, new, assisting of patient
toward, 84–85
Perfection, desire for, case study, 27–28
Perls, Fritz, 86
Personality disorder
borderline, 128
psychodynamics, 92
resistance, 131
Personality styles, psychodynamics, 92
PGC. *See* Practice Guidelines Coalition
Phobia, 235–239
multiple, 128
psychodynamics, 92
Political correctness, elimination of, 6
Political ideology, practice based on, 6
Pop psychology, elimination of, 6
Populations, future trends, 127–130

Positive alliance, between client, therapist, formation of, 83
Power, creative, 84
Practice
  best, defined, 1–19
  variability in, among psychotherapists, 5
Practice Guidelines Coalition, 4
Predetermined destiny, 242
Prescribing symptoms, as strategic intervention, 88
Present, emphasis on, in therapy, 85
Prevention, 135–136
Process instruction, technique, 166
Professional excellence, 18–19
Projections, interpretation of, as psychodynamic intervention, 88
Prolongation of therapy, conditions fostering, 44
Prostate cancer program, 129
Protocols
  drive toward, 2
  explosion in, 3
  by managed care companies, 3
Protracted period of time, psychotherapy during, 43–45
Provider groups, protocol production by, 3
Psychic space, schizophrenics allow into, 149
Psychodynamic interventions, 88
Psychodynamic nature of psychotherapy, 30–32
Psychodynamics
  to formulate treatment plan, 91
  understanding of, 91
Psychological treatments, as replacement for psychotherapy, 15–16
Psychopharmacology, psychotherapy and, 37–39
Psychotherapy
  effective, elements shared by, 82–86
  intermittent, throughout life cycle, 81–100
  as last resort, 52
  overview, 11–14
Puberty, focused psychotherapy, 102

R
Rage, as galvanizing emotion, 151

Reactive depression, 140
Reasoning, dichotomous, cognitive style, 210
Reassurance, giving of, vs. hope, 90
Reevaluation, of psychotherapy, 146
Reframing, as strategic intervention, 88
Reinforcement, schedules of, 88, 130
Relaxation, as behavioral intervention, 88, 130
Reliance, on medication, programs designed to reduce, 129
Repetition compulsion, 52–54, 54
Repression
  psychodynamics, 92
  as psychological defense mechanism, 93
Resiliency, phychotherapy and, 48–49
Resistance, 52–54, 99–100
  attacking, 99
  prescribing, as strategic intervention, 88
  strategic interventions to cut through, 131
Resources, eliciting, Eriksonian principle of, 237
Responsibility
  definition of, 83–84
  patient acceptance of, 43
Restructuring, cognitive, 130
Riskin, Jules, 157
Role playing, as behavioral intervention, 88
Romanticism, clinical, 16–18
Running hypotheses, creation of, in first session, 90

S
San Francisco Psychoanalytic Institute, 148, 153
Schedules of reinforcement, 130
Scheduling, flexibility of, 85
Schizophrenia
  allowing into psychic space, 149
  psychodynamics, 92
  speaking in patient's language with, 97
Schneider, Kirk J., 230–234
Seductive action, of hysteric, 106
Seeding technique, 165
Self-actualization, as goal of therapy, 83
Self-confidence, 131

Self-efficacy, 131, 141
  coping behavior, 132
Self-evaluation, 131
Self-perpetuation, of feelings, 98
Sensitivity to time, therapy and, 85–86
Session, first, ideal, 88–91
Settings, future trends, 127–130
Small therapeutic gain, achieving in first
  session, 90
Solace, psychotherapy as, 42
Solution-focused therapy, as form of
  focused psychotherapy, 81
Somaticizer programs, 129
Somatizers, resistance, 131
Soviet Union, psychiatry in, 6
Speaking in patient's language, with
  schizophrenics, 97
Spouse, death of, 140
  focused psychotherapy, 102
Squeamishness, in psychotherapist, 50–51
Stages of life, intermittent psychotherapy
  throughout, 102
Standardization
  advantages, disadvantages, 5–8
  trend toward, 2
Standards, guidelines, differentiated, 4–5
Strategic interventions, 88
  to cut through resistance, 131
Strategic nature of psychotherapy, 32–35
Strengths, of patient, emphasis on, 84
Stress management, 130
Substance abuse, case study, 33–34
Sullivan, Harry Stack, 149
Support systems, 130
Symbolic desensitization, 230–234
Symptom reduction, 73–77
Synchronization, of therapeutic goals,
  60–61
Syndromes, unverified, elimination of, 6
Systematic desensitization, as behavioral
  intervention, 88

T

Taking history, in first session, 89
Targeted group models, 132–136
  chronic medical diseases, 135
  management, 134–135
  prevention, 135–136

schizophrenics, 135
  treatment, 132–134
Targeted programs, elements of, 130–132
Techniques, psychotherapy as amalgam of,
  21–39
Theory, technique as dependent upon,
  86–87
Therapeutic alliance, 83
  establishing, 179
Therapeutic contract, 59
  in first session, 90
  formulation of, in first session, 89
Time
  protracted, psychotherapy during,
    43–45
  sensitivity to, therapy and, 85–86
Time-sensitive psychotherapies, 44
Timeliness, case study, 25–27
Tough love, provision of, 42
Toward standardization, trend, 2
Transactional analysis, 154
Transference
  interpretation of, as psychodynamic
    intervention, 88
  mimicking, as psychodynamic
    intervention, 88
  simulating, 62–64
Transference neurosis, 57
Transference relationship, 56–64
  dependency and, 58–59
Treatment outcomes, variability in, 5
Treatment plan, in first session, 89

U

Unacceptable behavior, patient in, 90–91
Unconscious destiny, acceleration of, 242
Unexpected, as strategic intervention, 88
Unverified syndromes, elimination of, 6

V

Variability in practice, among
  psychotherapists, 5
Victimization, elimination of, 6

W

Watzlawick, Paul, 156–158

Weakland, John, 157
Weekly solace, psychotherapy as, 42
Widows, bereavement, 128, 140
Withdrawal, psychodynamics, 92

Y

Young adulthood, focused psychotherapy,
    102

Younger therapists, 187
Yuppie syndrome. *See* Epstein-Barr
    syndrome

Z

Zeig, Jeffrey K., 235–239